Emotional Development in Psychoanalysis, Attachment Theory and Neuroscience

Emotional Development in Psychoanalysis, Attachment Theory and Neuroscience is a multi-disciplinary overview of psychological and emotional development from infancy through to adulthood. Uniquely, it integrates research and concepts from psychology and neurophysiology with psychoanalytic thinking, providing an unusually rich and balanced perspective on the subject. Written by leaders in their field, the chapters cover:

- Biological and neurological factors in the unconscious and memory
- The link between genetics and attachment
- The early relationship and the growth of emotional life
- The importance of a developmental framework to inform psychoanalytic work
- Clinical work

Drawing on a wide range of detailed case studies with subjects across childhood and adolescence, this book provides a ground-breaking insight into how very different schools of thought can work together to achieve clinical success in work with particularly difficult young patients.

Emotional Development in Psychoanalysis, Attachment Theory and Neuroscience represents the latest knowledge beneficial to child psychiatrists and child psycho-therapists, as well as social workers, psychologists, health visitors and specialist teachers.

Viviane Green is a member of the Association of Child Psychotherapists and the Association for Child Psychoanalysis. She is Head of Clinical Training at the Anna Freud Centre, London, and has developed and taught on child training programmes in Holland and Italy.

Emotional Development in Psychoanalysis, Attachment Theory and Neuroscience

Creating Connections

Viviane Green

Brunner-Routledge
Taylor & Francis Group
HOVE AND NEW YORK

First published 2003 by Brunner-Routledge
27 Church Road, Hove, East Sussex BN3 2FA

Simultaneously published in the USA and Canada
by Brunner-Routledge
29 West 35th Street, New York, NY 10001

Reprinted 2004

Brunner-Routledge is an imprint of the Taylor & Francis Group

Typeset in Times by Regent Typesetting, London
Printed and bound in Great Britain by T J International Ltd,
Padstow, Cornwall
Paperback cover design by Lisa Dynan

British Library Cataloguing in Publication Data
A catalogue record for this book is available
from the British Library

Library of Congress Cataloging in Publication Data

Emotional development in psychoanalysis, attachment theory, and
neuroscience : creating connections / edited by Viviane Green.
    p. cm.
Includes bibliographical references and index.
  ISBN 1-58391-134-0 (alk. paper) — ISBN 1-58391-135-9 (pbk. : alk.
paper)
  1. Psychoanalysis. 2. Emotions. 3. Attachment behavior. 4.
Neuropsychiatry. I. Green, Viviane, 1951-

  RC506.E455 2003
  616.89'17—dc21

                                                    2003001937

ISBN 1-58391-134-0 (hbk)
ISBN 1-58391-135-9 (pbk)

Contents

Figures

Contributors

Tessa Baradon received a masters degree in public health from the Haddassah Medical School in Jerusalem, where she founded and directed services for adolescents in crisis. After completing her training at the Anna Freud Centre, she established the Parent and Infant Project at the Anna Freud Centre, which she continues to manage. The Project has become a model for similar organisations both in the UK and abroad and extends its training programmes to a wide range of psychoanalytical and other professionals. Tessa Baradon lectures locally and abroad, with a particular focus on parent–infant mental health. Recent publications have addressed issues of technique and processes of change in parent–infant psychotherapy.

Peter Fonagy PhD FBA is Chief Executive of the Anna Freud Centre and Freud Memorial Professor of Psychoanalysis and Director of the Sub-Department of Clinical Health Psychology at University College London. He is a clinical psychologist and a training and supervising analyst in the British Psycho-Analytical Society in child and adult analysis. His clinical interests centre around issues of borderline psychopathology, violence and early attachment relationships. His work attempts to integrate empirical research with psychoanalytic theory. His research interests include the study of the outcome of psychoanalytic psychotherapy and the impact of early parent–child relationships on personality development. He holds a number of important positions, which include chairing the Research Committee and Vice-Presidency of the International Psychoanalytic Association, and Fellowship of the British Academy. He is on the editorial board of a number of major journals including *Development and Psychopathology*. He has published over 200 chapters and articles and has authored or edited several books. His most recent books include *What Works for Whom: A Critical Review of Psychotherapy Research* (With A. Roth, published 1996 by Guilford), *Attachment Theory and Psychoanalysis* (published by Other Press), *Evidence-Based Child Mental Health: A Comprehensive Review of Treatment Interventions* (with M. Target, D. Cottrell, J. Phillips and Z. Kurtz in press with Guilford) and *Affect Regulation, Mentalization and the Development of the Self* (with G. Gergely, E. Jurist and M. Target, published by Other Press).

Viviane Green is Head of Clinical Training at the Anna Freud Centre. She is an Honorary Lecturer at University College London. She helped set up a child psychotherapy training centre in Utrecht, Holland and has taught and supervised at the University of Padua, Italy. She has contributed chapters to *Psychoanalysis and Developmental Therapy* (edited by A. Hurry, Karnac Books, London, 1998) and *The Handbook of Child and Adolescent Psychotherapy: Psychoanalytic Approaches* (edited by M. Lanyado and A. Horne, Routledge, 1999).

Willem Heuves is a member of the Dutch Psychoanalytic Society and a member of the Association for Child Psychoanalysis. He is a lecturer at Leiden University and has had a long-standing interest in adolescence. He is widely published.

Marta Neil trained at the Anna Freud Centre. She holds posts in the Department of Psychological Medicine at Great Ormond Street Hospital for Children and in the Department of Child Psychiatry at Milton Keynes Hospital. She has a special interest in work with looked-after children and children who have experienced maltreatment and trauma. Together with Dr Jill Hodges she is involved in research using the Narrative Story Stem Technique to assess internal representations of parent–child interactions of children who have experienced emotional abuse.

Inji Ralph is a Child and Adolescent Psychotherapist who trained at the Anna Freud Centre, where she has been working since qualification. She teaches on the clinical training and on the MSc course in Psychoanalytic Developmental Psychology (University College London). She has worked in the NHS. Currently she also works in private practice and has a special interest in parent–infant psychotherapy.

Allan N. Schore is Assistant Clinical Professor of Psychiatry and Biobehavioural Sciences, University of California at Los Angeles Medical School, and is on the teaching faculties of the Institute of Contemporary Psychoanalysis and the Southern California Psychoanalytic Institute. He is the author of *Affect Regulation and the Origin of the Self: The Neurobiology of Emotional Development* (Lawrence Erlbaum, 1994) He is on the editorial board of *Neuro-Psychoanalysis* and is Special Editor of the *Infant Mental Health Journal*. He is currently publishing articles and chapters in a variety of fields: psychoanalysis, neuroscience, attachment theory, infant mental health, developmental psychology, developmental psychopathology and affect theory.

Mark Solms is Consultant Neuropsychologist at the Anna Freud Centre and a lecturer in Psychology at University College London. He is an Associate Member of the British Psycho-Analytical Society, Honorary Member of the New York Psychoanalytic Society and member of the British Neuropsychological Society. He has published widely in both neuroscientific and psychoanalytic journals. He is co-editor of the journal *Neuro-Psychoanalysis*, and co-chairperson of the International Neuro-Psychoanalysis Society. He received the 'International Psychiatrist' award from the American Psychiatric Association in 2001, and his book *Clinical Studies in Neuro-Psychoanalysis* (with Karen Kaplan-Solms) won the National Association for the Advancement of Psychoanalysis Gradiva Award (Best Book, Science Category) in 2001. He is the co-author with Oliver Turnbull of *The Brain and the Inner World: An Introduction to the Neuroscience of Subjective Experience*, published by Other Press.

Miriam Steele is the course organiser of the joint MSc course in Psychoanalytic Developmental Psychology at Anna Freud Centre/University College London. Miriam Steele's specialised area of research interest is in intergenerational patterns of attachment in normative and clinical populations. Her ongoing work includes a longitudinal study of attachment patterns in a group of 100 families comprising the London Parent Child Project. She is also involved in a study of attachment relationships in newly adopted maltreated children. She is widely published.

Oliver Turnbull is a Cambridge-trained neuropsychologist. He has published widely in neuroscientific journals, primarily on the topic of visuospatial disorders, laterality, and neuropsychological disorders involving false beliefs (confabulation) and denial of deficit (anosognosia). He is a senior lecturer in the Centre for Cognitive Neuroscience, School of Psychology, University of Wales, Bangor. He is also the Secretary of the International Neuro-Psychoanalysis Society, and the Research Digest Editor of the journal *Neuro-Psychoanalysis*. He is the co-author, with Mark Solms, of *The Brain and the Inner World: An Introduction to the Neuroscience of Subjective Experience*, published by Other Press.

Marie Zaphiriou Woods is a child and adult psychoanalyst and an Associate Member of the British Institute of Psychoanalysis. For many years she was the Consultant to the Anna Freud Centre Nursery. Currently, Marie is Consultant to the Centre's toddler groups and also supervises and teaches trainee child psychotherapists.

Acknowledgements

Thanks are due to many people who contributed to this book in various ways, in particular the staff and trainees at the Anna Freud Centre. Discussions on the psychoanalytic work undertaken by contributors, either at the Centre, within the National Health Service or other settings, provided the initial impetus for this book. The Anna Freud Centre has offered a rich culture to clinicians whereby clinical practice is both embedded in a 'tradition' and open to new developments in the fields represented in the first section. Special thanks are due to the following, who offered invaluable help and encouragement to the contributing authors: Jane Cheshire, Patricia Ellingham, Peter Fonagy, Dominique Green, Ann Horne, Anne Hurry, Pearl King, Nick Midgley, Nicky Parker, Anne Marie Sandler, Francesca Target.

Emotional development – biological and clinical approaches – towards an integration

Viviane Green

Emotional life, the very stuff of psychoanalysis, is now gaining prominence as a focus for legitimate scientific interest. A central aim behind this book was the wish to bring together under one roof some of the current psychoanalytic, attachment, neuropsychological and psychobiological perspectives in the belief that they have much to offer the individual who, for professional or personal reasons, is interested in emotional development. Emotional development takes place at the confluence of diverse and multiple processes and it seems apposite to draw on a variety of perspectives. In the first section the development of emotional life is viewed through different lenses, each highlighting a particular aspect of how the mind develops and functions. In the second section, the focus is at the psychic level, the individual's subjective experience as it reveals itself within the domain of a therapeutic relationship.

Integrating biological and clinical approaches: problems and possibilities

The link between the biological sciences and psychoanalysis is of course not new. From the outset the potential links between psychoanalysis (psychic life) and neurology (biology) had been of great interest to Freud. Many years later we are in a better position to understand the nature of these links but we are not yet clear as to how to integrate what are essentially very different paradigms, disciplines and traditions.

Whittle (1999) argues that subjectivity (within the domain of psychoanalysis) and science constitute utterly different enterprises, each with its own culture, methods and styles of thinking. Between these different parallel worlds, he writes, lies a yawning epistemological and methodological gap. While this may well be true it does not necessarily follow that what emerges from one field cannot inform the other. In some ways this book is an attempt to show that the gap may be neither so wide nor so unbridgeable. At the very least there are many clinicians peering over to the other side and indeed vice versa. All the authors in the first section straddle more than one discipline and as such are well placed to demonstrate that no single methodology alone can do justice to the complexities of the human mind.

The thrust of Whittle's article does not derogate the psychoanalytic enterprise, for he contends that in concerning itself with individual subjectivity psychoanalysis tells us more about human nature and speaks more directly to us as human beings than experimental psychology.

Echoing this sentiment and arguing for integration between, in this case, the cognitive neurosciences and psychoanalysis, Westen and Gabbard state:

> We will similarly do ourselves a disservice if we import more recent cognitive concepts such as implicit and procedural memory into psychoanalytic discourse without integrating them with decades of clinical thought and observation and carefully considering the ways in which they converge and diverge with regard to psychoanalytic thinking. Integration implies two-way influence . . . models in cognitive neuroscience stand to gain as much from psychoanalytic theory and data as vice versa.
>
> (Westen and Gabbard 2002:59)

Panksepp, in a spirit of consilience, views the time for integration as ripe when he states that:

> affective and cognitive neuroscientists are now in a position to link concrete neural entities to various abstract psychological and psychoanalytic concepts. Of course, we can anticipate that psychoanalytic theory and terminologies may need to be modified and fine-tuned when placed in the crucible of neuroscience. Likewise functional neuroscience may become more refined by being ground with the pestle of psychoanalytic thought.
>
> (Panksepp 1999)

This leaves a window for biology to be surprised by some of the findings from psychoanalysis. The challenge is for mainstream science to recognise that affective states probably reflect long-term causes of complex motivations and behaviour rather than simply being 'epiphenomenal flotsam'. The challenge for psychoanalysis, according to Panksepp, is to 'scientifically clarify the consistent patterns within the experiential side of life'.

The gap is diminishing and, at the very least, the work of integration is on the agenda. The problem now is to find ways in which integration can be approached in a manner that does not do a disservice to the integrity of a discipline. Psychoanalysis as both theory and practice is concerned about how we consciously and unconsciously experience, represent and shape our internal lives in ways that involve internal conflicts, compromises and adaptations. While psychoanalysis has generated hypotheses but has not been hypotheses testing the converse could be said of a scientific approach which does not address questions of subjective experiences, complex affects and motivations. The challenge for psychoanalysis is to continue to revise its metapsychological theories in the light of current knowledge from the neurosciences while holding on to its rich clinical tradition. For psychoanalysis integration is not a simple translation from one type of discourse into another. As Westen and Gabbard caution:

> an equally beguiling temptation . . . worth avoiding, is to imagine that rich clinical theories can be replaced by a description of neural pathways that mediate some of the processes described in those theories.
>
> (Western and Gabbard 2002: 59)

The movement or flow between biological and clinical approaches is by no means unproblematic. As yet there is no way of creating a seamless integration: clearly, clinical and biological approaches address and 'speak' about emotional life at entirely different levels. Nonetheless, it also seemed worth making some attempt to bring these related but distinct approaches together while acknowledging that a full integration is neither unproblematic nor wholly possible. This is reflected in the structure of the book and its division into two sections. Most chapters in the first section are focused principally on the neurosciences and attachment theory. For the sake of convenience the first section has been termed biological approaches. A more accurate term for some of the chapters in this section would be psycho-biological or neuropsychological. Attachment theory, with its roots in ethology, more accurately belongs to a sociobiological category. However, this more precise taxonomy seemed less immediately relevant than preserving a more general distinction between different frameworks: those within a broadly biological tradition and those within a clinical tradition.

Mental life and biological functioning (mind and brain) cannot be conflated, so there was a value in keeping the two parts of the book separate. Within individual chapters in each section both organic and psychic levels are addressed. The individual's psychic life – self and object representations, psychic structure, under-lying fantasy content and the manner in which meanings are ascribed – obviously emerges from organic foundations but cannot be reduced to them. They remain creations particular to an individual. Moving from the biological level to the psychic level is equally problematic. Individual chapters within each part retain a primarily clinical or attachment/biological focus while at the same time they convey elements of how the different levels can interpenetrate.

Biological approaches for the clinical mind

The term 'development' tends to suggest a unitary, one-directional process of unfolding. The simplicity of the term belies the intricacies of what are manifold, complex, intertwined processes. To get 'stuck' with just one account puts one in mind of the parable of the blind men and the elephant: the first feels the vast area of the torso, another the long trunk, the third a flapping ear, and each one in turn believes that his part represents the whole creature. There is of course not one definitive developmental 'story' but several, each account resting on its own discipline, offering its unique contribution and addressing questions of individual emotional growth at entirely different levels of explanation. Nonetheless there is a certain natural integration between certain psychodynamic assumptions and what we now know about the use-dependent nature of brain and emotional development. A psychodynamic view assumes that emotional development is a synergistic synthesis of many different interweaving strands. The internal landscape of the individual has been wrought from a dynamic interplay between exogenous and endogenous forces which are themselves subject to growth and change. In great part the inner affective landscape is wrought out of the experiences that have been offered and promoted or withheld by the early caregiving relationships. It is these which activate or stultify the psychic structures and processes giving rise to the individual's conscious and unconscious self and object representations.

The first part of the book takes a broadly psychobiological approach to the forces that drive and underpin development. In this first part, the ways in which development is influenced, optimised or compromised in the context of early relationships, is viewed from the 'outside', or through a second order of understanding. A biological approach which takes as a given that the brain is the substrate of mind (while not reducing mind to brain) and can demonstrate some of its mechanisms and workings offers us another way of thinking about and understanding what is occurring. A pervasive and almost superstitious fear is that thinking about ourselves in this explicitly organic way can invite a mechanistic view that squeezes out the mystery of being human, denigrating the importance of also understanding ourselves as creative generators and attributors of meaning to our experience. However, 'to understand the mechanics of the mind does not mean one has to approach the mind like a mechanic' (Westen and Gabbard 2002: 60). As Regina Pally points out in her introduction to *The Mind-Brain Relationship*:

> The idea that mental life is derived from biological events in neuronal circuits is the reigning doctrine of neuroscience, and therefore must be taken as a starting point for understanding the empirical research based on it. For those who criticise these attempts at integration as 'reductionist', I want to clarify that the emphasis here is that mental phenomena are derived from biological activity. There is no intention to equate the mental with the biological.
>
> (Pally 2000:2)

All the chapters in the first part spell out the ways in which development is conceived of as a dynamic process between the individual and the caregivers. What emerges unequivocally is a series of interdependencies whereby the organic and psychic foundations on which good enough development rest are contingent upon the milieu in which the individual is steeped. Development is no longer simplistically viewed as the product of nature and/or nurture. The very terms of the nature/nurture debate have been reconfigured. It is not a matter of biology/brain/genes on the one hand or environment/experience on the other, given that our brain development is now known to be experience dependent. The early emotional relationship qualitatively shapes the developing brain. We develop within the matrix of relationships in complex dynamic ways. Within child psychotherapy (as well as in other professions) it has long been axiomatic that early experiences have a formative impact on later development; 'the child is father to the man'. From a neuroscientific perspective we now know that the developing brain of the young infant undergoes critically sensitive periods for the development of circuits in the prefrontal cortex. Whether or not certain brain developments take place or not depends upon the nature of early caregiving experiences with significant consequences for emotional growth.

We are now in a better position to understand the specific ways in which this occurs. The organic strata for our sense of self and the ways in which it is carved out through early experiences are better understood. At a concrete level, current technologies such as EEG, scanners, imaging and mapping techniques have made it possible to literally get a 'picture' of brain development. A comparison of people reared in good enough conditions in contrast to those reared in early conditions where there is maltreatment, deprivation and trauma produces stark differences in early brain development.

Schore repeatedly stresses that the emotional relationship between child and caregiver is the environment for brain development and that brain development is an adaptation to that environment. Psychic life is rooted in embodied experience. He delineates the ways in which synaptic encoding occurs within the medium of the primary emotional relationship. As Seigal puts it:

> It is the human connections which shape the neural connections from which the mind emerges.
>
> (Seigal 1999)

Schore's chapter also outlines the psychobiological and emotional cost of protracted exposure and adaptation to an ongoing stressful caregiving relationship.

From a neuropsychoanalytic perspective Solms and Turnbull's chapter outlines a contemporary view of how memory systems develop and function and how memories are laid down. Here too, the brain is treated not simply as a biological organ, but also as a use-dependent organ.

Solms and Turnbull outline the developmental timetable for the effects of traumatic experiences on the memory systems. Included in this are the ways in which early relationship experiences are laid down in procedural memory as an encoding of the implicit 'rules' of relating. Their chapter alerts us to the complex ways in which the memory systems enable us to remember, store and 'forget' events. At the biological level it describes the ways in which these memory systems have different properties and substrates. It is a map of the mind where 'a given mental event can be declarative and explicit, declarative and implicit, procedural and explicit, or procedural and implicit' (Westen and Gabbard 2002: 80). Turnbull and Solms's chapter charts territory that is of direct relevance to clinicians. It reveals in more detail both the how and why of what lies within the conscious and unconscious domains. For clinicians it helps us make sense of experiences that are conscious and can be verbalised and those that are conveyed in other silent but powerful ways while remaining outside the patient's awareness. Furthermore, a neurodevelopmental timetable helps us understand why certain experiences can never be directly accessed. The links between affects and memory are also important. Psychic defence mechanisms, Westen and Gabbard (2002: 88) suggest, can be thought of as unconscious implicit procedures to self-regulate affects, particularly where there is a threat to self-esteem.

In all the chapters the need and reaching out for a relationship is taken as a fundamental motivation. What then arises out of that need is greatly dependent on the sort of relationship that is created between a caregiver and infant. The area of motivation is a complex one and lies outside the scope of this book, but each of the contributing authors suggests a more sophisticated view than one resting on a simple evolutionary reductionism which states we are equipped for attachment seeking for the purposes of survival. While this may be the *sine qua non* for brute survival, it is also clear that our emotional survival and well-being rest on far more than these imperatives alone. Research on affect, for instance (see Panksepp), suggests that we are also evolutionarily equipped to experience a variety of emotions including surprise, interest, fear, rage, joy, sadness, disgust, anguish and shame. Affects are understood to be part of a complex group of dynamic processes in the service of adaptation. A model of the mind as a multi-modular system with both discrete and cross-systemic features has both theoretical and clinical significance. To privilege one or two systems while demoting others is to ignore the current state of knowledge and to offer a narrow view of psychic organisation predicated on a limited number of possibilities. A biologically based broadening of understanding that ensues from such a multi-modal view can only enrich our understanding and offers a more wide-ranging account of underlying motivations and psychic organisation.

Two of the chapters in the first part are rooted in whole or part on attachment theory. Attachment theory robustly demonstrates, as Steele argues, the need for a secure base. It posits our drive for a warm, safe relationship as a fundamental motivator. Well-being, in the first instance, depends on the maintenance of a secure bond. Steele's chapter also outlines the different 'strategies' employed by the less or non-securely attached individuals when safety seeking is not unambiguously met by the caregiver. Attachment theory links the observable interrelational aspects between children and their caregivers and the transformation into an ensuing internal representational world. Our representational world will then colour how we approach and experience future relationships. As a counterbalance Steele also stresses how new relationship experiences, providing the representational world is not too rigidly 'set', can then make way for new representations.

Fonagy puts forward a different slant to attachment in a set of arguments that incorporate and give place to the twin developmental propellants of genetic heritage and attachment seeking. Genetic inheritance, Fonagy (*inter alia*) maintains, is mediated through the attachment relationship. As has been argued elsewhere (Rose 1997), to state that genes exert an important force on the course of development does not mean that the full developmental story has already been written within the DNA and then simply has to unfold in the manner of an inexorable Greek tragedy. Fonagy addresses the fallacious understanding that complex human behaviours can be attributed to single genes. Gene expression (genetic potential that may or may not be activated), Fonagy states, may also be partly dependent on environment. Our genetic developmental fate is also sculpted out of experiences, in a gene-environment interaction. The environment here is specifically defined as the attachment relationship. The formative feature that predicts the developmental outcome across an array of measures is, he argues, not attachment security per se but the features of the interpersonal environment which generate security. The central proposal is that we have an inbuilt biological evolutionarily advantageous potential for an interpersonal interpretive capacity: the capacity to 'read' and understand the mental states of others and our own. Where this capacity has been attenuated or severely distorted interpersonal difficulties arise. The therapeutic relationship can in part be understood as the medium within which mentalising and reflecting can begin to unfold.

In what ways can a biological perspective contribute to clinical understanding? The clinician may feel relief and pleasure that the perspectives offered in this first part expand our understanding of what has long been known clinically; that early relationships exert pivotal effects in shaping the course of emotional development.

The first part can shed light on clinically encountered phenomena. A therapeutic understanding of and approach to subjectivity is initially immersed in the immediacy of the experiential. An analytic way of reflecting enables a particular way of processing emotional communications. A biologically informed approach can also be the illuminating 'third space', a reality principle as it were, where we can step out of the intersubjective experiential realm and reflect on it through a second-order understanding. We are made aware of the ways in which development is circumscribed by biology. It describes and spells out for us what occurs at different stages of growth, what needs to occur for optimal growth and the effects of compromised growth. It offers the organic timetable which governs brain development and the biological substrate on which our emotional capacities rest.

A point of particular relevance for clinicians is the way in which a biological perspective can help anchor therapeutic hopes in the realm of the probable and possible. Broadly, the brain's wiring and communication system is not only extraordinarily complex but also constantly changing in response to the environment. As Steve Hyman in his chapter 'Susceptibility and second hits' writes:

> Scientists have been excited by recent findings on the degree to which neurons in many parts of the brain continue to undergo structural change not just through childhood and adolescence, as was once believed, but throughout life . . . new experiences, at whatever age, can cause the brain to physically alter its synapses – a characteristic known as plasticity. Indeed, those who compare the human brain to a digital computer do the brain a major disservice. No digital computer comes equipped with an army of Lilliputian technicians

who climb around and rewire the machine in response to every environmental stimulus.'

(Hyman 1999)

It is precisely because the brain is sculpted through experience and goes on being so (although not in the same way as in infancy) that a therapeutic relationship can elicit experiences and activate mental processes hitherto unknown, frozen or deeply buried. This theme is re-echoed in Steele's chapter, where it is argued that although attachment patterns show long-term resistance to change, alongside this are aspects of resilience which can be activated throughout life.

Alongside the plasticity is another biological reality. A neurological perspective on brain development also proposes that there are critical windows of time for certain developments to take place. A dark interpretation could be that if certain emotional experiences are withheld or curtailed during critical growth periods then there will be long-lasting consequences upon which therapy can have little impact. Perry strikes a moderate note when he suggests that:

the longer a child is in a deprived environment, the more severe the problems and the more resistant these emotional and behavioural problems are to intervention. Many will reach 'normal' landmarks in many areas if they receive love, attention and services, but I suspect they will not become what they could have.

(Perry, *Sunday Observer* 3 February 2002)

What does emerge unambiguously is a strong case for very early preventive interventions as illustrated by the work described in Baradon's chapter.

Somewhere, equidistant between a transcendental optimism and nihilistic pessimism, there is the possibility that while damage from the past cannot be undone, new relationship experiences in the present, such as those afforded by a therapeutic relationship, can still effect changes.

The clinical accounts in the second part cover the life span from infancy into adulthood to underscore the point that development is a process stretching into adulthood. Almost as if in illustration of Hyman's point, the Lilliputian technician within the brain's own circuitry seems to undergo metamorphosis into the therapist who is able to help establish or unfetter previously unsuspected psychic capacities. This is well illustrated in Woods' chapter about an adult from a deprived background who in the course of her analysis begins to experience herself and reflect on herself in a new way for the first time in her life. Ultimately, it may be, as Balbernie (2001) suggests, that we will discover not simply that there is a bidirectional impact in which later experiential changes impact on biology but more precisely how that effect is exerted.

The chapters in the first part suggest that, far from being reductionist, a biological approach can highlight the infinitely complex and subtle ways in which the mind's different systems work and interact. Yet, as a biological approach uncovers some workings it also contains within the heart of its explanations yet further questions and mysteries. Ultimately, we can only conclude that whatever psychodynamic model of the mind we hold it has to be one which is congruent with our present state of knowledge. Any psychoanalytic model of the mind which draws on a small range of organising principles (whether it be psychosexual theory, a limited number of positions or mental mechanisms) is unlikely to do justice to what is now known about the far greater complexity of how the human mind actually develops and works. To reiterate, the emerging picture is of the mind as a multi-modular system designed to manage a wide variety of biopsychological motivations. Some of the working of these systems – memory systems, attachment/safety seeking through to emotional regulatory systems – is outlined here.

Psychoanalytic and developmental approaches

A fuller understanding of emotional development necessitates incorporating the second order of understanding (the view from the 'outside') with a view of the individual as if from the inside, the world of subjective experience.

Psychoanalysis has concerned itself with individual subjectivity. It is the domain of experiences, the meanings given to them through conscious and unconscious mental processes and how these come to be represented in mental life. This is the area of interest to clinicians and, for many now, the area of intersubjectivity . . . the realm of what happens and is co-created between two people in a treatment relationship. The clinical accounts in the second part describe the many ways in which therapists work and reflect within the intersubjective realm and come to understand their patient's intrapsychic world. The transference and counter-transference relationship is the medium within which conscious and unconscious emotional processes between patient and therapist are communicated. It is within the therapeutic relationship that the individual's particular relationship history as laid down in procedural memory (see chapter by Solms and Turnbull) is activated and brought to life in a way that can be reflected on and elaborated. This is the very personal domain in which clinicians try to understand their patients.

Lying at the heart of the clinical approach is an interest in the world of the psyche, its internal object representations and relations. Inscribed within our representations are not simply traces of different dimensions of actual experiences but the transforming acts of feeling and mind (both conscious and unconscious) where meaning is ascribed and generated by the individual. The clinical accounts in the second part of the book implicitly ask questions such as: How does that person feel within their own skin? What does the subjective world feel like for a given individual? How has he made sense of his experiences? What psychic mechanisms help or hinder his capacity to function? What too of his wishes, pleasures, hopes, fears and sadness? What sort of internal figures inhabit his world and what feelings are embedded within and accrued around these figures? What too of his feelings about himself? The therapeutic relationship allows the gradual unfolding and discovery of the individual to his therapist and to himself. It is the experientially based developmental story as it reveals itself in the context of the transference and countertransference relationship. It is taken as given that this relationship is not reducible to one type of transference or countertransference but will encompass a wealth of experiences of self and self-and-other experiences. Also assumed is that while certain themes may predominate at one time or another, self-and-other experiences are not in a perpetual steady state. The very fluctuations are what alert the clinician to their patient's attempts to ward off painful affect in an attempt to regain psychic equilibrium.

The clinician seeking to understand his patient will bring certain explicit and implicit assumptions to bear on the nature of development and by extension his own role in the therapeutic process. The current flowing from the second-order explanations into the more directly clinically led focus on the individual's subjective world is apparent in several of the clinical accounts. The work of many of the authors who appear in the first part has already permeated clinical thinking in various ways. The ensuing clinical chapters reflect the manner in which clinicians have integrated some of the ideas from attachment theory and the biological sciences.

Anyone who works with children or is a parent is keenly aware that a maturational timetable is unfolding. In this very general sense we are all developmentalists. The child's or adult's possibilities, be they physical, emotional or cognitive, are broadly (while encompassing a wide range of individual variations) harnessed to age. As stated earlier, development is an ongoing process. Whereas there may be greater plasticity in the very early years, the treatment of an adult can also exert a great impact and promote the development of new psychic possibilities. For most psychodynamic clinicians the notion of emotional stages of development is a daily working tool. The clinician's own working models of roughly what to expect from children in different age groups is the implicit developmental framework which informs their understanding. Meaning in psychic life is in part ascribed in accordance with developmental level reached.

Historically, in many respects, classic Freudian theory is profoundly developmental. Freud's complementary series was later defined as involving the interplay between maturation and development. It outlines and emphasises the development of the ego and object relations. It charts the psychosexual stages negotiated in the process of growth. The oral, anal, phallic and genital stages posited by drive theory underlie and are contiguous with the notion of distinct phases: that of the under five, the Oedipal child, latency and adolescence. Each phase heralds the arrival of new psychic demands with concomitant changes in internal preoccupations, conflicts and fantasy life. These stages, broadly coincident with specific ages, are posited as a universal path although its overall shape and direction will differ between individuals.

Anna Freud's work, based on detailed observations of live children in clinical and natural settings, offered a longitudinal view. It is of crucial importance to stress that unlike the reconstructed child of adult analysis her conceptualisations arose in response to listening to and watching what children actually did and said and, of course, what they could not say but what might be expressed in their symptomatology. The inherent complexity of all the extrinsic and intrinsic forces that came together in the individual's child development found expression in Anna Freud's Profile and Developmental Lines. Etched in this view is a web of intricate interdependencies. Rose Edgcumbe's interesting paper, 'The history of Anna Freud's thinking on developmental disturbances' (1995), pinpoints how the developmental lines:

> attempted to describe in detail the myriad factors that have to interact successfully if a child is to complete its development satisfactorily in a whole range of areas – basic functions like eating and bodily care to much more sophisticated and complex areas of development such as the line from play to work, through to emotional and social independence.

The contributors offering clinical accounts work with an implicit notion of what is broadly age appropriate. The psychopathology of children can only be anchored in and evaluated against the background concept of age-appropriate developmental status in many areas of psychic growth (see R. Edgcumbe on Anna Freud).

Underpinning and running alongside the notion of age-appropriate development is a view that psychic development is not simply a purely linear progression. It is constituted of both progressive and regressive movements along a range of dimensions. Continuities and discontinuities, coupled with movement back and forth along the continuum, suggest that the pace and nature of development can vary enormously. In any given individual the balance between progressive and regressive forces will vary. Development could proceed unevenly with a child showing, for instance, good ego development but a restriction along the lines of object relationships. Another consideration is how far a child has active wishes to move forward and whether or not these wishes are supported by the parents or caregivers.

In the course of development new stages are reached, each one ushering in a new level of psychic organisation. Recent views of development suggest that good enough development entails the expansion of increasingly complex dynamic mental and emotional systems (Tyson 2002). In the clinical accounts all the authors have something of this developmental timetable in mind. The clinical accounts are divided according to age and each subsection also highlights the particular nature of a specific stage. Neil's chapter concerning a latency-aged boy poignantly shows how a physical condition necessitating medical interventions impinged on her patient Kieran's development. Kieran retained a pervasive fantasy life which, while used as a means of managing his experiences, also signalled his difficulties in moving into a more ordinary age-appropriate orientation and adaptation to others. The early medical interventions took place when he was 4 years old and were coincident with his entry into the Oedipal phase. It is therefore perhaps unsurprising that the Oedipal register in his fantasy life remained so prominent. This phase would have been highly traumatic for him and perhaps, as

Solms and Turnbull suggest, would mean that his experiences could not be engraved into memory in the ordinary way. In this sense Kieran's therapeutic treatment can in part be understood as his attempt to rework his traumatic experience in the presence of another who this time could help him bear the unbearable. This would in turn enable him to master and integrate that which had remained so disturbingly, highly affectively charged and saturated with terrifying meaning. Heuves' chapter on adolescence views individual cases in the light of the specific psychic tasks and conflicts during this period. Awareness of developmental issues also informs work with an adult. Thus, Zaphiriou Woods' understanding of the nature of the toddler phase is brought to bear on some of her adult patient's difficulties. In the transference she silently re-experiences the stubborn withholding of rage and her attempts to conceal this from herself and her analyst but which nonetheless find expression in her fantasy life.

Towards an integration

In this second part, reflecting themes in the first, there is a common understanding among the contributing clinicians that real relationships are the medium in which we initially develop and that our inner lives are carved through experience. At this level clinicians seek to understand how early relationship experiences shape the internal object world at the level of self and other representations. Intertwined with the belief that our attachment history reveals itself not only in our internal world but also in the manner in which we experience, manage and express our emotional lives is a more specifically psychoanalytic contribution. An internal representation is not a facsimile copy. The way in which we experience, represent and live out our internal life is transformed by and imbued with feelings and acts of mind such as fantasies and defences both conscious and unconscious. The more specific focus of the clinician is seeking to understand how individuals experience themselves and the important figures in their world and the way in which the patients create and attribute conscious and unconscious meaning as manifested in dreams, play, fantasies or stories, and brought to life in the therapeutic relationship itself. Subjective experience unfolding within the context of a treatment relationship is simultaneously a re-creation of the patient's internal world including his past and a living out of a new experience of the self and others in the present. At the risk of repetition it is important to stress that a psychoanalytic understanding of the internal representational world of figures (objects) is concerned with both the conscious and dynamically unconscious ways in which the mind creates and imbues experience of self and others with meaning and that these are permeated with a range of affects.

The contributions from attachment theory and the impact of the neurosciences have reverberated in the clinical accounts informing not only what the therapist observes but also the manner in which they cast their understanding of what is happening inter-psychically within the treatment relationship and intra-psychically within their patient's. Attachment theory gives us not only an observationally based description of the effects of insecure or disorganised attachment but also a way of understanding what happens within an individual when his attachment needs are thwarted. The neurosciences can now flesh out for us some of the physical correlates underlying some of these phenomena. Furthermore, as Schore's chapter illustrates, the neurosciences can help us understand the long-term impact on the individual when early stress responses are allowed to persist over protracted periods and the deleterious effects this subsequently has on the emotional regulatory system. How these features become organised within the inner representational world and come to manifest as clinical phenomena within treatment relationships is addressed in many of the accounts. The therapists describe the various ways in which their patients seem overwhelmed, freeze or panic. Ms A (see chapter by Woods), an adult, experiences going blank when feelings and thoughts seize up. From the attachment perspective these states can be understood as recapitulations of an earlier disorganised attachment. Schore's work suggests that such responses are the result of the failure of emotional regulatory mechanisms and the only self-protection left is to dissociate or shut down. This is vividly caught in Ms A's recollections of being literally immobilised and is represented in her fantasy of a shrouded baby. A more specifically psychoanalytic contribution, though, is to understand how these experiences come to be subjectively represented and expressed in the individual's psychic life. A psychoanalytic understanding is necessarily concerned with attachment status but also seeks to explore further the dynamically unconscious and conscious ways in which internal objects are imbued with affects and permeated with unconscious and conscious meaning.

   The attachment framework has for some time now been very influential and relevant to clinicians. As a theory it has offered a systematic way of understanding and measuring a primary, innate need. It lays emphasis on observable interactions that characterise the qualitative aspects of the *inter*-relationship between two people. As such it does not purport to be about *intra*-psychic life in its entirety. The need and search for establishing and maintaining a sense of psychic safety have long been recognised in psychoanalysis:

> Anxiety and other unpleasant affects arising from the outside as well as from the inside, are among the most powerful of behavioural motivators, as is the need to maintain an affective background of feelings of safety . . . this extension of the concept of motivation can allow a bridge to be made between psychoanalysis and attachment theory.
>
> (Sandler 1995)

The vicissitudes of what then occurs, whether attachment security needs are met or not, are in part what shapes our internal working models in relation to specific individuals. Representations are not only *schemas* but permeated with *contents* such as thoughts, conscious and unconscious wishes and feelings. It is the latter areas which are the more specific contributions from psychoanalysis. How does all this come together in the mind of a clinician?

Baradon's chapter shows clearly how a clinician's actual observations of mother–infant attachment behaviour are in part what enable her to focus on and infer the internal representations of the caregiver, which mediate her own attachment history and are reactivated in relation to her infant. In turn this will impact on how the infant will come to experience and represent her own sense of self and others. Baradon's psychodynamic understanding also allows her to pick up on not only the infant's attachment needs but also the more subtle feelings, fears and wishes with which the parent's internal working models are infused and which inform her attachment style. Her chapter also highlights the psychic and neuro-biological consequences for the child if attachment needs are repeatedly misunderstood or ignored. What is interesting is the way in which the therapist bridges and addresses both the infant/child and caregiver's states through picking up on the caregiver's internal representations and affective states. The clinical skill ultimately lies in the way in which all these different strands become threaded together in the mind of the clinician. In Baradon's chapter transference and countertransferential aspects remain the clinical tools but where the therapist situates herself rather differently. The transference and countertransference elements are processed in her mind and are then rerouted in the service of the caregiver/child relationship rather than in relation to the therapist. It is an intricate meshing process where the therapist has to hold the relationships between child and parent(s) in mind, leaving room for all the participants.

All the clinical accounts demonstrate the ways in which the therapist gradually comes to understand whether the child's (or the adult's) attachment relationships meet the basic conditions for offering safety. Where there are insufficient experiences of safe caregiving, intimacy becomes fraught with the dangers of whatever powerful feelings were stirred up earlier. The clinical chapters illustrate and elaborate on the ways in which, when this possibility for safe intimacy has been powerfully disrupted, another developmental course is set. Lack of safety is then repeated in the treatment relationship. In many instances what we witness is the child's or adult's need to recreate what they feel is safe simply because it is familiar. The devil you know is at least predictable and may be better than leaving room for the devil you don't know.

The chapter by Solms and Turnbull describes the mechanisms and developmental timetable for how these experiences are laid down in the different memory systems. They also address the conditions and the manner in which different types of memory are later re-experienced and/or retrieved or remain buried. Of particular interest to therapists is the way in which early trauma comes to organise aspects of memory in such a way that later triggers can evoke powerful feelings which are then no longer attached to the specific traumatic experience. The therapeutic relationship offers a later opportunity to integrate experiences in the context of a relationship where erstwhile there had been only overwhelming feelings of fear, terror, arousal and fragmentation. In the patient's subjective experience what remains are states of being with another which are unconsciously activated but lying outside the realm of what can be directly communicable. The patient repeatedly makes unconscious attempts to control the therapist by inviting or even overtly pressurising her into becoming the known and familiar figure. Paradoxically, alongside the familiar also lie powerful attendant feelings and fantasies often of an overwhelming or fearful nature.

In Ralph's chapter we read about Flora, a child whose young life has been marked by abuse followed by a series of disrupted attachments as she is removed from her parents to first one and then another set of foster parents. To even begin to trust another person is a task in itself. Her early experiences of emotional and sexual abuse meant that even when she was with her biological parents little safety was available. Attachment relationships gave rise to a central dynamic, to seduce or be seduced, giving rise to intolerable and disorganising levels of excitement and panic. Flora's early sexually abusive experiences meant that intimacy spelt overwhelming excitement and danger. During her treatment she re-enacted the repeated fear and anticipation of these states within both herself and her objects along with the impossibility of governing them. Through the use of countertransference her therapist not only absorbed but also metabolised the powerful transference re-enactments. Ralph describes how in the countertransference she was often left unable to think as Flora powerfully conveyed the full impact of her own feelings of being overwhelmed. Ralph, as the new developmental object, repeatedly disconfirmed Flora's previous experiences, thus providing a new experiential outcome for Flora of being with another. First experiencing then verbalising emotional experiences is the therapist's 'raid on the inarticulate'. The very process of verbalisation implies that there is someone who is engaged with trying to understand and make sense of the patient's experience. For many patients this is a new experience and in turn allows the possibility for a gradual internalization of a different self and object representation.

The therapist as a new developmental object

The therapist enters the child's developmental stream as both a transference figure and a new developmental object. Anne Hurry's chapter 'Psychoanalysis and developmental therapy' (1998) in the book of the same title captured and explored in depth the ways in which recent advances in our understanding of early child development, in particular the qualitative features of the early mother–infant bond as the template for future relationships, fashion our therapeutic understanding. Drawing on child developmental research, Hurry elaborates on the ways in which the psychoanalytic psychotherapeutic relationship effects change by the therapist, lending herself as both a transference figure and as a new developmental object, arguing cogently that there is no essential dichotomy between psychoanalysis and developmental help.

> Our understanding of developmental disturbances and of ways of treating them has been greatly enriched by findings from infant observational research, for the interactions that take place within the therapeutic developmental

> relationship are essentially similar to those that ordinarily take place between parents and the infant or child.
>
> (Hurry 1998:38)

A new developmental figure can also provide the scaffolding for a child or adult to establish emotional regulatory processes where previously there was dysregulation. Schore's chapter highlights the crucial importance of experience (maternal responses and mother–infant interactions) for the sensitive periods of brain development that underwrite the eventual capacity to self-regulate affect states. Also outlined are the adverse effects and consequences where maternal care provides less than average expectable conditions necessary for brain development and emotional growth. Consistently less than average expectable conditions leave the child hyper-vigilant in a persistent stress–response state. There is attendant cost to a whole range of other emotional capacities. One of Schore's important contributions has been to underscore the importance of affect regulation. The capacity to manage emotional states is understood as a neuropsychobiological developmental achievement arising out of the early mother–infant relationship. In this sense pathology can also be understood as maladaptive attempts at auto-regulation. Several of the authors in the clinical section pick up on the ways in which the therapist as a new developmental object offers the means within a relationship whereby powerful affects can be experienced, named and understood. Ultimately, the treatment relationship can offer the conditions for affective life to resurface and for regulatory processes to be reactivated.

Neil's chapter (particularly when describing Kieran's states of terror) is in part cast in the light of affect regulation, and integrated with more psychoanalytically based views. We see how previous ways of managing intolerable experiences gradually give way to more modulated responses. Kieran's fantasies represent, contain and regulate his immense anxieties about his brain tumour and the ensuing medical interventions. Kieran has to struggle to modulate his powerful feelings of helplessness and the arousal of a sense of sadism in himself and his objects. We read how he tries to arrive at a self-representation that will preserve his self-esteem and integrity as aims to feel powerful rather than humiliatingly helpless and frightened. His rich (even worryingly florid) fantasy life contains all these elements. Affects experienced in the presence of another are increasingly accessible for not only processing and naming but also incorporation into an awareness of self state and ultimately a degree of self-regulation. It is poignant to read how Kieran, once so terrified of needles, is finally able to bring down his anxiety to tolerable levels.

The counterpart to the patient's regulation within the treatment relationship includes the therapist's countertransference as the means for both allowing himself to experience affective movements into potentially dysregulatory states and the metabolising of disturbing experiences through his analytically reflective capacity. The clinical accounts illustrate the ways in which therapists come to know when their patients are overwhelmed through their own countertransferential responses. Elsewhere, Schore, drawing on a Kleinian perspective as a bridge, proposes an integrative model when he suggests that:

> projective identification is an early appearing yet enduring intrapsychic mech-
> anism that mediates the unconscious transmission of psychobiological states
> between the right brains of both members of an affect communicating dyad.
>
> (Schore 2002)

Other psychoanalytic bridges could also include a range of psychic processes such as externalisation and projection.

Attunement and the therapist as a present developmental object are key mutative therapeutic forces. There are links between the non-verbal aspects of communication within the therapeutic relationship and the rhythms and cadences of early mother–child interactions, 'the tiny building blocks of early communications' (Lanyado 2001) that shape our intimate experiences of being with another. These early interactions have also been of long-standing interest to child developmentalists such as Daniel Stern, whose research ratifies what has long been known clinically, that 'attunement' is a *sine qua non* for emotional health and growth. Lanyado reminds us that Winnicott's notions of 'holding' and Bion's concept of 'containment' come close to capturing a similar (but not identical) mental and emotional experience in the clinical relationship. Successive experiences of being with a safe enough/attuned or empathic figure in the context of a therapeutic relationship are precisely what makes possible the establishment of positive feelings but also allows the exploration of darker feelings about oneself and the other. Within the context of the transference–countertransference relationship such feelings can be brought into the realm of what can be thought about for perhaps the first time. The psychic scaffolding offered by the therapeutic relationship can enable the patient's intrapsychic capacities to come into being.

What, though, more precisely is meant by attunement? Synonyms that come to mind are usually words like mirroring, empathy, understanding or expressions such as being on the same wavelength. The emotional quality is of somehow recognising and resonating to a particular feeling. However, attunement may be a far more psychically complicated way of responding than simple mirroring. In brief, the adult's communication will contain the spectrum of feelings mentioned earlier, with the addition that the responder is not in the same place emotionally; that there is also a distance out of which a sense of difference between oneself and the other can be wrought. A playful or gentle teasing in the response would communicate that while the caregiver understands, names and gives reason for an infant's distress she herself is not overwhelmed (Lubbe 2000). Therapeutic attunement does not mean jettisoning an analytic reflective function. The part of attunement which in a sense requires the responder to remain both outside the child's experience while empathically 'within' it could be likened to the mutual coexistence of therapeutic empathy and the analytic reflective function.

In fact, as Steele points out, moments of misattunement occur more frequently than the converse. The important point is whether the mother–infant couple are able to keep re-engaging in the emotional 'dance'. Steele elaborates further when she emphasises the resilience and development-promoting aspects when a child needs to experience reaching out to find new ways of resecuring their emotional bonds. A similar point is made by Tronick (1998) when he describes the cycles of reaching out, perturbation, reparation and resumption of the relationship as an essential part of mother–infant interaction. It is in the breach that a further drive for fulfilment is created. In a re-echo of Winnicott, the good enough mother or developmental object is one who not only has to fail but also has to weather the emotional storms incurred through failure. For Leo, the elective mute child (chapter by Green), intrusive mothering was experienced as psychically over-whelming and disorganising, inducing anger and retaliatory rage. In these states he could only unconsciously aim to repeat and provoke similar experiences in the therapist's countertransference. It was partly as the result of several mutually experienced moments of intense frustration when Leo wished to communicate to his therapist and she could not understand him and she was no longer willing to second guess, that Leo began to relinquish his symptom.

The notion of the creative possibilities of a breach are also described by Stern *et al.* (1998). 'Now' moments, he suggests, are spontaneous occurrences in a relationship, which reveal each party to the other in an authentic way, resulting in a reconfiguration of each person's sense of the other. He emphasises how these moments arise out of periods of disequilibrium or destabilisation when something unexpected happens, revealing each person to the other in a new light. These are potentials within the transference/countertransference relationship. These 'now' moments provide not only a way of capturing the 'flow' of therapeutic change but situate the very nature of that change in the reconfiguration of the implicit relationship rather than exclusively in the verbalised aspects of the relationship.

Changes within this intersubjective domain effect alteration at the psychic level of self and object representations. Fonagy (1999) makes a useful distinction between mental representations and mental functions by comparing the former to music and the latter to the instrument that yields the tune. Change, he argues, is at the level of the altered mental representations (the tune) but these can only come into being when certain mental functions or capacities become available (the violin) . . . sometimes for the first time through the experience of being with some-one who is struggling to understand, make sense and give psychic meaning to one's experience. In just such a developmental move, Ms A (Woods) gradually becomes aware of the emotional experiences that resulted in curtailing the use of her mind and is subsequently able to 'reclaim' her capacities. She begins to explore other job possibilities. She begins to reality test in a different way. Her curiosity, 'allowed' and revived in the course of her analysis, enables her quite simply to wonder where the bus goes to next and to discover that it would in fact be closer to her analyst's house.

The crucial element seems to be that it is safe to discover the contents of one's own mind, feelings and thoughts and, by extension, to know another. The developmental corollary to the analyst's reflective function is the growth of the patient's discovery of his own reflective function. In all the clinical accounts we see these processes unfolding as the patients begin to reclaim their emotional and mental lives.

Biological and clinical approaches present us with different but complementary ways of approaching emotional development. Emotional life is the product of many internal and external forces. The psyche in its conscious and unconscious aspects is the world of mental and emotional capacities, representations and affects. While a more general developmental picture can be painted in the broad biological brushstrokes as outlined in the first part, every patient brings their own unique subjectively meaningful story as told in the second part. The clinical chapters illustrate the diverse ways in which a range of attenuated psychic capacities find new possibilities for growth within the therapeutic relationship. Bringing these approaches under the same roof may also mean that the house beneath is neither a neat bungalow, two-up, two-down nor a folly. The hope is that a 'structure' accommodating clinical and biological approaches enhances understanding.

References

Balbernie, R. (2001). 'Circuits and circumstances: the neurobiological consequences of early relationship experiences and how they shape later behaviour. *Journal of Child Psychotherapy 27* (3): 237–255.

Bion, W. R. (1962). *Learning from Experience*. London: Heinemann.

Bion, W. R. (1967). *Second Thoughts*. London: Heinemann.

Damasio, A. (1999). *The Feeling of What Happens: Body and Emotion in the Making of Consciousness*. New York: Harcourt Brace.

Edgcumbe, R. (1995). The history of Anna Freud's thinking on developmental disturbances. *Bulletin of the Anna Freud Centre 18*: 21–34.

Edgcumbe, R. (2000). *Anna Freud: A View of Development, Disturbance and Therapeutic Techniques*. London: Routledge.

Fonagy, P. (1999). The process of change and the change of processes: what can change in a 'good' analysis. www.psychematters.com/papers/fonagy.htm

Fonagy, P. and Target, M. (2000) Mentalisation and personality disorder in children: a current perspective from Anna Freud Centre. In Lubbe, T. (ed.), *The Borderline Psychotic Child*, 69–89. London: Routledge.

Fonagy, P., Gergely, G., Jurist, E. L. and Target, M. (2002). *Affect Regulation, Mentalisation, and the Development of the Self*. New York: Other Press.

Freud, A. (1980). *Normality and Pathology in Childhood*. London: Hogarth Press and the Institute of Psychoanalysis.

Freud, S. (1905). *Three Essays on the Theory of Sexuality*. S.E., 12.

Freud, S. (1911b). *Formulations on the Two Principles of Mental Functioning*. S.E., 12.

Freud, S. (1915c). *Instincts and their Vicissitudes*. S.E., 14

Freud, S. (1915e). *The Unconscious*. S.E., 14.

Freud, S. (1923b). *The Ego and the Id*. S.E., 19.

Freud, S. (1926). *Inhibitions, Symptoms and Anxiety*. S.E., 20.

Gardner, S. (1993). *Irrationality and the Philosophy of Psychoanalysis*. Cambridge, UK: Cambridge University Press.

Hurry, A (ed.) (1998). Psychoanalysis and developmental therapy. *Psychoanalysis and Developmental Therapy*. London: Karnac.

Hyman, S. (1999). Susceptibility and 'second hits'. In Conlan, R. (ed.), *States of Mind*, 9–28. Wiley: Chichester.

Jones, S. (1993). *The language of Genes*. New York: HarperCollins.

Klein, M. (1981). *The Writings of Melanie Klein,* Vol. 1, Money-Kyrle, R. E. (ed.). London: Hogarth Press.

Lanyado, M. (2001). The symbolism of the story of Lot and his wife: the function of the 'present relationship' and the non-interpretative aspects of the therapeutic relationship in facilitating change. *Journal of Child Psychotherapy 27* (1): 19–33.

Lubbe, T. (ed.) (2000). *The Borderline Psychotic Child.* London: Routledge.

Pally, R. (2000). *The Mind–Brain Relationship.* London: Karnac.

Panksepp, J. (1988). *Affective Neuroscience: The Foundations of Human and Animal Emotions.* Oxford: Oxford University Press.

Panksepp, J. (1999). Emotions as viewed by psychoanalysis and neuroscience: an exercise in consilience. *Neuro-Psychoanalysis 1* (1): 15–39.

Rose, S. (1997). *Lifelines: Biology, Freedom, Determinism.* London: Allen Lane/Penguin.

Sandler, J. (1995). On attachment to internal objects. Paper given at conference on Clinical Implications of Attachment: The Work of Mary Main, UCL, 1–2 July 1995.

Schore A. N. (2002). Clinical implications of a psychoneurobiological model of projective identification. In Alhanati, S. (ed.), *Primitive Mental States*, Vol. 2.1. London: Karnac.

Seigal, D. J. (1999) *The Developing Mind: Towards a Neurobiology of Interpersonal Experience*. New York: Guilford Press.

Solms, M. and Turnbull, O. (2002). *The Brain and the Inner World: An Introduction to the Neuroscience of Subjective Experience.* New York: Other Press.

Stern. D. (1985). *The Interpersonal World of the Infant: A View from Psychoanalysis and Developmental Psychology.* New York: Basic Books.

Stern, D. *et al.* (1998). The process of therapeutic change involving implicit knowledge: some implications of developmental observations for adult psychotherapy. *Infant Mental Health Journal 19* (3): 300–308.

Tronick, E. Z. (1998). Dyadically expanded states of consciousness and the process of therapeutic change. *Infant Mental Health Journal 19* (3): 290–299.

Tyson, P. and Tyson, R. (1990). *Psychoanalytic Theories of Development.* New Haven, CT: Yale University Press.

Tyson, P. (2002). *Journal of the American Psychoanlaytic Association 50.* (1): 32.

Westen, D. and Gabbard, O. G. (2002). Cognitive neuroscience, conflict and compromise. *Journal of the American Psychoanalytic Association 50* (1): 53–98.

Whittle, P. (1999). Experimental psychology and psychoanalysis: what we can learn from a century of misunderstanding. *Neuro-Psychoanalysis 1* (2): 233–245.

Part 1

Chapter 1

The human unconscious: the development of the right brain and its role in early emotional life

Allan N. Schore

Over the past few years a rapidly growing number of psychological and biological disciplines have been converging on the centrality of emotional processes in human development. Indeed these interdisciplinary studies are elucidating some of the fundamental psychobiological mechanisms that underlie the process of development itself. Contemporary developmental psychology, through attachment theory, is now focusing on the early ontogeny of adaptive socio-emotional functions in the first years of life. In current thinking development is 'transactional', and is represented as a continuing dialectic between the maturing organism and the changing environment. This dialectic is embedded in the infant–maternal relationship, and affect is what is transacted in these interactions. This very efficient system of emotional exchanges is entirely non-verbal, and it continues throughout life as the intuitively felt affective communications that occur within intimate relationships. Human development cannot be understood apart from this affect-transacting relationship. Indeed, it now appears that the development of the capacity to experience, communicate, and regulate emotions may be the key event of human infancy.

At the same time, developmental neurobiology is currently exploring the brain structures involved in the processing of socio-emotional information. Indeed, it is now held that 'the best description of development may come from a careful appreciation of the brain's own self-organizing operations' (Cicchetti and Tucker 1994: 544). There is widespread agreement that the brain is a self-organizing system, but there is perhaps less of an appreciation of the fact that 'the self-organization of the developing brain occurs in the context of a relationship with another self, another brain' (Schore 1996: 60). This relationship is between the infant's developing brain and the social environment, and is mediated by affective communications and psychobiological transactions. Indeed, neurobiology now refers to 'the social construction of the human brain'.

Recent models that integrate psychological and biological perspectives view the organization of brain systems as a product of interaction between (a) genetically coded programs for the formation of structures and connections among structures and (b) environmental influence (Fox *et al.* 1994). Influences from the social environment are imprinted into the biological structures that are maturing during the early brain growth spurt, and therefore have long-enduring psychological effects. The human brain growth spurt, which begins in the last trimester and is at least five-sixths postnatal, continues to about 18–24 months of age (Dobbing and Sands 1973).

Furthermore, DNA production in the cortex increases dramatically over the course of the first year and interactive experiences directly impact genetic systems that program brain growth (see Schore 1994; 2001a, b). We now know that the genetic specification of neuronal structure is not sufficient for an optimally functional nervous system – the changing social environment also powerfully affects the structure of the brain. This conception fits perfectly with Anna Freud's (1965) conception that psychic structure results from successive interactions between the infant's biologically and genetically determined maturational sequences on the one hand, and experiential and environmental influences on the other.

Thus, very current models hold that development represents an experiential shaping of genetic potential, and that genetically programmed 'innate' structural systems require particular forms of environmental input. According to Cicchetti and Tucker:

> The traditional assumption was that the environment determines only the psychological residuals of development, such as memories and habits, while brain anatomy matures on its fixed ontogenetic calendar. Environmental experience is now recognized to be critical to the differentiation of brain tissue itself. Nature's potential can be realized only as it is enabled by nurture
>
> (Cicchetti and Tucker 1994: 538).

Sander poses the central question, 'To what extent can the genetic potentials of an infant brain be augmented or optimized through the experiences and activities of the infant within its own particular caregiving environment?' (Sander 2000: 8). It has even been suggested that, 'within limits, during normal development a biologically different brain may be formed given the mutual influence of maturation of the infant's nervous system and the mothering repertory of the caregiver' (Connelly and Prechtl, 1981: 212). This critical 'mothering repertory' is expressed in her affect-regulating functions in a co-created attachment relationship with her infant. The development of the child's attachment outcome is thus a product of the child's genetically encoded biological (temperamental) predisposition *and* the particular caregiver affective-relational environment.

Indeed, neurobiology has now established that the infant brain 'is designed to be molded by the environment it encounters' (Thomas *et al.* 1997: 209). Recent psychoneurobiological conceptions of emotional development thus model how early socio-emotional experiences influence the maturation of biological structure, which in turn organizes more complex emergent function. This integrative perspective is expressed in the concept of the 'experience-dependent' maturation. The experiences required for the experience-dependent maturation of the systems that regulate brain organization in the first 2 years of life are specifically the social–emotional communications embedded in the affect-regulating attachment relationship between the infant and the mother.

The product of this growth-facilitating environment is the emergence of more complex affect-regulatory capacities and a shift from external to internal regulation. Thus, 'emotion is initially regulated by others, but over the course of early development it becomes increasingly self-regulated as a result of neurophysiological development' (Thompson 1990: 371). A large body of experimental and clinical work now indicates that the maturation of affects and the emergence of more complex communications represent essential goals of the first years of human life, and that the attainment of the essential adaptive capacity for the self-regulation of affect is a major developmental achievement.

Even more specifically, in a number of contributions I cite current findings in neuroscience which suggest that affect-regulating attachment experiences specifically influence the experience-dependent maturation of early developing regulatory systems of the right brain (Schore, 1994, 1996, 1997a, 1998d, 1999b, 1999d, 2000b, d, 2001a, b, c, d, e, in press a, b, c, d). These early interpersonal affective experiences have a critical effect on, as Bowlby (1969) speculated, the early organization of the limbic system, the brain areas specialized not only for the processing of emotion but also for the organization of new learning and the capacity to adapt to a rapidly changing environment (Mesulam 1998). The limbic system is expanded in the non-verbal right hemisphere, which is centrally involved in the processing of the physiological and cognitive components of emotions without conscious awareness and in emotional communications (Blonder *et al.* 1991; Spence *et al.* 1996; Wexler *et al.* 1992). It is now thought that "while the left hemisphere mediates most linguistic behaviors, the right hemisphere is important for broader aspects of communication' (Van Lancker and Cummings 1999: 95).

The right hemisphere is in a growth spurt in the first year-and-a-half (see Figure 1.1) and dominant for the first 3 (Chiron *et al.* 1997). A very recent MRI study of infants reports that the volume of the brain increases rapidly during the first 2 years, that normal adult appearance is seen at 2 years and all major fiber tracts can be identified by age 3, and that infants under 2 years show higher right than left hemispheric volumes (Matsuzawa *et al.*, 2001).

For the last 30 years psychoanalysis, the scientific study of the unconscious mind (Brenner 1980), has been interested in the unconscious processes mediated by the right brain, or as Ornstein (1997) calls it, 'the right mind' (Schore 1997c, 1999a, d). Recent experimental and clinical studies in developmental psychoanalysis and attachment theory have converged on the centrality of affective functions in the early years of human life, and this body of knowledge has been incorporated into clinical psychoanalysis, which is now 'anchored in its scientific base in developmental psychology and in the biology of attachment and affects' (Cooper 1987: 83). This advance has been paralleled in the 'decade of the brain' by studies in affective and social neuroscience which describe the right lateralized structural systems that mediate the non-conscious socio-emotional functions described by developmental psychoanalysts. Thus I have offered models of how

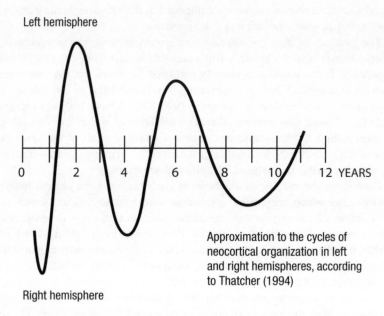

Left hemisphere

0   2   4   6   8   10   12 YEARS

Approximation to the cycles of
neocortical organization in left
and right hemispheres, according
to Thatcher (1994)

Right hemisphere

Figure 1.1 Hemispheric brain growth cycles continue asymmetrically throughout childhood, showing early growth spurt of the right hemisphere. (Adapted from Thatcher 1994)

attachment experiences influence right brain maturation (Schore 2000b) and linkages between the self-organization of the right brain and the neurobiology of emotional development (Schore 2000a).

In a number of works I am suggesting that the perspective of developmental neuropsychoanalysis, the study of the early structural development of the human unconscious mind, can make important contributions to a deeper understanding of how early attachment experiences indelibly impact the trajectory of emotional development over the course of the life span (Schore 1994, 1997b, c, 1999a, d, 2000a, b, 2001a, b, c, in press a, b, d). In a recent neuropsychoanalytic contribution I contend that the right brain acts as the neurobiological substrate of Freud's dynamic unconscious (Schore in press a). Knowledge of how the structural maturation of the right brain is directly influenced by the attachment relationship offers us a chance to more deeply understand not just the contents of the unconscious, but also its origin, dynamics, and structure.

The current paradigm shift from cognitive psychology to affective psychology, from purely mental states to states of mind/brain/body, and from the conscious verbal processing of the left verbal brain to the non-conscious processing of the right lateralized emotional brain, is particularly relevant to developmental psychoanalysis. It is now well-established that:

The infant's initial endowment in interaction with earliest maternal attunement leads to a basic core which contains directional trends for all later functioning.

(Weil 1985: 337)

Current psychoneurobiological models now indicate that the core of unconscious is a psychobiological affective core (Schore 1994).

Writing in the psychoanalytic literature Emde (1983) identifies the primordial central integrating structure of the nascent self to be the emerging 'affective core', a conception echoed in the neuroscience literature in Joseph's (1992) 'childlike central core' of the unconscious that is localized in the right brain and limbic system that maintains the self image and all associated emotions, cognitions, and memories that are formed during childhood. I would argue we currently know enough about the development of the right lateralized biological substrate of the human unconscious and that we now must go beyond purely psychological theories of emotional development.

And so in this chapter, I will present an overview of recent psychological studies of the social–emotional development of infants and neurobiological research on the maturation of the early developing right brain. I will focus on the structure–function relationships of an event in early infancy that is central to human emotional development: the organization, in the first year, of an attachment bond of interactively regulated affective communication between the primary caregiver and the infant. These experiences culminate, at the end of the second year, in the maturation of a regulatory system in the right hemisphere. I will then discuss the relationship between continued right brain maturation, more complex emotional development, and the expansion of the unconscious right mind over the life span.

Throughout, keep in mind Winnicott's dictum that the clinical encounter is always a mutual experience:

In order to use the mutual experience one must have in one's bones a theory of the emotional development of the child and the relationship of the child to the environmental factors.

(Winnicott 1971: 3)

But also consider Watt's recent injunction, in the journal *Neuropsychoanalysis*, regarding the nature of '(neuro) development':

In many ways, this is the great frontier in neuroscience where all of our theories will be subject to the most acid of acid tests. And many of them I suspect will be found wanting . . . Clearly, affective processes, and specifically the vicissitudes of attachment, are primary drivers in neural development (the very milieu in which development takes place, within which the system cannot develop).

(Watt 2000: 191)

Attachment processes as dyadic emotional communications

From birth onwards, the infant mobilizes its expanding coping capacities to interact with the social environment. In the earliest proto-attachment experiences, the infant uses its maturing motor and developing sensory capacities, especially smell, taste, and touch. But by the end of the second month there is a dramatic progression of its social and emotional capacities. Functional magnetic resonance imaging studies now demonstrate that a milestone for normal development of the infant brain occurs at about 8 weeks (Yamada *et al.* 2000). At this point a rapid metabolic change occurs in the primary visual cortex of infants, reflecting the onset of a critical period in which synaptic connections in the occipital cortex are modified by visual experience. The mother's face is the primary source of visuo-affective information for the developing infant.

It is at this very time that face-to-face interactions, occurring within the primordial experiences of human play, first appear. Such interactions:

> emerging at approximately 2 months of age, are highly arousing, affect-laden, short interpersonal events that expose infants to high levels of cognitive and social information. To regulate the high positive arousal, mothers and infants . . . synchronize the intensity of their affective behavior within lags of split seconds.
>
> (Feldman *et al* 1999: 223)

These dyadic experiences of 'affect synchrony' occur in the first expression of positively charged social play, what Trevarthen (1993) terms 'primary inter-subjectivity', and at this time they are patterned by an infant-leads-mother-follows sequence. This highly organized dialogue of visual and auditory signals is transacted within milliseconds, and is composed of cyclic oscillations between states of attention and inattention in each partner's play. In this communicational matrix both synchronously match states and then simultaneously adjust their social attention, stimulation, and accelerating arousal to each other's responses (see Figure 1.2).

Within episodes of affect synchrony parents engage in intuitive, non-conscious, facial, vocal, and gestural preverbal communications:

> [T]hese experiences provide young infants with a large amount of episodes – often around 20 per minute during parent–infant interactions – in which parents make themselves contingent, easily predictable, and manipulatable by the infant.
>
> (Papousek *et al.* 1991: 110)

In such synchronized contexts of 'mutually attuned selective cueing', the infant learns to send specific social cues to which the mother has responded, thereby

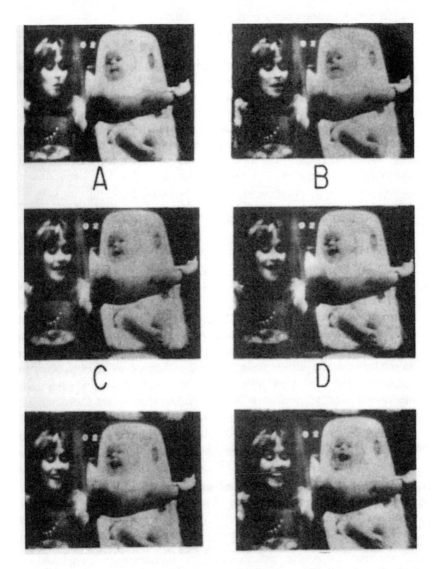

Figure 1.2 Affect synchrony: mother and infant are seated face to face, looking at each other. At point A, mother shows a 'kiss-face', and infant's lips are partially drawn in, resulting in a tight, sober-faced expression. At point B, mother's mouth has widened into a slightly positive expression, and infant's face has relaxed with a hint of widening in the mouth, also a slightly positive expression. At point C, both mother and infant show a slight smile, further widened at point D. At point E, the infant breaks into a 'full gape smile'. At point F, the infant has shifted the orientation of his head further to his left, and upward, which heightens the evocativeness of the gape smile. Total time under 3 seconds. (From Beebe and Lachmann 1988). Copyright © 1988 The Analytic Press. Reprinted with permission

reflecting 'an anticipatory sense of response of the other to the self, concomitant with an accommodation of the self to the other' (Bergman, 1999: 96). These are critical events, because they represent a fundamental opportunity to practice the interpersonal coordination of biological rhythms. According to Lester, Hoffman, and Brazelton 'synchrony develops as a consequence of each partner's learning the rhythmic structure of the other and modifying his or her behavior to fit that structure' (Lester *et al.* 1985: 24).

Since the mother's psychobiological attunements to the dynamic changes of the infant's affective state are expressed in spontaneous non-verbal behaviors, the moment-to-moment expressions of her interactive regulatory functions occur at levels beneath awareness. This microregulation continues, as soon after the 'heightened affective moment' of an intensely joyful full gape smile the baby will gaze avert in order to regulate the potentially disorganizing effect of this intensifying emotion (see Figure 1.3). In order to maintain the positive emotion the intuitive mother takes her cue and backs off to reduce her stimulation. The period immediately after a 'moment of meeting', when both partners disengage (box D), provides 'open space', in which both can be together, yet alone in the presence of the other. This allows for the organization of the infant's nascent capacity for auto-regulation.

In this mutually regulated process of affect synchrony the more the contingently responsive mother tunes her activity level to the infant during periods of social engagement, the more she allows him to recover quietly in periods of disengagement, and the more she attends to the child's re-initiating cues for re-engagement, the more synchronized their interaction. The synchronizing caregiver thus facilitates the infant's information processing by adjusting the mode, amount, variability, and timing of the onset and offset of stimulation to the infant's actual integrative capacities. These mutually attuned synchronized interactions are fundamental to the healthy emotional development of the infant.

Intersubjective resonance, affect synchrony, and interactive repair

Furthermore, in the visual, auditory, and gestural emotional communications embedded within synchronized face-to-face transactions both members of the dyad experience a state transition as they move together from low arousal to a heightened energetic state of high arousal, a shift from quiet alertness into an intensely positive affective state. What dyadic psychobiological mechanism could account for these 'mutual regulatory systems of arousal'? Sander (1991) describes the context of a specifically fitted interaction between the infant and mother as a *resonance* between two systems attuned to each other by corresponding properties. In describing the unique nature of an emotionally communicating mother–infant dyad, Trevarthen also describes a resonance process:

Corresponding generative parameters in . . . two subjects enable them to

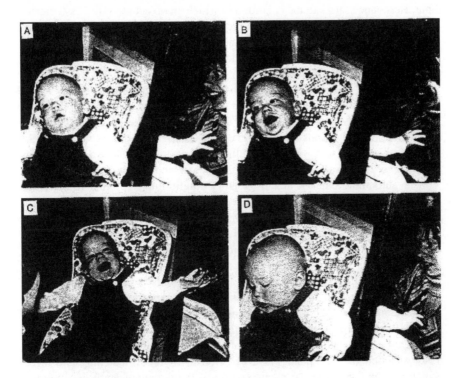

Figure 1.3 Sequence of attuned interaction: (A) the infant looks at the mother and the mother shows an exaggerated facial expression; (B) the infant and the mother smile; (C) the infant laughs, the mother relaxes her smile; and (D) the infant looks away, the mother ceases her smile and watches her infant. (From Field and Fogel 1982) Lawrence Erlbaum Associates Inc.

resonate with or reflect on one another as minds in expressive bodies. This action pattern can become 'entrained', and their experiences can be brought into register and imitated. These are the features that make possible the kind of affectionate empathic communication that occurs, for instance, between young infants and their mothers.

(Trevarthen 1993: 126).

In physics, a property of resonance is sympathetic vibration, which is the tendency of one resonance system to enlarge and augment through matching the resonance frequency pattern of another resonance system. Resonances often have chaos associated with them, and thus they are characterized by non-linear dynamical factors: relatively small input amplitudes engender a response with a surprisingly large output amplitude (Schore 1997a, 2000c). This 'small input' represents extremely brief but biologically significant facial and bodily signals transmitted within the dyad, and the 'large output' responses are intense emotional states in both. Resonance refers to the condition in which an object or system is subjected to an oscillating signal having a frequency at or close to that of a natural vibration of the object or system and the resulting *amplification* of the natural vibration. According to Tomkins (1984), affect acts as an 'analog amplifier' that extends the duration of whatever activates it.

In other words, an amplification of positively valenced states especially occurs in moments of affect synchrony when *external sensory stimulation frequency coincides with the organism's genetically encoded endogenous rhythms.* The behavioral manifestations of these endogenous rhythms are expressed in the infant's quiet alert state, one in which the eyes are open and have a 'bright shiny appearance'. This state is one of maximal interest, and reflects an internal condition of autonomic balance and 'regulatory equilibrium'. In order to act as an amplifier of the infant's state, the caregiver must first match the infant's rhythmic expressions of this state, what Stern (1983) describes as moment-to-moment state sharing, feeling the same as the other, and then dynamically engage in state complementing, responding in one's unique way to stimuli coming from the other.

In light of the observation that these resonant interactions are patterned by an infant-leads-mother-follows sequence, recall Winnicott's (1971) description of the infant's expression of a 'spontaneous gesture', a somato-psychic expression of the burgeoning 'true self', and the attuned mother's 'giving back to the baby the baby's own self'. But the *Oxford Dictionary* also defines resonance as a shared feeling or sense. The transfer of emotional information is thus intensified in resonant contexts. The phenomena of resonant rhythmic matching and affect synchrony thus underlie the maximization of the communication of emotional states within an intimate dyad, and represents the psychobiological underpinning of empathy.

In other words, when an attuned dyad co-creates a resonant context within an attachment transaction, the behavioral manifestation of each partner's internal state is monitored by the other, and this results in the coupling between the output of one partner's loop and the input of the other's to form a larger feedback configuration and an amplification of the positive state in both. Infant researchers refer to the delight the infant displays in reaction to the augmenting effects of his mother's playful, empathically attuned behavior, her mulitmodal sensory amplification and resonance with the child's feelings. Stern (1985) describes a particular maternal social behavior which can 'blast the infant into the next orbit of positive excitation', and generate 'vitality affects'.

In order to enter into this communication, the crescendos and decrescendos of the mother's affective state must be in resonance with similar crescendos and decrescendos of the infant's internal states of arousal. In these synchronized attachment transactions the dyad is co-creating 'mutual regulatory systems of arousal'. Since arousal levels are known to be associated with changes in metabolic energy the emotion-regulating caregiver is modulating the child's energetic state. It is well established that energy (state) shifts are the most basic and fundamental feature of emotion and that when a system is attuned at the 'resonant' frequency energy transfer is maximum and the system becomes synchronized (Schore, 1997a, 2000c). Thus such energy-infused heightened affective moments allow for a sense of vitalization, and thereby increased complexity and coherence of organization within the infant.

In this system of non-verbal emotional communication the infant and mother co-create a context which allows for the outward expression of internal affective states in infants. In order to optimize this regulatory context, the mother must access her reflective function to monitor her own internal signals and differentiate her own affective state, as well as modulating non-optimal high levels of stimulation which would induce supra-heightened levels of arousal in the infant. The burgeoning capacity of the infant to experience increasing levels of accelerating, rewarding affects is thus at this stage amplified and externally regulated by the psychobiologically attuned mother, and depends upon her capacity to engage in an interactive emotion-communicating mechanism that generates these in herself and her child.

But we know that the primary caregiver is not always attuned: developmental research shows frequent moments of misattunement in the dyad – ruptures of the attachment bond. Although short-term dysregulations are not problematic, prolonged negative states are toxic for infants, and although they possess some capacity to modulate low-intensity negative affect states, these states continue to escalate in intensity, frequency, and duration. How long the child remains in states of intense negative affect is an important factor in the etiology of a predisposition to psychopathology. Active parental participation in state regulation is critical to enabling the child to shift from the negative affective states of hyper-aroused protest or hypo-aroused despair to a re-established state of positive affect. Again, the key to this is the caregiver's capacity to monitor and regulate her own affect, especially negative affect.

In this essential regulatory pattern of 'disruption and repair' (Beebe and Lachmann 1994) the 'good-enough' caregiver who induces a stress response in her infant through a misattunement reinvokes in a timely fashion her psychobiologically attuned regulation of the infant's negative affect state that she has triggered. The reattuning, comforting mother and infant thus dyadically negotiate a stressful state transition of affect, cognition, and behavior. This recovery mechanism underlies the phenomenon of 'interactive repair', in which participation of the caregiver is responsible for the reparation of dyadic misattunements (Schore 1994, 1996). If attachment is the regulation of interactive synchrony, stress (dysregulation) is defined as an asynchrony in an interactional sequence, and a period of synchrony following this allows for stress recovery: re-regulation. It is now thought that the process of re-experiencing positive affect following negative experience is critical to the child's learning that negativity can be tolerated and endured and that infant resilience is best characterized as the capacity of the child and the parent for transition from positive to negative and back to positive affect. Resilience in the face of stress is an ultimate indicator of attachment capacity.

Over the course of the first year the arousal regulation of positive affective states in interactive play and negative states in interactive repair underlies the formation of an attachment bond between the infant and primary caregiver. An essential attachment function is to promote the synchrony or regulation of biological and behavioral systems on an organismic level, and attachment can be defined as the regulation of biological synchronicity between organisms (Wang 1997; Schore 2000a, b). To put this another way, attachment is the dyadic (interactive) regulation of emotion (Sroufe 1996). The baby becomes attached to the psychobiologically attuned regulating primary caregiver who not only minimizes negative affect but also maximizes opportunities for positive affect.

These data underscore an essential principle overlooked by many emotion theorists: affect regulation is not just the dampening of negative emotion. It also involves an amplification, an intensification of positive emotion, a condition necessary for more complex self-organization. Attachment is more than the re-establishment of security after a dysregulating experience and a stressful negative state: it is also the interactive amplification of positive affects, as in play states. Regulated affective communications with a familiar, predictable primary caregiver create not only a sense of safety, but also a positively charged curiosity that fuels the burgeoning self's exploration of novel socio-emotional and physical environments.

Attachment dynamics and the developmental neurobiology of the right brain

Research now suggests that 'learning how to communicate represents perhaps the most important developmental process to take place during infancy' (Papousek and Papousek, 1997: 42). But how do these emotional communications impact the developing brain? Trevarthen's (1993) work on maternal–infant protoconversations bears directly on this problem. Coordinated with eye-to-eye messages are auditory vocalizations, tactile stimuli, and body gestures that induce the positive affects of excitement and pleasure within the dyad. But Trevarthen also focuses on internal structure–function events (see Figure 1.4), stating that "the intrinsic regulators of human brain growth in a child are specifically adapted to be coupled, by emotional communication, to the regulators of adult brains" (Trevarthen 1990: 357). Furthermore, the resonance of the dyad ultimately permits the intercoordination of positive affective brain states.

Trevarthen's description of 'emotional communication' that triggers instant emotional effects is paralleled by Buck's characterization of 'spontaneous emotional communication':

> Spontaneous communication employs species-specific expressive displays in the sender that, given attention, activate emotional preattunements and are directly perceived by the receiver . . . The 'meaning' of the display is known directly by the receiver . . . This spontaneous emotional communication constitutes a *conversation between limbic systems* . . . It is a biologically-based

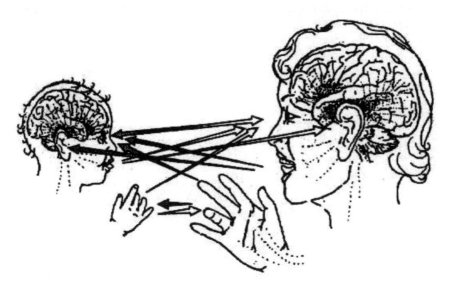

Figure 1.4 Channels of face-to-face communication in protoconversation. Proto-conversation is mediated by eye-to-eye orientations, vocalizations, hand gestures, and movements of the arms and head, all acting in coordination to express interpersonal awareness and emotions. (Adapted from Trevarthen 1993)

> communication system that involves individual organisms *directly* with one another: *the individuals in spontaneous communication constitute literally a biological unit . . .* The direct involvement with the other intrinsic to spontaneous communication represents an *attachment* that may satisfy deeply emotional social motives.
>
> (Buck 1994: 266, my italics)

Buck localizes this biologically based spontaneous emotional communication system to the right hemisphere, in accord with other research that indicates a right lateralization of spontaneous gestures and emotional communication.

These emotionally charged, psychobiologically attuned face-to-face inter-actions occur in the context of mother–infant play and interactive repair, and they increase over the second and third quarters of the first year, a time of limbic maturation. The learning mechanism of attachment, imprinting, is defined as synchrony between sequential infant–maternal stimuli and behavior. These events are critical to the experience-dependent maturation of the limbic system, the brain circuits that process socio-emotional information. In recent work I offer evidence to show that a progression of right lateralized limbic structures are imprinted in synchronized emotional transactions over the course of the first 2 years. In the first quarter of the first year socio-emotional experiences impact the experience-dependent maturation of the right amygdala; second and third quarters, the right anterior cingulate; and last quarter through the second half of the second year, the right orbitofrontal areas (Schore 2001a).

In light of the principles that the right hemisphere is in a growth spurt at this time, that it, more than the later maturing left, is densely connected into the limbic system, and that it is centrally involved in processing faces, right lateralized limbic structures are specifically impacted by an array of more and more complex attachment experiences. Thus:

> The emotional experience of the infant develops through the sounds, images, and pictures that constitute much of an infant's early learning experience, and are disproportionately stored or processed in the right hemisphere during the formative stages of brain ontogeny.
>
> (Semrud-Clikeman and Hynd 1990: 198)

Using EEG and neuroimaging data, Ryan and his colleagues conclude that 'the positive emotional exchange resulting from autonomy-supportive parenting involves participation of right hemispheric cortical and subcortical systems that participate in global, tonic emotional modulation' (Ryan et al. 1997: 719).

Furthermore, Tronick et al. (1998) are now describing how microregulatory social–emotional processes of communication generate expanded intersubjective states of consciousness in the infant–mother dyad. In such there is 'a mutual mapping of (some of) the elements of each interactant's state of consciousness into each of their brains' (Tronick and Weinberg 1997: 75). They argue that the infant's self-organizing system, when coupled with the mother's, allows for a brain organization which can be expanded into more coherent and complex states of consciousness. I suggest that Tronick is describing an expansion of what the neuroscientist Edelman (1989) calls primary consciousness, which relates visceral and emotional information pertaining to the biological self, to stored information processing pertaining to outside reality. Edelman lateralizes primary consciousness to the right brain.

These dyadically synchronized affectively charged transactions elicit high levels of metabolic energy for the tuning of developing right brain circuits involved in processing socio-emotional information. It has been suggested that 'mothers invest extra energy in their young to promote larger brains' (Gibbons 1998: 1346). In terms of self-organization theory, the mutual entrainment of their right brains during moments of affect synchrony triggers an amplified energy flow which allows for a coherence of organization that sustains more complex states within the infant's right brain.

But evidence is now appearing that supports the idea that the organization of the mother's brain is also being influenced by attachment transactions. A neurobiological study of early mammalian mother–infant interactions reports increased dendritic growth in the mother's brain (Kinsley et al. 1999). The authors conclude that events in late pregnancy and the early postpartum period:

> may literally reshape the [mother's] brain, fashioning a more complex organ that can accommodate an increasingly demanding environment . . . To

consider the relationship of a mother caring for her young as unidirectional disregards the potentially rich set of sensory cues in the opposite direction that can enrich the mother's environment. By providing such stimuli, [infants] may ensure both their own and their mother's development and survival.

(Kinsley *et al*. 1999: 137)

The right brain and the psychobiology of attachment

The matter of survival is an essential goal of the infant's developing adaptive capacities, and so a focus on emotional development brings us back to the level of a biological organism, the domain of the body. Basic survival functions involve the regulation of right brain brain/mind/body states. In an important article Lieberman (1996) writes that current models of development are almost exclusively focusing on cognition. She states, 'The baby's body, with its pleasures and struggles, has been largely missing from this picture' (Lieberman 1996: 289). Once again, information about the development and dynamic operations of the right hemisphere is critical to a deeper understanding of the evolution of the organismic substrate of the corporeal/social/emotional self (Schore 1994; Devinsky 2000).

This hemisphere is pre-eminently concerned with the analysis of direct information received from the body. Right hemispheric functions are centrally involved in allowing the individual to emotionally understand and react to bodily stimuli, to identify a corporeal image of self and its relation to the environment, and to distinguish self from non-self (Devinsky 2000). These developmental advances are specifically influenced by the attachment relationship. Thus emotion-regulating attachment transactions, in addition to producing neurobiological consequences, are also generating important events in the infant's bodily state, that is, at the psychobiological level (Henry 1993; Schore 1994). Winnicott (1986: 258) proposed that 'The main thing is a communication between the baby and mother in terms of the anatomy and physiology of live bodies.'

These body-to-body communications also involve right brain to right brain interactions. Indeed, most human females cradle their infants on the left side of the body (controlled by the right hemisphere). This tendency is well developed in women but not in men, is independent of handedness, and is widespread in all cultures (Manning *et al*. 1997). It has been suggested that this left-cradling tendency 'facilitates the flow of affective information from the infant via the left ear and eye to the center for emotional decoding, that is, the right hemisphere of the mother' (Manning *et al*. 1997: 327). As the neurologist Damasio (1994) indicates, this hemisphere contains the most comprehensive and integrated map of the body state available to the brain.

Over 25 years ago Basch speculated that 'the language of mother and infant consist of signals produced by the autonomic, involuntary nervous system in both parties' (Basch 1976: 766). This conception is consonant with a large body of developmental psychobiological research that describes the attachment relationship in terms of the mutual regulation of vital endocrine, autonomic, and central nervous systems of both mother and infant by elements of their interaction with each other. Hofer (1990) emphasizes the importance of 'hidden' regulatory processes by which the caregiver's more mature and differentiated nervous system regulates the infant's 'open', immature, internal homeostatic systems. Buck's (1994) neuropsychological description of attachment as a conversation between limbic systems is thus isomorphic to Hofer's psychobiological character-ization of the adult's and infant's individual homeostatic systems that are linked together in a superordinate organization.

Importantly, Hofer describes the latter relational context as a mutually regulat-ing 'symbiotic' state. These matters bear upon the concept of symbiosis, which has had a controversial history in recent developmental psychoanalytic writings. This debate centers around Mahler et al.'s (1975) reference to a normal symbiotic phase during which the infant 'behaves and functions as though he and his mother were a single omnipotent system – a dual unity within one common boundary' Mahler et al. 1975: 8). Although the symbiotic infant is dimly aware that the mother is the source of his pleasurable experiences, he is in a 'state of undifferentiation, a state of fusion with the mother, in which the "I" is not differentiated from the "not-I"' (p. 9).

This latter definition of symbiosis departs from the classical biological concept and is unique to psychoanalytic metapsychology. Current evidence may not directly support any inferences about the limits of the infant's awareness, nor about an entire stage that describes the infant's behavior only with this characteri-zation. However, moments of face-to-face affective synchrony do begin at 2–3 months, the advent of Mahler's symbiotic phase, they do generate high levels of positive arousal, and such mutually attuned sequences can be portrayed as what Mahler et al. (1975) call instances of 'optimal mutual cueing'. Indeed, in her earliest writings Mahler (1968) did emphasize the affective nature of these inter-actions, describing 'the emotional rapport of the mother's nurturant care, a kind of social symbiosis'.

But even more importantly, Hofer's work as well as recent brain research calls for a return of the definition of symbiosis to its biological origins. The *Oxford Dictionary* offers the derivation from the Greek, 'living together', and defines symbiosis as an interaction between two dissimilar organisms living in close physical association, especially *one in which each benefits the other* (my italics). An even more basic definition from biological chemistry suggests that 'symbiosis is an association between different organisms that leads to a reciprocal enhance-ment of their ability to survive' (Lee *et al.* 1997: 591). Recall Buck's (1994) description of an emotionally communicating dyad as 'literally a biological unit', a conception that echoes Polan and Hofer's (1999) description of the dyad as a self-organizing regulatory system composed of mother and infant as a unit. These conceptions suggest that instances of positively charged, psychobiologically attuned attachment transactions of affect synchrony are an example of biological symbiosis.

The construct of symbiosis is thus reflected in the conception of attachment as the interactive regulation of biological synchronicity between organisms. In discussing the central role of facial signalling in attachment, Cole asserts, 'it is through the sharing of facial expressions that mother and child become as one. It is crucial, in a more Darwinian biological context, for the infant to bond with her mother to ensure her own survival' (Cole 1998: 11). Recall Bowlby's (1969) assertion that the development of attachment has consequences that are vital to survival and that the infant's capacity to cope with stress is correlated with certain maternal behaviors. The early developing right hemisphere is dominant for both attachment and the control of vital functions that support survival and enable the organism to cope with stressors (Wittling and Schweiger 1993; Schore 1994, 2001a, b, e, 2002c).

Organization of a regulatory system in the right brain

What are the unique functional capacities of the socio-emotional right hemisphere? Neuroimaging studies show that the right hemisphere is specialized for processing faces that are familiar to an individual (Nakamura *et al.* 2000) and is faster than the left in performing valence-dependent, automatic, pre-attentive appraisals of emotional facial expressions (Pizzagalli *et al.* 1999). These are matched at levels beneath awareness against a right cortical 'non-verbal affect lexicon', a vocabulary for non-verbal affective signals such as facial expressions, prosody (emotional tone of the voice), and gestures (Borod *et al.* 1998; Bowers *et al.* 1993; Dimberg *et al.* 2000; George *et al.* 1996). In line with Bowlby's (1969) speculation that the mother–infant bond occurs within a context of 'facial expression, posture, tone of voice', an individual's unique affect lexicon is constructed in attachment experiences. But in addition, somatosensory processing and the representation of visceral and somatic states, and body sense are under primary control of the 'non-dominant' hemisphere (Coghill *et al.* 2001; Damasio 1994; Devinsky 2000).

Indeed, the right cortical hemisphere (see Figure 1.5), more so than the left, contains extensive reciprocal connections with both the limbic system that rapidly processes emotional information and the autonomic nervous system that generates the somatic components of emotional states. This unique anatomy is responsible for its dominance for the processing and expression of emotional information at levels beneath conscious awareness. This relaying of sensory information into the limbic system allows incoming social information to be associated with positively or negatively valenced motivational and emotional states, in accord, as Freud speculated, with a calibration of degrees of pleasure–unpleasure (see Schore 2001a, 2002a).

Emotions are now conceptualized as action dispositions that are governed by two opponent motivational systems: an appetitive system that promotes approach behaviors and an aversive system that promotes avoidance behaviors. Defense responses increase when the aversive system is primed, and decrease when the appetitive system is primed, and the activation of both is modulated by arousal

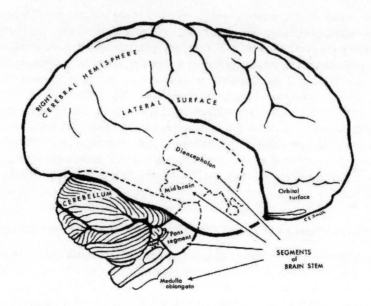

Figure 1.5 Relationships of brain stem structures to the orbital surface of the right hemisphere. (From Smith, 1981)

level (Lang 1995). In accord with this principle, in recent writings I suggest that the processing of social, emotional, and bodily information by the dual corticolimbic–autonomic circuits of the right brain along a basic appetitive–aversive dimension is ultimately expressed in a behavioral predisposition involving engagement, approach and attachment, or a set disposing disengagement, avoidance, escape, and defense (Schore 1994, 1996, 2001a).

Furthermore, authors now refer to a 'rostral limbic system', a hierarchical sequence of interconnected limbic areas in orbitofrontal, insular cortex, anterior cingulate, and amygdala (see Schore 2001a). These three-tiered, right vertically organized limbic circuits allow for cortically processed information concerning the external environment (such as visual and auditory stimuli emanating from the emotional face of an attachment object) to be integrated with subcortically processed information regarding the internal visceral environment (such as concurrent changes in the bodily self state). When the higher cortical and lower subcortical limbic levels are resonantly intercommunicating, both top-down and bottom-up, the right brain, the system unconscious, acts as an efficient, cohesive system that can rapidly and relatively flexibly cope with the dynamically shifting demands of the inner and outer worlds, and yet adaptively maintain a coherent subjective experience despite changes in interpersonal and intrapersonal contexts.

The right hemisphere stores, in implicit-procedural memory (Hugdahl 1995), an internal working model of the attachment relationship that determines the individual's characteristic approach to affect regulation. In the securely attached individual this representation encodes an expectation that homeostatic disruptions will be set right, allowing the child to self-regulate functions which previously required the caregiver's external regulation. Throughout life these unconscious internal working models are used as guides for future action. A body of studies reveals that the right hemisphere is the substrate of affectively laden auto-biographical memory (Fink *et al.* 1996), and that 'self-related' material and 'self-recognition' are processed in the right hemisphere (Keenan *et al.* 2001).

Furthermore, the activity of this 'non-dominant' hemisphere, and not the later maturing 'dominant' verbal–linguistic left, is instrumental to the perception of the emotional states of other selves, that is, for empathy (Schore 1994, 1996, 1999a, 2000b). A very recent neuroimaging study reports that 'recognizing emotions from visually presented facial expressions requires right somatosensory cortices', and in this manner 'we recognize another individual's emotional state by internally generating somatosensory representations that stimulate how the individual would feel when displaying a certain facial expression' (Adolphs *et al.* 2000: 2683). Empathy is, of course, a moral emotion, and a number of authors have stressed the importance of right hemispheric emotional–imagistic processes in moral development (Vitz 1990, Schore 1991, 1994, 1998b). Attachment experiences thus directly impact the neurobiological substrate of moral development.

Thus, both the receptive and expressive aspects of the adaptive capacity to empathize with another's state are acquired in infant–maternal right hemispheric biologically based spontaneous emotional communications that occur within 'conversations between limbic systems'. Very recent studies indicate that joint attention, affectively charged dyadic transactions which allow the infant to appre-ciate that 'the other person is a locus of psychological attitudes toward the world, that the other is "attending" in such a way that shared experiences are pos-sible' (Hobson 1993: 267), also involves the right hemisphere (Kingstone *et al.* 2000).

In the course of the second year the infant acquires the ability to generate a 'the-ory of mind', in which an individual imputes mental states to self and to others and predicts behavior on the basis of such states. The human 'right mind', from its very beginnings, is not just directed towards evaluating the overt behavior of others, but in attempting to understand the mind of other humans (Schore, 1998a). Furthermore, evidence is now accumulating which suggests a critical role for early right hemispheric functions in language development, especially affective language (Locke 1997, Schumann 1997, Snow 2000).

The right brain contains a circuit of emotion regulation that is involved in 'intense emotional–homeostatic processes', and in the regulation of not only the biologically primitive negative emotions such as rage, fear, terror, disgust, shame, and hopeless despair, but also intensely positive emotions such as excitement and joy (Schore 1994, 1996, 1997a, 1999b, 2001a, b). This hemisphere contains 'a unique response system preparing the organism to deal efficiently with external challenges', and so its adaptive functions mediate the human stress response (Wittling 1997: 55). It therefore is centrally involved in the vital functions that support survival and enable the organism to cope actively and passively with stress.

In securely attached individuals the highest levels of the right brain, the orbitofrontal cortex (Schore 1994, 1998a, 2001a, b), function in integrating and assigning emotional–motivational significance to cognitive impressions, the association of emotion with ideas and thoughts (Joseph 1996), in the processing of affect-related meanings (Teasdale *et al.* 1999), and in the generation of a theory of mind with an affective component (Stone *et al.* 1998: 651). Its functions are most observable in contexts of uncertainty, in moments of emotional stress (Elliott *et al.* 2000), when it supports the early mobilization of effective behavioral strategies in novel or ambiguous situations (Savage *et al.* 2001). This 'senior executive' of the social–emotional brain thus acts as a coping mechanism that efficiently monitors and autoregulates the duration, frequency, and intensity of not only positive but also negative affect states, and thereby a central feature of the developing personality. Indeed, it is now thought that 'the orbitofrontal cortex is involved in critical human functions, such as social adjustment and the control of mood, drive and responsibility, traits that are crucial in defining the "personality" of an individual' (Cavada and Schultz 2000: 205).

This right lateralized self system matures in the middle of the second year, allowing for an expansion of the individual's affect array and the emergence of a capacity to reflect upon and regulate these emotional states. The regulatory core of the self is thus non-verbal and unconscious. The functioning of the 'self-correcting' right hemispheric system is central to self-regulation, the ability to flexibly regulate emotional states through interactions with other humans – interactive regulation in interdependent, interconnected contexts via a two-person psychology, and without other humans – autoregulation in independent, autonomous contexts via a one-person psychology. The adaptive capacity to shift between these dual regulatory modes, depending upon the social context, emerges out of a history of secure attachment interactions of a maturing biological organism and a psychobiologically attuned social environment.

Continued right brain maturation and emotional development

The right hemisphere, the neurobiological locus of the corporeal and emotional self, continues its growth phase through the second year. At 19–28 months the two hemispheres first integrate and coordinate visual information (Liegeois *et al.* 2000). This developmental advance allows facial visuoaffective and somatic signals processed by the right hemisphere into complex subjective affective states to be then communicated to the left for further semantic processing. This bihemispheric activity would allow for the emergence of narratives of the child's emotional experiences.

The right hemisphere, *the biological substrate of the human unconscious*, ends its first and most extensive growth phase in the second year, when the left hemisphere begins one (Thatcher 1994). But during this time the right is still dominant – Chiron *et al.* (1997) report that between 1 and 3 years resting cerebral blood flow shows a right hemisphere predominance, which then shifts to the left in the fourth year. They conclude: 'right-to-left asymmetry seems to be related to the consecutive emergence of functions dedicated first to the right (visuospatial abilities), and then to the left posterior associative cortex (language abilities)' (p. 1064).

I suggest that the onset of left hemispheric dominance, the usual organizational pattern of most adult brains, results from the growth of left prefrontal callosal axons over to the right. Levin (1991) points out that callosal transmission begins at 3½ years, a period of intense interest to Freud:

> Thus, the beginning of the oedipal phase, a psychological and neuroanatomical watershed in development, coincides with the onset of the ability (or inability) of the hemispheres to integrate their activities (p. 21) . . . the development of this defensive function, which Freud called the repression barrier, is accomplished by the increasing and reversible dominance of the left over the right hemisphere, which is known to occur during brain maturation.
>
> (Levin 1991: 194)

Basch (1983) also proposes that 'in repression it is the path from episodic to semantic memory, from right to left [brain], that is blocked' (p. 151).

This means that at this point in development each hemisphere is capable of forming independent self representations, one stored in explicit memory and accessible to language functions in the left, and another stored in implicit memory in the right. The right hemisphere contains an affective–configurational representational system: one that encodes self-and-object images unique from the lexical–semantic mode of the left (Watt 1990). Such a dual hemispheric system (Siegel 1999) allows for competition between the right and left brain (right mind–left mind) systems, and the presence of *conflict*, especially, as Brenner (1982) suggests, involving sexual and aggressive forces that are active at this time.

The right hemisphere continues into subsequent (but much less prolific) growth phases at later points of the life span (Thatcher 1994; Epstein 2001). It is now thought that the effectiveness of newly formed and pruned networks in these later stages is limited by the adequacy of already formed, underlying networks, and therefore maturation is optimal only if the preceding stages were installed optimally (Epstein 2001). Thus, the ongoing maturational potential of an individual right brain, the locus of the emotional and corporeal self, and the dynamic unconscious, is related to its attachment-influenced early organization. As in infancy, this further growth of right-lateralized cortical–subcortical systems is experience dependent.

This expansion occurs as the developing individual is presented with the stresses that are intrinsic to later stages of life, childhood, adolescence, and adulthood, as described by Erikson (1950; Seligman and Shanok 1995). Each of these ontogenetic expansions allows for more complex right brain representations, yet the earliest-forming strategies of affect regulation, co-created in attachment transactions of affective synchrony that regulate positive affect and interactive repair that regulate negative affect, provide the fundamental coping mechanisms for dealing with the stressors inherent in later novel, more challenging socio-emotional environments (Schore 2001a).

For example, as the toddler becomes a young child, age-appropriate interactions with peers depend upon an efficient right hemispheric ability to engage in relational, non-verbal affective transactions with other children. This capacity involves the abilities to non-consciously yet efficiently read faces and tones of voice and therefore the intentionalities of peers and teachers, to empathically resonate with the states of others, to communicate emotional states and regulate interpersonal affects, and thus to cope with the novel ambient interpersonal stressors of early childhood. In light of the fact that both the right and left hemispheres enter into subsequent growth spurts from ages 4 through 10 and that the frontal lobes continue to reorganize, the cognitive–emotional advances of late childhood reflect more complex connections within the right and between the emotional right and verbal–linguistic left hemisphere.

The brain undergoes a significant reorganization during adolescence, and this maturation contributes to the multiple psychological changes seen at this time of transition between childhood and adulthood. Spear notes, 'adolescence is second only to the neonatal period in terms of both rapid biopsychosocial growth as well as changing environmental characteristics and demands' (Spear 2000: 428). These data suggest that the right brain circuits that support emotional modulation, self-regulation, and stress coping mechanisms are resculpted. However, during disequilibrating stage transitions when right lateralized autoregulatory systems are reorganizing, the child–adolescent with a secure attachment can access emotionally available parents for interactive regulation. In this manner, the original attachment objects can continue to scaffold the individual's developing nascent, more complex regulatory capacities.

In securely attached individuals, or those in interaction with securely attached individuals who can act as interactive regulators, unconscious internal working models can become more complex. The experience-dependent expansion of the right brain is reflected in the growth of the biological substrate of the human unconscious over the life span (Schore 2001c, 2003a, b). In an updated conception, the unconscious is characterized as 'a cohesive, continually active mental structure that takes note of life's experiences and reacts according to its scheme of interpretation' (Winson 1990: 96).

As mentioned, the non-dominant(!) right brain plays a fundamental role in the maintenance of 'a coherent, continuous, and unified sense of self' (Devinsky 2000). This self system, described in the psychoanalytic literature by Kohut's self psychology (1971), as well as in the neuropsychoanalytic literature (Schore 1994), continues to develop more complexity, efficiency, and flexibility over the stages of the life span. The continuing ontogeny of this self-regulating and self-correcting dynamic system allows for an expansion of the boundaries of the emotion communicating self. The early right brain capacities of non-consciously processing socio-emotional information and bodily states are not only central to the origin of the self, but they are also required for the ongoing development of the self over the life span.

In cases wherein emotional development is relationally impaired, various self pathologies (Kohut 1977) and attachment disorders (Bowlby 1969) reflect deficits in the structural organization of the right brain. The psychotherapy of such 'developmental arrests' (Stolorow and Lachmann 1980) is directed toward the mobilization of fundamental modes of development (Emde 1990) and the completion of interrupted developmental processes (Gedo 1979). This remobilization of the development of the 'right mind' (Ornstein 1997), the locus of social/emotional self (Schore 1994; Devinsky 2000), can occur within the growth-facilitating environment of an affect-regulating therapeutic relationship which optimizes the 'laying down of psychological structure' (Kohut 1984: 98).

In neuropsychiatric writings Rotenberg describes:

> [T]he importance of the emotional relationships between psychotherapist and client can be explained by the restoration, in the process of such relationships, of . . . right hemispheric activity. In this way the emotional relationships in the process of psychotherapy are covering the deficiency caused by the lack of emotional relations in early childhood.
>
> (Rotenberg 1995: 59)

In a number of works I have modeled how right-hemisphere-to-right-hemisphere communications in the therapeutic alliance (as in the infant–mother dyad) can directly access, regulate, and alter the development of unconscious structures (Schore 1994, 1997b, 1998c 1999c, 2001c, 2002b, d). In this fashion, the therapeutic relationship 'heals by drawing into itself those methods of processing and regulating affect relied on by the patient for psychological survival and then transforming them', thereby inducing change in 'the patient's unconscious affect-regulating structures' (Spezzano 1993: 215–216).

A co-constructed therapeutic context that enhances intersubjective resonance and focuses on emotional communication and affect regulation is an essential element of developmental (Hurry 1998) therapy. A relational growth-facilitating environment which mobilizes the attachment mechanisms of psychobiological attunement, affect synchrony, and the interactive repair is essential to the therapeutic transformation of an insecure into an 'earned secure' (Phelps et al. 1998) attachment. Very recent formulations suggest that the goal of attachment-focused psychotherapy is the mutual regulation of affective homeostasis and the restructuring of interactive representations encoded in implicit–procedural memory (Amini et al. 1996).

Recall that the limbic system is specialized for the processing of emotion, the organization of new learning, and the capacity to adapt to a rapidly changing environment (Mesulam 1998), all components of the psychotherapeutic experience. Affectively charged interactive moments within the therapeutic alliance are thus necessary elements of a therapeutic corrective emotional experience. According to Andreasen, the editor of the *American Journal of Psychiatry*, psychoanalytic intensive therapy 'may be viewed as a long-term rebuilding and restructuring of the memories and emotional responses that have been embedded in the limbic system' (Andreasen 2001: 314).

Brown (1993) asserts that the process of emotional development, as it continues in adulthood, brings the potential to observe and understand the processes of our own minds. 'Adult affective development is the potential for self-observation and reflection on the very processes of mental functioning' (p. 42). This involves not simply the affective content of experience but of the very processes by which affect comes into experience – how it is experienced by the self and what informs the self about its relationship to internal and external reality. 'Psychotherapy is one medium of adult affective development in the sense that it serves the purpose of disciplined conscious reflection on affective processes' (p. 56).

I suggest Brown is describing a developmental progression in the complex operations of the right brain: the sense of a corporeal and emotional self (Devinsky 2000; Schore 1994), the storage of internal working models of the attachment relationship that guide appraisals of experience (Schore 1994), the processing of socio-emotional information that is meaningful to the individual (Schore 1998a), the mobilization of the vital functions that enable the organism to cope actively and passively with stress (Wittling 1997), the ability to empathize with the emotional states of other humans beings (Schore 1996), the mediation of emotional–imagistic processes in moral development (Vitz 1990), the appreciation of humor, a mechanism for coping with daily stress (Shammi and Stuss 1999), the solution of insight-related, yet-to-be-solved problems (Beeman and Bowden 2000), the support of narrative comprehension (Robertson and Gernsbacher 2001), the cerebral representation of one's own past and the activation of autobiographical memory (Fink *et al.* 1996), the establishment of a 'personally relevant universe' (Van Lancker 1991), and 'the capacity to mentally represent and become aware of subjective experiences in the past, present, and future' (Wheeler *et al.* 1997: 331). Emotional development is thus central to the expansion of the self over the course of the life span.

References

Adolphs, R., Damasio, H., Tranel, D., Cooper, G. and Damasio, A.R. (2000). A role for somatosensory cortices in the visual recognition of emotion as revealed by three-dimensional lesion mapping. *Journal of Neuroscience 20*: 2683–2690.

Amini, F., Lewis, T., Lannon, R. *et al.* (1996). Affect, attachment, memory: contributions toward psychobiologic integration. *Psychiatry 59*: 213–239.

Andreasen, N. C. (2001). *Brave New Brain*. New York: Oxford University Press.

Basch, M. F. (1976). The concept of affect: a re-examination. *Journal of the American Psychoanalytic Association 24*: 759–777.

Basch, M. F. (1983). The perception of reality and the disavowal of meaning. *Annual of Psychoanalysis 11*: 125–154.

Beebe, B. and Lachman, F. M. (1988). Mother–infant mutual influence and precursors of psychic structure. In Goldberg, A. (ed.), *Progress in Self Psychology,* Vol. 3, 3–25. Hillsdale, NJ: Analytic Press.

Beebe, B. and Lachmann, F. M. (1994). Representations and internalization in infancy: three principles of salience. *Psychoanalytic Psychology 11*: 127–165.

Beeman, M. J. and Bowden, E. M. (2000). The right hemisphere maintains solution-related activation for yet-to-be-solved problems. *Memory & Cognition 28*: 1231–1241.

Bergman, A. (1999). *Ours, Yours, Mine: Mutuality and the Emergence of the Separate Self.* Northvale, NJ: Analytic Press.

Blonder, L. X., Bowers, D. and Heilman, K. M. (1991). The role of the right hemisphere in emotional communication. *Brain 114*: 1115–1127.

Borod, J., Cicero, B. A., Obler, L. K., Welkowitz, J., Erhan, H. M., Santschi, C., Grunwald, I. S., Agosti, R. M. and Whalen J. R. (1998). Right hemisphere emotional perception: evidence across multiple channels. *Neuropsychology 12*: 446–458.

Bowers, D., Bauer, R. M. and Heilman, K. M. (1993). The nonverbal affect lexicon: theoretical perspectives from neuropsychological studies of affect perception. *Neuropsychology 7*: 433–444.

Bowlby, J. (1969). *Attachment and Loss. Vol. 1: Attachment.* New York: Basic Books.

Brenner, C. (1980). A psychoanalytic theory of affects. In Plutchik, R. and Kellerman, H. (Eds), *Emotion: Theory, Research and Experience*, Vol.1. New York: Academic Press.

Brenner, C. (1982). *The Mind in Conflict.* Madison, CT: International Universities Press.

Brown, D. (1993). Affective development, psychopathology, and adaptation. In Ablon, S. L., Brown, D., Khantzian, E. J., Mack J. E. (eds), *Human Feelings: Explorations in Affect Development and Meaning*, 5–66. Hillsdale, NJ: Analytic Press.

Buck, R. (1994). The neuropsychology of communication: spontaneous and symbolic aspects. *Journal of Pragmatics 22*: 265–278.

Cavada, C. and Schultz, W. (2000). The mysterious orbitofrontal cortex. Foreword. *Cerebral Cortex 10*: 205.

Chiron, C., Jambaque, I., Nabbout, R., Lounes, R., Syrota, A. and Dulac, O. (1997). The right brain hemisphere is dominant in human infants. *Brain 120*:1057–1065.

Cicchetti, D. and Tucker, D. (1994). Development and self-regulatory structures of the mind. *Development and Psychopathology 6* : 533–549.

Coghill, R. C., Gilron, I. and Iadorola, M. J. (2001). Hemispheric lateralization of somatosensory processing. *Journal of Neurophysiology 85*: 2602–2612.

Cole, J. (1998). *About Face.* Cambridge, MA: MIT Press.

Connelly, K. J., and Prechtl, H. F. R. (1981). *Maturation and Development: Biological and Psychological Perspectives.* Philadelphia: Lippincott.

Cooper, A. M. (1987). Changes in psychoanalytic ideas: transference interpretation. *Journal of the American Psychoanalytic Association 35*: 77–98.

Damasio, A. R. (1994). *Descartes' Error.* New York: Grosset/Putnam.

Devinsky, O. (2000). Right cerebral hemisphere dominance for a sense of corporeal and emotional self. *Epilepsy & Behavior 1*: 60–73.

Dimberg, U. and Petterson, M. (2000). Facial reactions to happy and angry facial expressions: evidence for right hemsphere dominance. *Psychophysiology 37*: 693–696.

Dimberg, U., Thunberg, M. and Elmehed, K. (2000). Unconscious facial reactions to emotional facial expressions. *Psychological Science 11*: 86–89.

Dobbing, J. and Sands, J. (1973). Quantitative growth and development of human brain. *Archives of Diseases of Childhood 48*: 757–767.

Edelman, G. (1989). *The Remembered Present: A Biological Theory of Consciousness.* New York: Basic Books.

Elliott, R., Dolan, R. J. and Frith, C. D. (2000). Dissociable functions in the medial and lateral orbitofrontal cortex: evidence from human neuroimaging studies. *Cerebral Cortex 10*: 308–317.

Emde, R. N. (1983). The pre-representational self and its affective core. *Psychoanalytic Study of the Child 38:* 165–192.

Emde, R. N. (1990). Mobilizing fundamental modes of development: empathic availability and therapeutic action. *Journal of the American Psychoanalytic Association* 38: 881–913.

Epstein H. T. (2001). An outline of the role of brain in human cognitive development. *Brain and Cognition 45*: 44–51.

Erikson, E. (1950). *Childhood and Society.* New York: W. W. Norton.

Feldman, R., Greenbaum, C. W. and Yirmiya, N. (1999). Mother–infant affect synchrony as an antecedent of the emergence of self-control. *Developmental Psychology, 35*: 223–231.

Field, T. and Fogel, A. (1982). *Emotion and Early Interaction.* Hillsdale, NJ: Erlbaum.

Fink, G. R., Markowitsch, H. J., Reinkemeier, M., Bruckbauer, T., Kessler, J. and Heiss, W.-D. (1996). Cerebral representation of one's own past: neural networks involved in autobiographical memory. *Journal of Neuroscience, 16*: 4275–4282.

Fox, N. A., Calkins, S. D. and Bell, M. A. (1994). Neural plasticity and development in the first two years of life: evidence from cognitive and socioemotional domains of research. *Development and Psychopathology 6*: 677–696.

Freud, A. (1965). *Normality and Pathology in Childhood.* New York: International Universities Press.

Gedo, J. E. (1979). *Beyond Interpretation.* New York: International Universities Press.

George. M. S., Parekh, P. I., Rosinsky, N., Ketter, T. A., Kimbrell, T. A., Heilman, K. M., Herscovitch, P. and Post, R. M. (1996). Understanding emotional prosody activates right hemispheric regions. *Archives of Neurology 53*: 665–670.

Gibbons, A. (1998). Solving the brain's energy crisis. *Science 280*: 1345–1347.

Henry, J. P. (1993). Psychological and physiological responses to stress: the right hemisphere and the hypothalamo-pituitary–adrenal axis, an inquiry into problems of human bonding. *Integrative Physiological and Behavioral Science 28*: 369–387.

Hobson, R. P. (1993). Through feeling and sight to self and symbol. In Neisser, U. (ed.), *The Perceived Self: Ecological and Interpersonal Sources of Self-Knowledge*, 254–279. New York: Cambridge University Press.

Hofer, M. A. (1990). Early symbiotic processes: hard evidence from a soft place. In Glick, R. A. and Bone, S. (eds), *Pleasure Beyond the Pleasure Principle*, 55–78. New Haven, CT: Yale University Press.

Hugdahl, K. (1995). Classical conditioning and implicit learning: the right hemisphere hypothesis. In Davidson, R. J. and Hugdahl, K. (eds), *Brain Asymmetry*, 235–267. Cambridge, MA: MIT Press.

Hurry, A. (1998). Psychoanalysis and developmental therapy. In Hurry, A. (ed.), *Psychoanalysis and Developmental Therapy*, 32–73. London: Karnac.

Joseph, R. (1992). *The Right Brain and the Unconscious: Discovering the Stranger Within.* New York: Plenum Press.

Joseph, R. (1996). *Neuropsychiatry, Neuropsychology, and Clinical Neuroscience*, 2nd edn. Baltimore: Williams & Wilkins.

Keenan, J. P., Nelson, A., O'Connor, M. and Pacual-Leone, A. (2001). Self-recognition and the right hemisphere. *Nature 409*: 305.

Kingstone, A., Friesen, C. K. and Gazzaniga, M. S. (2000). Reflexive joint attention depends on lateral and cortical connections. *Psychological Science 11*: 159–166.

Kinsley, C. H., Madonia, L., Gifford, G. W., Tureski, K., Griffin, G. R., Lowry, C., Williams, J., Collins, J., McLearie, H. and Lambert, K. G. (1999). Motherhood improves learning and memory. *Nature 402*: 137.

Kohut, H. (1971). *The Analysis of the Self*. New York: International Universities Press.

Kohut, H. (1977). *The Restoration of the Self*. New York: International Universities Press.

Kohut, H. (1984). *How Does Analysis Cure?* Chicago: University of Chicago Press.

Lang, P. J. (1995). The emotion probe: studies of motivation and attention. *American Psychologist 50:* 372–385.

Lee, D. H., Severin, K., Yokobayashi, Y. and Reza Ghadiri, M. (1997). Emergence of symbiosis in peptide self-replication through a hypercyclic network. *Nature, 390*: 591–594.

Lester, B. M., Hoffman, J. and Brazelton, T. B. (1985). The rhythmic structure of mother–infant interaction in term and preterm infants. *Child Development, 56*: 15–27.

Levin, F. (1991). *Mapping the Mind*. Mahweh, NJ: Analytic Press.

Lieberman, A. S. (1996). Aggression and sexuality in relation to toddler attachment: implications for the caregiving system. *Infant Mental Health Journal 17*: 276–292.

Liegeois, F., Bentejac, L. and de Schonen, S. (2000). When does inter-hemispheric integration of visual events emerge in infancy? A developmental study on 19- to 28-month-old infants. *Neuropsychologia 38*: 1382–1389.

Locke, J. L. (1997). A theory of neurolinguistic development. *Brain and Cognition 58*: 265–326.

Mahler, M. S. (1968). *On Human Symbiosis and the Vicissitudes of Individuation, Vol. 1: Infantile Psychosis*. New York: International Universities Press.

Mahler, M., Pine, F. and Bergman, A. (1975). *The Psychological Birth of the Human Infant*. New York: Basic Books.

Manning, J. T., Trivers, R. L., Thornhill, R., Singh, D., Denman, J., Eklo, M. H. and Anderton, R. H. (1997). Ear asymmetry and left-side cradling. *Evolution and Human Behavior 18*: 327–340.

Matsuzawa, J., Matsui, M., Konishi, T., Noguchi, K., Gur, R. C., Bilker, W. and Miyawaki, T. (2001). Age-related changes of brain gray and white matter in healthy infants and children. *Cerebral Cortex 11*: 335–342.

Mesulam, M.-M. (1998). From sensation to cognition. *Brain 121*: 1013–1052.

Ornstein, R. (1997). *The Right Mind: Making Sense of the Hemispheres*. New York: Harcourt Brace.

Nakamura, K., Kawashima, R., Ito, K., Sato, N., Nakamura, A., Sugiura, M., Kato, T., Hatano, K., Ito, K., Fukuda, H., Schorman, T. and Zilles, K. (2000). Functional delineation of the human occipito-temporal areas related to face and scene processing: a PET study. *Brain 123*: 1903–1912.

Papousek, H. and Papousek, M. (1997). Fragile aspects of early social integration. In Murray, L. and Cooper, P. J. (eds), *Postpartum Depression and Child Development*, 35–53. New York: Guilford Press.

Papousek, H., Papousek, M., Suomi, S. J. and Rahn, C. W. (1991). Preverbal communication and attachment: comparative views. In Gewirtz, J. L. and Kurtines, W. M. (eds), *Intersections with attachment*, 97–122. Hillsdale, NJ: Erlbaum.

Phelps, J. L., Belsky, J. and Crnic, K. (1998). Earned security, daily stress, and parenting: a comparison of five alternative models. *Development and Psychopathology 10*: 21–38.

Pizzagalli, D., Regard, M. and Lehmann, D. (1999). Rapid emotional face processing in the human right and left brain hemispheres: an ERP study. *NeuroReport 10*: 2691–2698.

Polan, H. J. and Hofer, M. A. (1999). Psychobiological origins of infant attachment and separation responses. In Cassidy, J. and Shaver, P. R. (eds), *Handbook of Attachment: Theory, Research, and Clinical Applications*, 162–180. New York: Guilford Press.

Robertson, D. A. and Gernsbacher, M. A. (2001). A common network of brain supporting narrative comprehension. Paper presented at Cognitive Neuroscience Society Annual Meeting, New York, March 2001.

Rotenberg, V. S. (1995). Right hemisphere insufficiency and illness in the context of search activity concept. *Dynamic Psychiatry* 150/151: 54–63.

Ryan, R. M., Kuhl, J. and Deci, E. L. (1997). Nature and autonomy: an organizational view of social and neurobiological aspects of self-regulation in behavior and development. *Development and Psychopathology 9* : 701–728.

Sander, L. (1991). Recognition process: specificity and organization in early human development. Paper presented at University of Massachussetts conference, *The Psychic Life of the Infant*.

Sander, L. (2000). Where are we going in the field of infant mental health? *Infant Mental Health Journal 21*: 5–20.

Savage, C. R., Deckersbach, T., Heckers, S., Wagner, A. D., Schacter, D. L., Alpert, N. M., Fischman, A. J. and Rauch, S. L. (2001). Prefrontal regions supporting spontaneous and directed application of verbal learning strategies: evidence from PET. *Brain 124*: 219–231.

Schore, A. N. (1991). Early super-ego development: The emergence of shame and narcissistic affect regulation in the practicing period. *Psychoanalysis and Contemporary Thought* 14: 187–250.

Schore, A. N. (1994). *Affect Regulation and the Origin of the Self: The Neurobiology of Emotional Development*. Mahwah, NJ: Erlbaum.

Schore, A. N. (1996). The experience-dependent maturation of a regulatory system in the orbital prefrontal cortex and the origin of developmental psychopathology. *Development and Psychopathology 8*: 59–87.

Schore, A. N. (1997a). Early organization of the nonlinear right brain and development of a predisposition to psychiatric disorders. *Development and Psychopathology 9*: 595–631.

Schore, A. N. (1997b). Interdisciplinary developmental research as a source of clinical models. In Moskowitz, M., Monk, C., Kaye, C. and Ellman, S. (eds), *The Neurobiological and Developmental Basis for Psychotherapeutic Intervention*, 1–71. Northvale, NJ: Aronson.

Schore, A. N. (1997c). A century after Freud's project: is a rapprochement between psychoanalysis and neurobiology at hand? *Journal of the American Psychoanalytic Association 45*: 841–867.

Schore, A. N. (1998a). The experience-dependent maturation of an evaluative system in the cortex. In Pribram, K. (ed.), *Brain and Values: Is a Biological Science of Values Possible?* 337–358. Mahwah, NJ: Erlbaum.

Schore, A. N. (1998b). Early shame experiences and infant brain development. In Gilbert P.

and Andrews, B. (eds), *Shame: Interpersonal Behavior, Psychopathology, and Culture*, 57–77. New York: Oxford University Press.

Schore, A. N. (1998c). Affect regulation: a fundamental process of psychobiological development, brain organization, and psychotherapy. Unpublished address, Tavistock Clinic, London, July 1998.

Schore, A. N. (1998d). The relevance of recent research on the infant brain to pediatrics. Unpublished address, Annual Meeting of the American Academy of Pediatrics, Scientific Section on Developmental and Behavioral Pediatrics, Section Program, Translating neuroscience: early brain development and pediatric practice, San Francisco, CA, October 1998.

Schore, A. N. (1999a). Commentary on emotions: neuro-psychoanalytic views. *Neuro-Psychoanalysis, 1*: 49–55.

Schore, A. N. (1999b). Parent–infant communications and the neurobiology of emotional development. Unpublished address, Zero to Three 14th Annual Training Conference, Anaheim, CA, December 1999.

Schore, A. N. (1999c). Psychoanalysis and the development of the right brain. Unpublished address, First North American International Psychoanalytic Association Regional Research Conference, 'Neuroscience, Development and Psychoanalysis'. Mount Sinai Hospital, New York, December 1999.

Schore, A. N. (1999d). The right brain, the right mind, and psychoanalysis. On-line at the website for *Neuro-Psychoanalysis*: http://www.neuro-psa.com/schore.htm

Schore, A. N. (2000a). Foreword to the reissue of *Attachment and Loss, Vol. 1: Attachment* by Bowlby, J. New York: Basic Books.

Schore, A. N. (2000b). Attachment and the regulation of the right brain. *Attachment & Human Development 2*: 23–47.

Schore, A. N. (2000c). The self-organization of the right brain and the neurobiology of emotional development. In Lewis, M. D. and Granic, I. (eds), *Emotion, Development, and Self-Organization*, 155–185. New York: Cambridge University Press.

Schore, A. N. (2000d). Healthy childhood and the development of the human brain. Unpublished keynote address, Healthy Children Foundation Conference, Luxembourg and World Health Organization, Luxembourg, November 2000.

Schore, A. N. (2001a). The effects of a secure attachment relationship on right brain development, affect regulation, and infant mental health. *Infant Mental Health Journal, 22*: 7–66

Schore, A. N. (2001b). The effects of relational trauma on right brain development, affect regulation, and infant mental health. *Infant Mental Health Journal 22*: 201–269.

Schore, A. N. (2001c). The Seventh John Bowlby Memorial Lecture, 'Attachment, the self-organizing brain, and developmentally oriented psychoanalytic psychotherapy'. *British Journal of Psychotherapy 17*: 299–328.

Schore, A. N. (2001d). Plenary Address: Parent-infant emotional communication and the neurobiology of emotional development. In *Proceedings of Head Start's Fifth National Research Conference, Developmental and Contextual Transitions of Children and Families: Implications for Research, Policy, and Practice*, 49–73.

Schore, A. N. (2001e). Regulation of the right brain: a fundamental mechanism of attachment, trauma, dissociation, and psychotherapy, Parts 1 and 2. Unpublished addresses, conference, 'Attachment, Trauma, and Dissociation: Developmental, Neuropsychological, Clinical, and Forensic Considerations', University College of London Attachment Research Unit and Clinic for the Study of Dissociative Disorders, London, June 2001.

Schore, A. N. (2002a). The right brain as the neurobiological substratum of Freud's dynamic unconscious. In Scharff, D. and Scharff, J. (eds), *The Psychoanalytic Century: Freud's Legacy for the Future.* 61–88 New York: Other Press.

Schore, A. N. (2002b). Clinical implications of a psychoneurobiological model of projective identification. In Alhanati, S. (ed.), *Primitive Mental States, Vol. lll: Pre- and Peri-natal Influences on Personality Development*, 1–65 London: Karnac.

Schore, A. N. (2002c). Dysregulation of the right brain: a fundamental mechanism of traumatic attachment and the psychopathogenesis of posttraumatic stress disorder. *Australian and New Zealand Journal of Psychiatry 36*: 9–30.

Schore, A. N. (2002d). Neurobiology and psychoanalysis: convergent findings on the subject of projective identification. In Edwards, J. (ed.), *Being Alive: Building on the Work of Anne Alvarez*, 57–74. London: Brunner-Routledge.

Schore, A. N. (2003a). *Affect Dysregulation and Disorders of the Self.* New York: W. W. Norton.

Schore, A. N. (2003b). *Affect Regulation and the Repair of the Self.* New York: W. W. Norton.

Schumann, J. H. (1997). *The Neurobiology of Affect in Language.* Malden, MA: Blackwell.

Seligman, S. and Shahmoon-Shanok, R. (1995). Subjectivity, complexity, and the social world: Erikson's identity concept and contemporary relational theories. *Psychoanalytic Dialogues 5*: 537–565.

Semrud-Clikeman, M. and Hynd, G. W. (1990). Right hemisphere dysfunction in nonverbal learning disabilities: social, academic, and adaptive functioning in adults and children. *Psychological Bulletin 107*: 196–209.

Shammi, P. and Stuss D. T. (1999). Humour appreciation: a role of the right frontal lobe. *Brain 122*: 657–666.

Siegel, D. J. (1999). *The Developing Mind: Toward a Neurobiology of Interpersonal Experience.* New York: Guilford Press.

Smith, C. G. (1981). *Serial Dissection of the Human Brain.* Baltimore/Munich: Urban & Schwarzenberg.

Snow, D. (2000). The emotional basis of linguistic and nonlinguistic intonation: implications for hemispheric specialization. *Developmental Neuropsychology 17*: 1–28.

Spear, L. P. (2000). The adolescent brain and age-related behavioral manifestations. *Neuroscience and Biobehavioral Reviews 24*: 417–463.

Spence, S., Shapiro, D. and Zaidel, E. (1996). The role of the right hemisphere in the physiological and cognitive components of emotional processing. *Psychophysiology 33*: 112–122.

Spezzano, C. (1993). *Affect in Psychoanalysis: A Clinical Synthesis.* Hillsdale, NJ: Analytic Press.

Sroufe, L. A. (1996). *Emotional Development: The Organization of Emotional Life in the Early Years.* New York: Cambridge Universty Press.

Stern, D. N. (1983). Early transmission of affect: Some research issues. In Call, J., Galenson, E. and Tyson, R. (eds), *Frontiers of Infant Psychiatry*, 52–69. New York: Basic Books.

Stern, D. N. (1985). *The Interpersonal World of the Infant.* New York: Basic Books.

Stolorow, R. D. and Lachmann, F. M. (1980). *Psychoanalysis of Developmental Arrests.* New York: International Universities Press.

Stone, V. E., Baron-Cohen, S. and Knight, R. T. (1998). Frontal lobe contributions to theory of mind. *Journal of Cognitive Neuroscience 10*: 640–656.

Teasdale, J. D., Howard, R. J., Cox, S. G., Ha, Y., Brammer, M. J., Williams, S. C. R. and

Checkley, S. A. (1999). Functional MRI study of the cognitive generation of affect. *American Journal of Psychiatry 156*: 209–215.

Thatcher, R. W. (1994). Cyclical cortical reorganization: origins of human cognitive development. In Dawson, G. and Fischer, K. W. (eds), *Human Behavior and the Developing Brain* 232–266. New York: Guilford Press.

Thomas, D. G., Whitaker, E., Crow, C. D., Little, V., Love, L., Lykins, M. S. and Lettermman, M. (1997). Event-related potential variability as a measure of information storage in infant development. *Developmental Neuropsychology 13*: 205–232.

Thompson, R. A. (1990). Emotion and self-regulation. In *Nebraska Symposium on Motivation*, 367–467. Lincoln: University of Nebraska Press.

Tomkins, S. (1984). Afffect theory. In Ekman, P. (ed.), *Approaches to Emotion*. Hillsdale, NJ: Erlbaum.

Trevarthen, C. (1990). Growth and education of the hemispheres. In Trevarthen, C. (ed.), *Brain Circuits and Functions of the Mind*, 334–363. Cambridge: Cambridge University Press.

Trevarthen, C. (1993). The self born in intersubjectivity: The psychology of an infant communicating. In Neisser, U. (ed.), *The Perceived Self: Ecological and Interpersonal Sources of Self-Knowledge*, 121–173. New York: Cambridge University Press.

Tronick, E. Z. and Weinberg, M. K. (1997). Depressed mothers and infants: failure to form dyadic states of consciousness. In Murray, L. and Cooper, P. J. (eds), *Postpartum Depression in Child Development*, 54–81. New York: Guilford Press.

Tronick, E. Z., Bruschweilwe-Stern, N., Harrison, A. M., Lyons-Ruth, K., Morgan, A. C., Nahum, J. P., Sander, L. and Stern, D. N. (1998). Dyadically expanded states of consciousness and the process of therapeutic change. *Infant Mental Health Journal 19*: 290–299.

Van Lancker, D. (1991). Personal relevance and the human right hemisphere. *Brain and Cognition, 17*: 64–92.

Van Lancker, D. and Cummings, J. L. (1999). Expletives: neurolingusitic and neuro-behavioral perspectives on swearing. *Brain Research Reviews 31*: 83–104.

Vitz, P. C. (1990). The use of stories in moral development. *American Psychologist 45*: 709–720.

Watt, D. (1990). Higher cortical functions and the ego: explorations of the boundary between behavioral neurology, neuropsychology, and psychoanalysis. *Psychoanalytic Psychology 7*: 487–527.

Watt, D. (2000). The dialogue between psychoanalysis and neuroscience: alienation and reparation. *Neuro-Psychoanalysis 2:* 183–192.

Wang, S. (1997). Traumatic stress and attachment. *Acta Physiologica Scandinavica, Supplement 640*: 164–169.

Weil, A. P. (1985). Thoughts about early pathology. *Journal of the American Psychoanalytic Association 33:* 335–352.

Wexler, B. E., Warrenburg, S., Schwartz, G. E. and Janer, L. D. (1992). EEG and EMG responses to emotion-evoking stimuli processed without conscious awareness. *Neuropsychologia 30:* 1065–1079.

Wheeler, M. A., Stuss, D. T. and Tulving, E. (1997). Toward a theory of episodic memory: the frontal lobes and autonoetic consciousness. *Psychological Bulletin 121*: 331–354.

Winnicott, D. (1971). *Playing and Reality*. New York: Basic Books.

Winnicott, D. (1986). *Home is Where We Start From*. New York: W. W. Norton.

Winson, J. (1990). The meaning of dreams. *Scientific American,* November: 86–96.

Wittling, W. (1997). The right hemisphere and the human stress response. *Acta Physiologica Scandinavica, Supplement 640*: 55–59.

Wittling, W. and Schweiger, E. (1993). Neuroendocrine brain asymmetry and physical complaints. *Neuropsychologia 31*: 591–608.

Yamada, H., Sadato, N., Konishi, Y., Muramoto, S., Kimura, K., Tanaka, M., Yonekura, Y., Ishii, Y. and Itoh, H. (2000). A milestone for normal development of the infantile brain detected by functional MRI. *Neurology 55*: 218–223.

Chapter 2

Memory, amnesia and intuition: a neuro-psychoanalytic perspective

Oliver Turnbull and Mark Solms

This chapter describes how inherited memory mechanisms are modified and individualised during development, and how our personal experiences are organised into predetermined categories of knowledge and behaviour (some conscious and some unconscious) to shape our everyday lives. These links enable individuals to fine-tune their need-satisfying activities in relation to the idiosyncrasies of the specific environment that they are born into. The survival value of such memory systems is obvious, for their content adapts the individual to the specific world that he or she inhabits. However, while the *content* of the memory systems is unique to each individual, memories are organised according to a regular, standard pattern. This 'standard' pattern of organisation of human memory, across a number of subsystems, will be the main theme of this chapter. We begin with an introductory tour of these subsystems, before moving on to some related topics of special interest to psychoanalysis.

The term 'memory' covers many different mental functions. Sometimes we think of memory as the act of *remembering*. This aspect of memory is *reminiscence*, the bringing to mind of some previously learned fact or experienced event. At other times the term 'memory' refers not to the process of bringing stored knowledge to mind but rather to the stored knowledge itself. This meaning of 'memory' denotes the part of the mind that contains *traces of influence* from the past which persist in the present. The term 'memory' is also used in connection with the *process* of acquiring knowledge – that is, the process of learning or memorising.

Because the function of memory covers so many different things, cognitive scientists today divide it up into a number of component functions.[1] We will discuss several ways of dividing up this complex topic.

Encoding, storage, retrieval and consolidation

Three stages in the processing of memory are frequently referred to in the specialist literature (see Figure 2.1).[2] The acquiring of new information is called encoding, retaining the information is described as storage, and bringing the information back to mind is retrieval. Placing the functions of memory in the

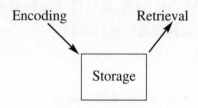

Figure 2.1 Encoding, storage and retrieval.

sequence of encoding, storage and retrieval provides a simple way of dividing it up. However, these three concepts by themselves do little justice to the complexities of the neurobiology of memory.

The simple classification already runs into trouble as soon as the concept of consolidation is introduced (see Figure 2.2). This has become an important concept in memory research, as it seems to cast significant light on how memory is actually organised in the brain. Compelling evidence for the existence of consolidation first came to light from studies of the way in which memory breaks down following brain damage.

It is almost invariably the case that memory is not affected globally following brain damage. It hardly ever happens that someone's memory is completely destroyed – in fact, when a patient suffers from a total amnesia, we readily entertain a diagnosis of hysteria. The neuropsychological reality is that particular *aspects* of memory are vulnerable to brain injury or disease, while other aspects are almost indestructible. The most vulnerable memories are the recent ones, the memories of events that occurred (or facts that were learned) just a few hours, days, months or weeks before the brain was damaged. As a rule, the more remote the memory, the less likely it is to be disrupted by neurological pathology. The discovery of this *temporal gradient* (as it is often called) is attributed to Ribot, and it is therefore described as Ribot's law. It is perhaps surprising that the most recent memories – the freshest ones – are the most vulnerable, while the more remote memories are the most durable. The fact that this is indeed the case suggests that something *entrenches* memories over time. This 'something' is the process of

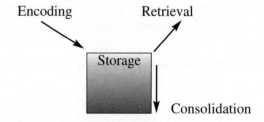

Figure 2.2 Encoding, storage, retrieval, consolidation.

consolidation. Memories are continually being consolidated to deeper and deeper levels of storage. At this moment, very little consolidation of the material you are reading is taking place; tonight (while you are sleeping) a fair amount of consolidation should take place; and over the next few days, weeks, months and years, the process of consolidation will continue. Consolidation is perhaps best conceptualised as an aspect of the encoding stage of memory process that continues into the storage stage (see Figure 2.2).

Short- and long-term storage

Our diagram of memory processes is complicated further by the fact that the storage aspect must be divided into short-term and long-term components (Figure 2.3). The distinction between short- and long-term memory is probably the most important division within the memory systems of the brain. It is also an important source of terminological confusion. For many people, the term 'short-term memory' denotes memories laid down over the last few hours or days. People say, 'My short-term memory is so bad, I can barely remember what happened yesterday!' In technical usage, however, we would say that this person is describing a difficulty with their *recent* memory. In technical parlance, 'short-term memory' (abbreviation: *STM*) refers to information that is in your consciousness *right now*, derived from events that probably occurred just a few seconds ago. Both recent and remote memory are aspects of 'long-term memory' (abbreviation: *LTM*). If a patient can't remember what happened yesterday, therefore, there is something wrong with their *long-term* memory. Long-term memory begins a few seconds ago. It is partly as a result of this ambiguity (amongst other reasons) that the term 'short-term memory' is falling out of use in cognitive science today, and being replaced by the terms immediate memory and, increasingly, working memory.

Short-term (or immediate or working) memories, then, are memories of events (or facts) that you are holding in mind *at this moment*. They may be there because you have just learned them or experienced them (because they have just happened *to* you) and therefore haven't yet disappeared from your consciousness. Or they may be there because you are *actively* holding them in mind, wanting to keep them in conscious awareness, or because you actively brought them to mind (from LTM). This reveals that short-term memory has an active and passive aspect to it.

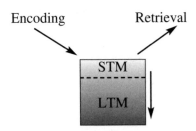

Figure 2.3 STM and LTM

We (OT and MS) tend to use the term 'immediate memory' to refer to the passive (perceptual) aspect of short-term memory, and we reserve the term 'working memory' for the active (cognitive operation) aspect. As we use these two terms, then, they refer respectively to the externally and internally generated *current contents of consciousness*.

The contents of consciousness are held in what cognitive scientists often refer to as a 'buffer', where it can (if we wish it to) be sustained by continuous rehearsal. The mechanism of working memory can hold information in this buffer for as long as you like (until you fall asleep, that is!). For this reason, the buffer of STM can be regarded as the medium of our consciousness. To be more precise, it is the medium of our *extended consciousness* (see Damasio, 1999, or Solms and Turnbull, 2002, for more detail). Cognitive scientists use terms like 'ultra-short-term' and 'iconic' memory to denote the momentary effects of external perceptual stimuli in *core consciousness,* which exists only in the moment, and does not extend over time.

As you read these lines, and register them in core (perceptual) consciousness, the information they contain is held in the buffer of your short-term memory. Within a few seconds, as you read on and must thereby encode *more* information, the lines you read a few moments ago will have to be transferred out of the STM buffer, to make way for the new information. This is due to the fact that although you can keep information in mind for an extended period of time, the STM buffer of consciousness has a very limited *capacity* (roughly seven units of information).[3]

This leads to the question of what happens to the material that has been bumped out of the buffer. You cannot encode and store absolutely everything you experience. Indeed, attentional mechanisms exclude a good deal of information at even the perceptual stage. The mechanism of consolidation continues this sifting process within the memory storage systems themselves. Consolidation is therefore not only a process of entrenching what is *kept* in memory, it is also a process of getting rid of the memories you do *not* want to keep. This introduces an important distinction between passive and active forgetting ('trace decay' versus 'repression').[4] We will return to this issue later in the chapter.

Earlier, we suggested that a fair amount of consolidation of what you are reading here will occur tonight. Many neuroscientists believe that the function of sleep (and of REM or dreaming sleep in particular) is intimately bound up with the process of consolidation. This theory is controversial. One especially mischievous claim is that dreams are the 'dustbins' of memory (Crick and Mitchison, 1983). According to this view, memories are consolidated during REM sleep, and the ones that are selected for erasure appear briefly in your dreams, on their way to oblivion. Hence the most *irrelevant* facts of the day turn up in your dreams, and this is why dreams are so readily *forgotten*. Psychoanalysts hold quite different views on the nature and function of dreaming (see Solms, 1997a, 2000, or Solms and Turnbull, 2002, for a summary).

The physiology of consolidation: cells that fire together . . .

The physiology of short-term memory is not very well understood, but neuro-scientists agree that it differs radically from that of long-term memory. Short-term memory appears to involve reverberating circuits – groups of interconnected cells firing together in closed (self-reactivating) loops. The maintenance of the firing pattern *is* the (neural correlate of the) holding in mind of the information. Once a particular reverberating circuit has been established, it is more likely to become activated *again* for the reason that 'cells that fire together, wire together'. This is Hebb's law. The process of 'wiring together' is what transforms short-term memories into long-term ones. It seems to involve a two-stage process. Initially, the cell changes are purely *physiological*, in that the synapses connecting the cells in the circuit become more 'permeable' (i.e., their thresholds decrease, making the cell more likely to fire in response to stimuli at synapses that caused them to fire previously). This in turn sets off a second, more permanent, *anatomical* process. The continual firing of cells at certain junctions activates genetic mechanisms in the cells, which promotes the growth of further synapses at those junctions. Thus the cells *literally* grow and 'wire together' at constantly activated junctions.[5]

This relatively recent discovery, which won Eric Kandel the 2000 Nobel Prize for physiology and medicine, has very important implications for our understand-ing of memory. It demonstrates that temporary, reverberating circuits have a permanent, trophic effect on the cells involved, producing an increased density of neural tissue. This trophic effect is activity dependent; and it continues throughout life.

Forgetting, repression and infantile amnesia

The process of 'wiring together' inevitably has a flip side: if the process is activity dependent, then what happens if a particular circuit falls into *dis*use? What hap-pens to synapses that are *not* active? What happens is that they *atrophy*; they literally *die*. This 'use it or lose it' rule plays an important part in early brain development. We are all born with more synapses than we need. These synapses represent the *potential* connections between neurons that *might* be needed to create internal maps and models of the world we find ourselves in. In a sense, they repre-sent all the possible worlds we could find ourselves in. The *actual* environment we are born into results in only a subset of these connections being activated. These connections are then strengthened; and the ones that are not used fall by the wayside. This process is commonly referred to as neuronal 'pruning'.

But the process does not end in early childhood. Although that is when the vast bulk of excess neural tissue is shed, the 'use it or lose it' principle continues to operate throughout life. As a result, connections that may have been activated frequently in childhood (and therefore preserved) can subsequently fall away at later stages of development, for the simple reason that they are no longer required.

This fact forms the basis of a prevalent argument against the psychoanalytic theory of 'infantile amnesia'.

This argument is usually formulated in the following way: people don't rely on the same memory circuits in adulthood as they did in childhood because their circumstances change so radically. Since the childhood memories are no longer used, they atrophy. Infantile amnesia is therefore a simple matter of memory decay – the disintegration of ancient connections that have fallen into disuse. There is therefore (it is argued) no need to postulate an active 'repressing' force to explain our universal inability to recall the events of earliest childhood, and there is no point in trying to 'recover' them.

There are several substantial problems with this claim, two of which are worth briefly mentioning. The first is the fact that *conscious* and *unconscious* remembering are two entirely different things. The *activation of a memory trace* is not at all synonymous with *conscious remembering*. The fact that you are not consciously aware and mindful of the events of early childhood therefore does not mean that the traces they left are not constantly being activated. On the contrary, it is quite likely that the networks that survived the great pruning processes of early childhood serve as *templates* around which all later memories are organised. These deeply consolidated 'trunk' circuits would be activated on a very regular basis, even if the events that forged them in the first place are not consciously brought to mind in the process – and even if the events that forged them *cannot* be brought to consciousness any longer. This introduces some important points about the functional architecture of human memory, which we will turn our attention to in the next section. For now we will just mention that the distinction between *conscious* and *unconscious* memory mechanisms is very well established in contemporary neuroscience (see Solms and Turnbull, 2002, for a summary). Nobody doubts that a long-term memory trace can be activated without an attendant experience appearing as a conscious reminiscence. In fact most memory processes take this form. Such memory processes are described as 'implicit'. When a long-term trace is activated *and* brought to conscious awareness (i.e., when, in addition to being activated, it becomes available to the temporary 'buffer' of working memory, mentioned above) we say that it has been rendered explicit. The technical terms 'implicit memory' and 'explicit memory' in contemporary neuroscience are synonymous with the psychoanalytic terms 'unconscious' and 'conscious' memory respectively.

A second reason to question the claim that early childhood memories are simply 'forgotten' invokes Ribot's law, which states that the oldest memories are the most robust memories. Any account of infantile amnesia must explain why it violates Ribot's law. In psychoanalysis, the explanation is that early childhood memories *are* very robust; they only *appear* to be forgotten, when in fact they are just unavailable to conscious awareness. The question then becomes: why are they not available to conscious awareness? (The answer, in psychoanalysis, is *repression*). It is not clear how the alternative account explains this violation of Ribot's law.

Mnemonic diversity

Freud is supposed to have said that once a memory is laid down it can never be forgotten. This was never *really* his opinion, but he certainly did emphasise the remarkable persistence of memory.[6] And long-term memory is indeed a very durable thing.

The reason that long-term memories are so enduring is that they are generally encoded in several places – in a sense, memories are 'everywhere' in the brain. From the earlier discussion on the nature of connections between cells, it should come as no surprise to learn that memories have *a widely distributed anatomical representation*. For this reason, there is a great deal of redundancy in the mnemonic process. Memories involve connections between vast assemblies of neurons, and removing one or another piece of the assembly will not get rid of the whole. It may degrade it slightly, but it is very difficult to obliterate an entire network. (By the same token, degraded traces can be 'reconstructed', although the reconstructed version may not always be entirely accurate; see below.) A second, related reason why long-term memory is so robust is that *memories are encoded in more than one way*. There is a plurality of memory subsystems, not just one 'filing cabinet'. So even if one 'file' is lost or degraded, much of the information it contained may be stored elsewhere, in different ways, in other 'files'.

We will now introduce some of the better-known 'filing cabinets' of human memory. There is some controversy in the field about whether these represent *entirely* independent categories, but this classification system is very widely used, and is likely to remain useful. The categories may be visualised as subsystems of the 'storage' component of memory depicted in Figures 2.1 and 2.2.

Semantic memory

Semantic memory is 'a network of associations and concepts that underlies our basic *knowledge of the world* – word meanings, categories, facts and propositions, and the like'.[7] This knowledge is stored in the form of third-person information, of the kind that one might find in an encyclopaedia. It comprises bits of objective information about the world and its workings – facts such as 'dogs have four legs' and 'London is the capital of Britain'. There is nothing 'subjective' about semantic memory, in the sense that it does not represent *experiences*. It contains information that we typically share with other members of our society, especially our peer group. However, it also stores *objective* personal information – such as 'I was born on 17th July 1961' and 'I live in Bangor, Wales'. Much of our semantic knowledge is encoded during the primary school years of childhood, but most of it is acquired even earlier than that. One should remember that semantic memory includes a lot of extremely 'general' knowledge. Indeed, we often forget that we once had to *learn* it. For example, semantic memory contains grammatical rules of language, the knowledge that objects drop when you let go of them, that cups break but balls bounce, and that leaves blow in the wind. When your hands dart out to catch a falling cup, in anticipation of the fact that it might break, that movement is based on *memory*; you reach downwards because you know from endlessly repeated experiences what is likely to happen. The habitual hand movements themselves (in this example) are classified under the heading of 'procedural memory', a sort of 'bodily' memory that we discuss below; but the *abstract rule* 'cups can break when they drop' is encoded in semantic memory.

Categories of knowledge and perception

Semantic memory can be divided into several sub-components, so that there are specific aspects of our semantic memory that can be disrupted in relative isolation. This property of semantic memory is known as material specificity. The rules of language, mathematical rules, the knowledge of the shapes and attributes of various categories of object, are stored in different networks of the brain and are therefore vulnerable to being damaged separately. Much of the difference between the mental functions of the left and right cerebral hemispheres is dependent on material specificity (see Solms and Turnbull, 2002, for a summary, especially in relation to psychoanalysis). Material specificity is, to some extent, dependent on modal specificity.[8] For example, circuits in the medial occipitotemporal part of the cortex, especially on the right, categorise information that enables us to recognise individual *faces*, and circuits on the lateral convexity of the left temporal lobe (and adjacent parts of the parietal and occipital lobes) categorise information that enables us to retrieve specific *names*.[9] The 'face' circuits encode visual-specific images whereas the 'name' circuits encode auditory-specific images. However, categorical knowledge about faces and names (and the connections between them) is also stored and classified *abstractly*. To the extent that memory networks are encoded as concrete, modality-specific images rather than abstract, material-specific connections and categories, neuroscientists tend to classify them under the heading of *perceptual* rather than memory mechanisms (see below). The abstract connections between objects (or their properties) are generally classified as semantic memories.

Anatomy of semantic memory

Since semantic memory is concerned with 'objective' facts, and represents the world from a 'third-person' point of view (even information about your self, such as 'I was born on 17th July 1961'), it is encoded in the exteroceptive *cerebral cortex*. The network of associations and concepts that comprise semantic memory takes the form of a 'directory' of connections between the concrete images that are represented in the modality-specific cortex.[10] These directories can, therefore, to a large extent be 'localised' in the cortical 'association' areas that link the various unimodal cortices with one another (Figure 2.4). This applies especially to the posterior temporal and inferior parietal regions, which form the hub of the functional unit of the brain that Luria called the unit for 'receiving, analysing *and*

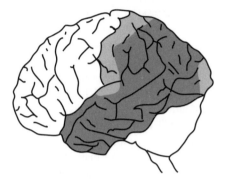

Figure 2.4 Posterior 'association' cortex.

storing information' (see Luria 1973). However, as previously stated, the reader should not mistake these nodal points in the associative networks for the networks themselves. The memory traces *themselves* are very widely distributed in the cerebral cortex, as they must of necessity include all the concrete, unimodal images that the semantic directories link up.

The remembered present

The ambiguity at the borders between semantic memory and perception is reflected in some curious anomalies in our clinical categorisation of patients with damage to these regions of the brain. For example, although patients who are unable to remember names tell us that there is something wrong with their 'memory', we (neurologists and neuropsychologists) consider them to have something wrong with their 'language' functions. Accordingly, we classify these patients under the nosological heading of 'aphasia' ('anomic aphasia', to be precise) rather than 'amnesia'. Likewise, inability to recognise familiar faces is classified as a perceptual disorder (an 'agnosia' – 'prosopagnosia' to be precise) rather than a memory disorder (an amnesia). Similarly, the inability to recall the movement one makes to catch a falling cup is a disorder of skilled movement ('ideomotor or ideational apraxia') rather than an amnesia. *All* the aphasias, agnosias and apraxias are, in reality, disorders of *memory* (in its broadest sense), but we classify them as disorders of language, perception, skilled movement, etc. This is, in part, because these categories of knowledge are so overlearned that we overlook the fact that we ever did learn them.

As a result, much of what we take for granted as 'the way the world *is*' – as we *perceive* it – is in fact what we have *learned* about the world – as we *remember* it. This is best demonstrated by the fact that the way the world 'is' can suddenly change – often dramatically – for people whose brains are damaged. As a result, and not surprisingly, some patients have great difficulty recognising that it is them*selves* rather than the *world* that has changed. This can also be demonstrated neurodevelopmentally. It is possible to 'engineer' a cat that cannot *see* horizontal lines by depriving it of this type of experience in crucial developmental periods. The visual cortex of such cats is organised in a way that lacks horizontal information. If you confront a cat deprived from birth of horizontal visual experiences with a horizontal line (by say, putting a horizontal bar in its path), it will behave as if the object does not exist and walk straight into it. This is evidence of the fact that much of what we take to be perception is in fact memory. Another example of memory-based perception is *accent*, which reflects differences between the learned features of different languages. Japanese people have great difficulty distinguishing between 'r' and 'l' sounds because, in the phonologically meaningful surround that their brain develops, this distinction does not (meaningfully) exist. Even if they are later put into an environment where it does have significance, they perceive the world differently – at least as far as that tiny little detail is concerned.

The title of Gerald Edelman's popular book, *The Remembered Present* (1989), captures very well what perception is about. We all automatically reconstruct the reality we perceive from models we have stored in our memories. We do not perceive the world anew every moment of the day, and try afresh to discriminate recognisable objects and decipher meaningful words from the undifferentiated din of stimuli that constantly impinge on us. This, presumably, is what newborn babies have to do in the first moments of extrauterine life. We adults *project* our expectations (the products of our previous experience) onto the world all the time, and in this way we largely *construct* rather than perceive (in any simple sense) the world around us. Thus the world of our everyday experience is doubly removed from the 'reality itself' that philosophers speak of (see Solms and Turnbull, 2002, for a summary) – first by the interposition of our perceptual apparatus (which is designed to *sample* and *represent* certain selected features of the world) but also by our memory (which, on the basis of past experience, organises and transforms those selected features into recognisable *objects*).

Aleksandr Luria (the famous Russian neurologist) argued[11] that the hierarchical arrangement of perception and memory reverses during the maturational process. For a small infant everything depends on the senses, and cognition is driven by concrete perceptual reality. During the course of development, however, deeply encoded and abstract knowledge derived from these early learning experiences comes to govern the perceptual processes. We therefore see what we expect to see, and we are either surprised, or fail to notice, when our expectations are contradicted. Experimental studies show that we frequently see things that are not there, simply because we expect them to be there. The best-known example of this is the 'blind spot', which is located in each eye at the point where the optic nerve enters the retina. For this reason, objectively, we have a hole in our vision (near the middle of the visual field) when we close one eye. Subjectively, however, this region is 'filled in' with the texture, colour, movement, etc., appropriate to what we *expect* to experience in that part of the visual field under prevailing circumstances. This is an example of what cognitive scientists call 'top-down' influences on visual perception. (Only newborns can be argued to rely exclusively on the bottom-up perceptual mechanisms.)

These facts are obviously important for psychotherapists whose daily work is concerned, perhaps above all else, with helping their patients to become aware of the internalised models that govern their life experiences – and render the present as if it were the past. It is not certain whether the findings of neuroscience in relation to the top-down influences of memory mechanisms on perception apply also to the complex relational phenomena of *transference* and the like that analysts study. However, it seems a reasonable working assumption that these mechanisms explain at least *part* of these more complex phenomena. (Here we have fertile soil for future interdisciplinary research (see Solms and Turnbull 2002).

Procedural memory

Procedural memory is a kind of 'bodily' memory. It is memory for habitual *motor* skills, or more generally *perceptuomotor* or *ideomotor* skills. It 'allows us to learn skills and know how to *do* things':[12] knowledge about how to walk, how to stack blocks in towers, how to write, or play the piano. As we said above, many of these skills are so overlearned that we do not normally think of them as aspects of *memory*. However, *being* learned skills, retrieved when appropriate, that is what they are. They depend on the right sort of experience, and a great deal of practice. Constant repetition in the learning phase is especially important for procedural memory – which has far deeper evolutionary roots than semantic memory does. All levels of ideomotor ability, from walking through playing the piano, are skills that are learnt gradually. Skills like riding a bicycle are also extremely resistant to decay with time. An aphorism that is therefore frequently applied to procedural skills is that they are 'hard to learn, hard to forget'.

There is a degree of overlap between procedural and semantic memory, as many motor skills are encoded and stored in both procedural and semantic forms. A useful way to distinguish them is to think of the difference between one's concrete skill in *playing* a particular game and (say) one's abstract knowledge of the *rules* of that game.

The distinction between procedural and semantic memory is underscored by the fact that they can break down independently of each other with brain damage. It is quite common for neurological patients to lose habitual abilities but retain abstract knowledge about the skills they have lost. Accordingly, functional imaging studies (e.g. PET and fMRI imaging)[13] reveal that different parts of the brain are activated in procedural and semantic memory tasks. However, the parts of the brain that are activated in procedural memory tasks do not constitute the *entire* motor system. For example, cortical motor (and ideomotor) structures in the parietal and frontal lobes are engaged in procedural *learning*. However, once a skill becomes *habitual* (i.e., more deeply consolidated in procedural memory) the motor programme representing it is progressively consolidated into subcortical structures, involving mainly the basal ganglia and cerebellum (see Figure 2.5).

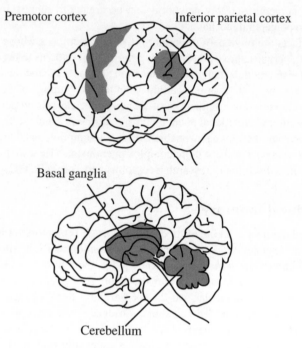

Premotor cortex   Inferior parietal cortex

Basal ganglia

Cerebellum

Figure 2.5 (A) Premotor and inferior parietal cortex.
(B) Cerebellum and basal ganglia.

Procedural memory and the unconscious

An important feature of procedural memory is that it functions *implicitly*. Habitual behaviour is executed automatically (and therefore unconsciously) almost by definition. As soon as a procedural memory is rendered explicit, it becomes something else; it is translated into a semantic or episodic form (episodic memory is discussed in the next section). It is widely known that game-playing skills can improve without a commensurate increase in abstract and explicit knowledge of how one is *supposed* to move when playing the game. This knowledge, which *instructors* of (say) tennis or golf have, is *not* acquired merely by practice at the procedural aspects of playing the sport. Many extremely competent players have no knowledge of the detailed movements required to execute a particular shot. In fact, a well-known form of gamesmanship in such sports is to *ask* your opponent how exactly they hold the racquet, or what position their elbow takes during a stroke. The experienced player knows that explicitly thinking about what was previously a well-rehearsed movement often causes a steep decline in performance levels. In contrast, top sportsmen describe their best, or peak, experiences as them being 'in the zone' – a situation of complete automaticity, in which they do not think *at all* about how to execute the stroke, and the racquet, bat or club seems simply an extension of their body.[14]

Typically, procedural memories will be associated with both semantic *and* episodic memories. That is, the same experiences will have been encoded in different ways simultaneously – as a set of experiential episodes, as a set of abstract facts, and as a set of habitual responses. This is a manifestation of the redundancy in memory that we mentioned before. As a result, it is quite possible (indeed commonplace) for a person's behaviour to be heavily determined by influences and events of which they are totally unconscious.

This is obviously relevant to some of the phenomena that psychotherapists deal with. It adds another dimension to what we said about 'transference' and the like in relation to perceptual memory. Transference clearly encompasses aspects of procedural memory too; in fact, probably even more so. It is uncertain to what extent this applies to other phenomena of interest to psychotherapists – such as the 'bodily memories' that some traumatised patients display. However, as we discussed previously, some automatic emotional behaviours (like unconscious fear reactions to conditioned noxious stimuli) certainly do seem to function very much like procedural memories. Perhaps future interdisciplinary collaboration between analysts and neuroscientists will help us to differentiate more precisely between such 'procedural' memory subsystems.

Episodic memory and consciousness

Episodic memory involves the literal 're-experiencing' of past events – the bringing back to awareness of previous experiential episodes. This is what most of us think of as memory proper. When we say '*I remember* . . . [anything]' we are speaking of an *episodic* memory. According to Schacter's definition, the episodic memory system 'allows us *explicitly* to recall the personal incidents that *uniquely* define our lives'.[15] The emphasis here falls on the twin facts that these memories are intrinsically *subjective* and that they are intrinsically *conscious* (hence the *I* and the *remember*).

Why should our memories of personal life events necessarily be conscious? Herein lies an important problem. These memories are conscious because they involve reliving of past *moments of experience*. We know what 'moments of experience' are made of (see Solms and Turnbull, 2002, for a summary); they consist in momentary couplings of perceptions of the state of the self with concurrently perceived events in the outside world – and we know that *consciousness* (or 'core consciousness') is both the medium and the message of such couplings. Episodic memory, then, constitutes the essential tissue of the 'autobiographical self' (see Damasio 1999). Extended consciousness is 'extended' precisely because it *extends* the quality of consciousness backwards onto *past* self–object couplings. It involves the reliving of past moments (or past self–object 'units') of core consciousness.

But does that really mean that autobiographical knowledge is necessarily conscious? Psychotherapists routinely report that their patients 'recover' memories of personal life events of which they were previously unconscious. Were these memories not then previously encoded as 'episodes'? Did they previously exist only as semantic beliefs and procedural habits? If that is so, all so-called *recovered memories* would in fact be *reconstructed* memories, in the sense that they would be made from raw material which was not, in itself, 'episodic'. On the one hand, it certainly seems plausible that a personal episode can leave a neural trace (a self–world connection) which links two veridical representations (a state of the self with concurrent events in the world) which only becomes conscious once the *link* (as opposed to the *representations* themselves) is activated once more. On the other hand, it is questionable whether a *state* of the self can be 'represented' without necessarily being 'reactivated'. In other words, states of the self might be intrinsically conscious. (One cannot say the 'I' in 'I remember . . .' without simultaneously *being* it.) The *sense* of self (of 'I was there . . .'; 'it happened to me . . .') appears to be *necessarily* conscious. This implies that although *external events* can be encoded unconsciously in the brain (as semantic, perceptual or procedural traces), the episodic *living* of those events apparently cannot. Experiences are not mere traces of past stimuli. Experiences have to be *lived*. It is the *reliving* of an event as an *experience* ('I remember . . .') that necessarily renders it conscious. And it is the sense of self (of 'being there') that combines the traces into an experience.

Thus we seem to have rediscovered, from a neuroscientific standpoint, the obvious fact that what *we feel* about our experiences is what renders them susceptible to repression. Even though we may have a perfectly good semantic, perceptual or procedural record of an event, the multiple exteroceptive traces of that event have to be brought back into concurrent connection with (and by) the sentient, feeling self if the event is going to be consciously relived (i.e., remembered episodically). Anything that impedes such connections can banish a memory from extended consciousness.

All of this suggests that when psychoanalysts speak of unconscious memories of personal events, what they are really referring to is something that the stored memories of the events in question *would be like* if they *could* be re-experienced. Unconscious memories of events (unconscious episodic memories) are 'as if' episodic memories. They do not exist *as experiences* until they are reactivated by the *current* self. In the interim they only exist, as such, in the form of procedural and semantic traces (habits and beliefs).

Anatomy of episodic memory

The structures that are most important for episodic memory are quite different from those that serve semantic and procedural memory. Episodic memory involves conscious activation (i.e., arousal by the core brainstem structures – see Solms and Turnbull, 2002, for a summary) of stored patterns of cortical connectivity (i.e., facilitated synaptic networks) representing previous perceptual events.[16] The directories of such links between the stored cortical patterns and various states of the brainstem self seem to be encoded, above all, through the

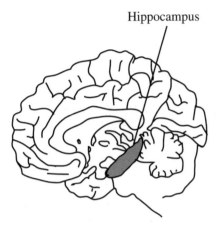

Hippocampus

Figure 2.6 The hippocampus.

hippocampus. The hippocampus is a folded piece of primitive cortex that lies on the inner surface of the forebrain within the temporal lobe (Figure 2.6). It is densely interconnected with a group of other structures loosely termed the 'limbic system'.

It is a matter of no small importance for understanding episodic memory that the network of structures that comprise the limbic system were first identified (by James Papez in the 1930s) not in connection with the functions of *memory* but rather in connection with *emotion*. This underscores the fact that episodic memories are not simply stored, but rather *lived*. The essence of episodic memory is that it is *conscious*, and the essence of self-generated states of consciousness is that they are intrinsically *emotional* (see Solms and Turnbull, 2002, for summary). This is why we say that consciousness is both the medium and the message of episodic memory; we retrieve events in an episodic form in order to remember what they *felt* like.

The effects of hippocampal lesions

Patients with bilateral damage to the hippocampus are not unconscious. Core consciousness is completely intact in these cases. What they lose is a crucial component of *extended* consciousness; the ability to extend conscious awareness to the neural traces of past events. *The traces themselves are still there* (implicitly, in procedural and semantic form) but these patients are unable to consciously (explicitly) *revive* them. For this reason, the behaviour of these patients is still *influenced* by past experience; all that they lack is the ability to reflect consciously upon the experiences. A famous case of Claparede's is often cited in this connection.[17] Claparede concealed a pin in his hand when he greeted this amnesic patient, pricking her hand as he shook it. When he next attempted to greet the patient, she withdrew her hand, *even though she had no conscious recollection of ever having met Claparede before*. The event had disappeared from her (episodic) memory but its effects remained. This is an example of the dissociation between episodic and procedural memory. When asked why she refused to take Claparede's hand, the patient explained that 'one has the right to withdraw one's hand' (or something to that effect), thereby demonstrating the dissociation between episodic and semantic memory. She knew what to *do* (procedural memory), and she recalled relevant *abstract facts* (semantic memory), but she was unable to bring the appropriate *actual experience* (episodic memory) back to mind.

A further distinction needs to be drawn here. Claparede's patient would have been able to recall the actual experience of her hand being pricked *if it had occurred a long time before the onset of her brain damage*. Patients with hippocampal lesions lose (primarily) the ability to recall events that occur *after* the damage. This demonstrates that the hippocampus is centrally implicated not so much in the *retrieval* of past experiences as in the *encoding* of experience in an explicitly retrievable form (see Figure 2.1). It appears as if the role of the hippocampus is to create the (self–object) directory links referred to above. Inability to consciously recall personal events which occur after brain damage is called anterograde amnesia. Difficulty remembering such events that occurred prior to the damage is called retrograde amnesia. Typically, the episodic memory cut-off point does not coincide *precisely* with the moment the brain was damaged; the period of amnesia for personal events usually extends some way beyond the onset of the damage. This reflects Ribot's law, and is attributable to the fact that recent memories (those encoded just before the onset of amnesia) are not yet deeply enough entrenched to withstand the effects of hippocampal damage. The retrospective erasure of prior memories provides striking evidence of the existence (and importance) of the process of *consolidation* discussed above, and of the involvement of the hippocampus in this ongoing dynamic process.

The role of the hippocampus in episodic memory is also evident from the effects of hippocampal *stimulation*. Just as hippocampal lesions *deprive* perceptual traces of a sense of 'I was there' or 'that happened to me', so hippocampal stimulation can *produce* an artificial sense of 'I was there' or 'that happened to me'. This is the presumed physiological basis of the *déjà vu* phenomenon, some forms of hallucination (e.g., in complex partial seizure disorders), and (quite possibly) certain forms of 'false memory'.

HM

No account of the neuropsychology of episodic memory is complete without at least a passing reference to the celebrated case of 'HM'. Alongside Phineas Gage, HM is perhaps the most famous clinical case in the history of behavioural neuroscience. He suffered from an intractable seizure disorder which had its epicentre in the hippocampus (as seizure disorders often do, due to the low firing threshold of limbic neurons). In the 1950s a Canadian neurosurgeon by the name of Scoville sensibly decided to remove the diseased hippocampal tissue that was producing the seizures. Today this operation is still very successful in treating cases of intractable epilepsy. As a direct result of what Scoville discovered, however, the operation that is performed today differs in one very important respect from the operation that he performed on HM. Scoville removed *both* HM's left and right hippocampi. As a direct consequence of this operation – the effects of which were later documented by Brenda Milner, a neuropsychologist colleague of Scoville's – HM never laid down another episodic memory. This case first drew the attention of neuroscientists to the critical role of the hippocampus in memory.

HM still has good access to his pre-morbid memories. This means that he is only able to recall the life he led until shortly before his operation, including his child-hood and early adulthood. He is, therefore, subjectively still living in the 1950s. He also has normal immediate memory. Thus, he can hold onto roughly seven units of information at a time, but as soon as the information is shunted from his STM buffer into LTM, and replaced by a new chunk of conscious information, he can never bring the original information back to consciousness again. HM has been very extensively studied by neuropsychologists. This has provided abundant opportunity for him to demonstrate the integrity of his semantic and procedural memory abilities. For example, he has shown strong improvement in his scores on a wide variety of standard psychological tests, even though none of these tests *feel familiar* to him, and even though he does not recognise a single one of the profes-sionals who have worked with him at such close quarters over all these years. [18]

Today, when the hippocampus is removed for the treatment of complex partial epilepsy, neurosurgeons resect only *one* hippocampus, and we expend a great deal of effort to ensure that it is the diseased rather than the healthy one that is removed. If both hippocampi are diseased, then the operation is absolutely contraindicated (on the assumption that it is better to have epilepsy than to never lay down another episodic memory again). There are also several other disease processes that preferentially affect this region. For example, this type of amnesia is frequently found after *herpes simplex encephalitis*, a viral illness that tends to selectively attack hippocampal tissue. This type of amnesia is also a common consequence of *hypoxia* (which occurs with smoke inhalation, anaesthetic accidents and near-drowning incidents, among other things). Perhaps the best-known disorder causing this type of amnesia is *Alzheimer's disease*, where the pathological process very commonly begins in the region of the hippocampus, and affects the hippocampus more severely than most other structures of the brain.

Forgetting, repression and infantile amnesia revisited

A central point to grasp is that the multiplicity of LTM storage systems makes it a commonplace for experiences to influence our behaviour and beliefs without us *consciously remembering* the experiences in question. The fact that you cannot explicitly bring something to mind does not mean that you do not know (uncon-sciously, implicitly) what happened, and act accordingly. What you remember, consciously or unconsciously, depends solely on which memory systems are engaged when the memories are being encoded and retrieved. Only when the episodic memory system is involved in the encoding (and early consolidation) of an experience can we explicitly remember that experience. If this system is not engaged, the event will disappear from consciousness, even though its implicit effects on behaviour and beliefs may well endure.

This suggests a possible physiological mechanism for (at least some forms of) repression. Facts about the forgetting of stressful experiences have come to light in recent years which are of obvious relevance for psychotherapists. The first such fact is that stressful experiences can impair hippocampal (and therefore episodic memory) functioning. In stressful situations the body unleashes a cascade of events that culminates in the adrenal glands releasing steroid hormones (gluco-corticosteroids). These hormones help us to mobilise energy where we need it (e.g., increase cardiovascular activity) and to dampen down processes that need to be inhibited in stressful situations. But, useful as they are, excessive exposure to glucocorticosteroids can also damage neurons – and hippocampal neurons in particular, since these neurons contain an unusually high concentration of gluco-corticoid receptors. Schacter (1996) reviews convincing evidence to the effect that prolonged stress (e.g. in war veterans and victims of childhood sexual abuse) results in elevated glucocorticosteroids. This is associated with various abnormalities of memory which may reflect hippocampal dysfunction. Moreover, brain imaging studies reveal that hippocampal volume is significantly decreased in such populations. Furthermore, experiments on normal subjects also show that pharmacological manipulation of steroid hormone levels can produce temporary episodic memory impairment, even in healthy volunteers. These facts suggest that hippocampal uncoupling might well be an important component in the repression (i.e., unavailability to consciousness) of traumatic memories. These memories are not encoded in a form that leaves them accessible to subsequent conscious recall, due to hippocampal dysfunction during the traumatic moment itself.

A similar line of reasoning applies to infantile amnesia. The hippocampus is not fully functional in the first 2 years of life. This suggests that it is not *possible* for someone to encode episodic memories during the first 2 years of life. Naturally, this does not imply that these early years are unimportant, or that we have *no memory* of the first 2 years of life. It implies only that the memories that we *do* encode during the very early years will take the form of habits and beliefs (procedural and semantic knowledge) rather than explicit, episodic memories. Infantile knowledge is stored as 'bodily memory' and implicit knowledge about how the world works. We therefore have every reason to accept that early experience has a decisive impact on personality development (considering the evidence of 'neuronal pruning' and the like; see above) but it seems highly unlikely that anyone can explicitly remember any event that happened to them in the first 24 months of life. When one is faced with an episodic memory dating from those very early years in a psychotherapeutic setting, it seems prudent to regard it as a 'reconstruction' derived from sources other than episodic memory (or possibly constructions derived from *later* episodes, projected backwards onto the first two years).[19] Many of the characteristics that Freud attributed to 'screen memories' seem to apply here.

This has important implications for the 'recovery' of repressed and infantile memories. On present knowledge, it seems reasonable to assume that *episodic* early infantile memories can never be recovered in any veridical sense. Our earliest experiences can only be *reconstructed*, through inferences derived from implicit (unconscious) semantic and procedural evidence. The same applies, to a lesser extent, to traumatic memories. It appears reasonable to assume that in some extreme cases traumatic events simply are not encoded in episodic memory, and therefore (as in cases with structural hippocampal damage) they can never be retrieved as such. However, it seems likely that such events will more commonly be encoded in a *degraded* episodic form, with the result that greater effort will be required to revive them, and the final product will be more or less unreliable – cobbled together from vague episodic traces, and partly constructed from other sources.

Retrieval disorders

So far, we have focused almost exclusively on the encoding and storage stages of memory (see Figure 2.1). Although the amnesia associated with hippocampal damage takes the form of an inability to retrieve post-morbid episodic memories, this is not due to any abnormality in the brain's retrieval mechanisms per se. These memories cannot be retrieved because they were not encoded in an appropriate episodic form in the first place. The memory disorders associated with abnormalities of retrieval take an entirely different form.

Figure 2.6 reminds us that the hippocampus is part of a complex circuit of (limbic) structures. Nestled within the temporal lobe, which is part of the functional unit for 'receiving, analysing and storing information', the hippocampus may be described as the *perceptual* end of the limbic system. Through a thick bundle of axons (the fornix), which course around the diencephalon, the hippocampus projects to a group of structures nestled within the 'motor' part of the brain – the functional unit for 'programming, regulating and verifying activity'.

These densely interconnected structures include the dorsomedial nucleus of the thalamus, the mammillary bodies, the basal forebrain nuclei, and the ventromesial frontal cortex itself, which surrounds all these nuclei. These structures are damaged by a variety of disease processes, but perhaps most commonly by the vitamin B deficiency associated with chronic alcoholism (Wernicke's encephalopathy) and by ruptured aneurysms of the anterior communicating artery. These pathologies produce a striking neuropsychological condition known as Korsakoff's psychosis. The fact that it is described as a 'psychosis' immediately indicates a cardinal difference from the amnesia associated with hippocampal lesions. If you ask a patient like HM where he first met you, he will almost certainly respond that he 'doesn't know' or 'can't remember'. Put the same question to a patient with Korsakoff's syndrome, however, and – even if you have never met the patient before in your life – he or she is likely to respond with a statement like 'What do

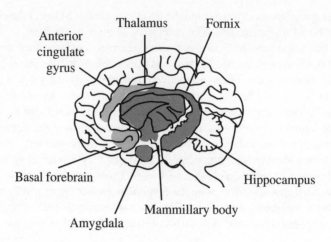

Figure 2.7 The hippocampus and its connections.

you mean, where did I first meet you . . . we've known each other for years; just yesterday, you were sitting right here and we had a drink together!' These patients do not *forget*; they *misremember*, and often in the most grandiose fashion. This type of misremembering is called confabulation.

Confabulation is the primary distinguishing characteristic between the encoding and retrieval forms of the amnestic syndrome. Korsakoff patients do not forget, or have gaps in their reminiscences. Rather, their reminiscences contain material that does not belong there. Careful studies of these patients have revealed that their false memories do not come from thin air. Rather, they are fragments of real memories jumbled up in an inappropriate manner. (Later we will discuss some important implications of these studies for psychoanalysis.) The term achronogenesis, which means disorder of time source, is sometimes used to describe these memory errors. Patients suffering from achronogenesis may tell you about something that happened 10 years ago as if it had happened yesterday. It turns out that a problem of time tagging is not the only characteristic of confabulatory errors. Another very interesting feature of these patients is their inability to distinguish between memories and non-memories. Dreams, memories for real experiences, and daytime thoughts are frequently confused with one another.[20]

An example of this phenomenon will capture the nature of the difficulty more clearly. In a standard clinical assessment of memory, one of these patients was read the following story:

> On December 6th, last week, a river overflowed in a small town 10 miles from Oxford. Water covered the streets, and entered the houses. Thirteen people were drowned, and 600 people caught colds, because of the dampness and cold weather. In trying to save a boy, who was caught under a bridge, a man cut his hand.

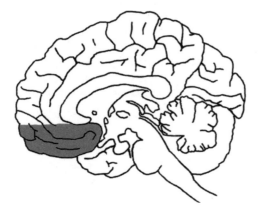

Figure 2.8 The ventromesial quadrant of the frontal lobes.

The patient was then asked to retell the story, and he replied:

> There was a flood, I think it happened in Streatham [which is where he lived] . . . was it in the High Street? What happened to Jack and that shop of his in the High Street? I don't remember . . . but I remember the day I was there with him. And there was a doctor there, asking me stupid questions about my memory – didn't he realise that people who have suffered strokes can't remember!

There are clearly some elements of the original story there, but the story rapidly becomes muddled. This includes tangential associations and confusion of memories from the past with thoughts from the present – as is demonstrated by the comment about doctors and their silly questions.

The *contents* of such patients' confabulations, and the *types* of errors they habitually make, have important implications for psychoanalysis. We have discussed a number of striking examples elsewhere (see Kaplan-Solms and Solms 2000). They can be observed with especial clarity in patients with lesions to the ventromesial quadrant of the frontal lobes (Figure 2.8). Bilateral damage to this part of the brain produces a state of mind that shows several properties reminiscent of what Freud described as 'the special characteristics of the system Ucs'. These functional characteristics were listed as follows: 'exemption from mutual contradiction, primary process (mobility of cathexis), timelessness, and replacement of external by psychical reality' (Freud 1915: 187).

Exemption from mutual contradiction

One such patient was an English gentleman in a neurological rehabilitation unit, who had lived abroad for some years. A close friend of his had died some 20 or 30 years previously, while they were both living in Kenya. One day he excitedly informed the staff that he had met a friend of his in the hospital. 'Can you believe it?' he said, 'Phil Adams[21] is here in the same unit as me. You know the chap I told you about who died in Kenya 20 years ago? It is wonderful to see him again.' When questioned as to how Phil Adams could be in the hospital if he had died in Africa 20 years before, the patient stopped for a moment and said: 'Yes, that must cause interesting legal problems – being dead in one country and alive in another.' This man was clearly quite capable of accepting two mutually exclusive facts as being simultaneously true.

Timelessness

A second patient – a woman who suffered from damage in the same brain region – had experienced several instances of medical difficulties prior to the stroke for which she had been admitted on this occasion. One was a deep vein thrombosis (in her leg), another a hysterectomy. To this woman, her current hospitalisation was one and the same as the others. She would speak as if she was in the neurological ward for the purposes of a hysterectomy, but in virtually the next sentence she would suggest that her admission was due to a deep vein thrombosis, and then again, also, for a stroke. Indeed, she even seemed to think she was hospitalised at all the locations of the previous admissions simultaneously – so that she was in King's College Hospital, the Royal Free Hospital, and the Royal London Hospital, all at the *same* time. A series of separate temporal events had thus become merged into a single experience.

Timelessness of a different kind was displayed by the gentleman with the dead friend, described above. His wife always came to visit him at 5 p.m., which was visiting time. For this reason, the patient was constantly of the opinion that it was 5 p.m. – even straight after breakfast, or before lunch. During one lunch-time, when his error was being corrected by a staff-member for the umpteenth time, he noticed a 'No Smoking' sign on the wall, which took the form of a red circle with a diagonal line through it. Mistaking this sign for a clock, he retorted: 'Look . . . it *is* 5 o'clock!'

Replacement of external reality by psychical reality

In these cases, the demands of the internal world of the drives take precedence over the constraints of external reality, and inner wishes displace outer perceptions. An example of this kind of error is the above-mentioned case where the 'No Smoking' sign *became* a clock showing 5 p.m., because this accorded with the patient's wishes. His inner reality dominated over his external perception in a way that we do not normally allow. In the same way, his *wish* to meet his dead friend (or to be among friends) distorted his *perception* of a stranger in the hospital (someone whose features probably reminded him of his friend). Even when he recalled the fact of his friend's death, the external evidence could be put to one side in the service of maintaining the wish.

Primary process (mobility of cathexis)

This can be defined as a situation in which feelings invested in one object are transferred to other objects without adequate constraint – usually in cases where the objects have some feature in common (sometimes quite a superficial feature). Such 'mobility of cathexis' is apparent in the example where the patient conflates a stranger with his long-dead friend. Perhaps a better example comes from another patient, who clearly recognised her husband when he visited her in hospital, and treated him as such. Yet, when he was not there, she regularly referred to the man in the bed next to hers as being her husband, and behaved accordingly towards him. Again, the wish-fulfilling properties of such conflations are clear. She wanted her husband to be there. When he was, that was fine; but when he wasn't, it was not at all difficult to ignore or modify her conception of reality to fit with her requirements.

This is not the place for a detailed discussion of the issues raised by such patients (see Kaplan-Solms and Solms 2000). However, it seems clear that these typical features of confabulation are also the special functional characteristics that Freud attributed to the system Unconscious.[22] Considering them again in the context of memory retrieval mechanisms allows us to draw some interesting conclusions about the organisation of memory.

A second type of memory organisation?

We have said that the hippocampus is critically implicated in the *encoding* of episodic memories, and that when it is damaged episodic memories literally disappear (as such). However, when the diencephalic and ventromesial frontal structures that support episodic memory *retrieval* are damaged, the memories do not disappear – they merely lose their veridical and rational organisation. This is because the structures that normally systematise the retrieval process in accordance with the requirements of reality and reason (Freud's 'reality principle' and 'secondary process') are damaged. This suggests something very important about long-term memory, and unconscious memory systems in general. The way that long-term memories are organised, and interconnected *unconsciously,* may differ dramatically from the way in which we normally retrieve them consciously. The associative links that form between them may therefore be very different from what we would imagine from the point of view of the healthy, reflective ego. The features of veridicality and rationality that we normally value so highly appear to be *add-on* features that only make their appearance during the *retrieval* process, under the goal-directed control of the functional unit for programming, regulation and verification of activity (see Luria 1973). This functional unit also loses its influence over our memory processes at night, while we are sleeping (Solms 1997a, 2000).

Psychoanalysts have long believed that the organising principles of unconscious cognition are entirely different from those of conscious (and preconscious) mental life. Using the memory errors of neurological patients as a source of evidence in this regard offers us an opportunity to investigate these organising principles from a completely different perspective to that which was used to discover the principles – that is, from the free associations of neurologically normal patients on the psychoanalytic couch.[23] Although the evidence provided here is by no means unproblematic, and open to criticism and reinterpretation, it suggests a novel line of approach to the investigation of unconscious memory systems. We (authors of this chapter) are currently conducting a systematic series of investigations of confabulatory amnestic patients from this point of view, using a range of neuropsychological techniques.

The point we are making here is simply that there is a great difference between the retrieval of information (conscious remembering) and the way in which the information is actually stored and organised unconsciously. The implicit effects that unconscious memory associations exert on our everyday cognition and behaviour might be equally unexpected from the viewpoint of explicit ego functioning. It is important to remind ourselves here of a point we made near the beginning of this chapter, namely that memory traces may be unconsciously activated all the time; one does not have to explicitly retrieve a memory in order for it to be active, and for it to influence cognition and behaviour.

Forgetting, repression and infantile amnesia – again

We have just learned that frontal cortex is crucial for the retrieval of memory in a *realistic, rational* and *orderly* way. Frontal cortex, no less than the hippocampus, is poorly developed in the first 2 years of life. In fact, there is a substantial growth spurt in frontal cortex at around 2 years of age, and then a second spurt at about 5 years – and frontal cortical volume continues to expand throughout the whole of adolescence. In the first few years the level of organisation of the frontal system ('the unit for programming, regulating and verifying activity') may be considered so poor that the organised retrieval process we have just discussed is, to all intents and purposes, not available to the young child. The goal-directed, rational, realistic, selective and chronologically sequenced way of remembering that we rely upon as adults is thus not characteristic of those early years of life. As a result, the reminiscences of young children are not all that different from those of adults suffering from Korsakoff's syndrome.[24] Since the goal-directed frontal system plays an important part in *controlling* encoding and consolidation processes too, it seems highly likely that the memory traces of young children are actually *stored* differently from the way they are stored in adult brains. If something is encoded in one form, it is more difficult to retrieve it accurately in another form, thus reinforcing what we said earlier about the reconstructed nature of childhood episodic memories. These facts, no less than those pertaining to the maturation of the hippocampus, shed important new light on the phenomenon of infantile amnesia.

All of these considerations raise the possibility that what Freud called 'primary repression' or 'biological repression' (i.e., the natural development of a repression barrier around the fifth year of life) may have a lot to do with normal frontal lobe maturation. These considerations also suggest that it would be a mistake to think of repression solely in terms of *encoding* mechanisms (i.e., failure of *hippocampal* memory mechanisms). *Retrieval* mechanisms, and the *frontal lobes*, obviously also play an important part in the developmental and clinical phenomena that Freud conceptualised under the rubric of 'repression'. Also, in certain individuals and in certain situations, the retrieval processes run by the frontal lobes might well be selectively *biased* in the type of material that is promoted for conscious representation in the episodic memory system. But here too the reader should not forget what we said earlier about failures of episodic memory: the fact that something is not *consciously* remembered does not mean that it not remembered at all. Presumably 'repressed' memories, no less than other forms of implicit memory, continue to exert a definite effect on cognition and behaviour, throughout life, via the procedural and semantic memory systems.

The frontal lobes, emotion and memory

In recent years we have become increasingly aware of the neurobiology of the various core emotion systems, whose biological basis lies in a range of subcortical structures (see Panksepp 1998). These systems are involved in the process of learning about the *consequences* of our actions – the better to predict these consequences in the future. Much progress has been made in relation to the learning involved in one emotion (fear) and Joseph LeDoux's (1996) book, *The Emotional Brain*, provides an excellent summary of this field. We are also beginning to understand something of the way in which the output of these systems interacts with cognitive processes, and the manner in which it enters conscious experience. The anatomical basis for this interaction are the ventromesial frontal lobe structures described above (see Figure 2.8). It is in this brain region that the fibre pathways from the various subcortical emotion systems begin to interact with the cortical systems of the frontal lobes which are so central to cognition. This offers a mechanism by which core emotional information can access the highest-order and most sophisticated parts of the mental apparatus – and knowledge on this topic has helped us to resolve a long-standing problem in neuropsychology.

Neurological patients with ventromesial frontal lesions, especially after high-velocity motor vehicle accidents, have long been a puzzle to the neuropsychological community. Such patients show relatively normal intelligence, and often show near-normal performance on a range of 'executive' tasks. However, in spite of such apparently normal performances, they choose unsuitable friends, enter inadvisable relationships and engage in inappropriate activities (Bechara *et al.* 2000). This behaviour typically leads to financial losses, career termination, and loss of affection of family and friends. The role of emotion, and especially for emotion *learning*, has recently changed our understanding of the behaviour of such patients. Indeed, it has changed our understanding of many aspects of mental life. It appears that the poor judgement and decision-making abilities of these patients follow from an *inability* to use emotion-learning systems, which provide information about the possible outcome of decisions (see Damasio 1994, 1996).

This literature has suggested a biological basis for the substantial role of emotion in cognition, and this aspect of mental life can now be reliably assessed using the Iowa Gambling Task (Bechara *et al.* 1994). In this task the subject is faced with four decks of cards, and asked to choose any deck, in any sequence. They win or lose money with each turn. Some decks have frequent high gains, but also occasional substantial losses. Sustained playing of these decks leads to overall financial *loss*. Other decks have more modest payouts, but lead only to small and infrequent losses, so that sustained playing of the decks leads to small but consistent *gains*. The game is complex, and participants do not appear, *subjectively*, to understand the contingencies of the game. Nevertheless, participants quite rapidly develop a 'feeling' about which decks are good or bad, which probably derives from small activations of emotion in the seconds *preceding* the choice of a high-risk 'bad' deck – when the participant is *imagining* which deck they might choose (see Damasio 1994, 1996). Activation of the autonomic nervous system is the physiological correlate of this emotional experience, and can be directly measured using galvanic skin response (GSR; see Damasio 1994, 1996). In other words, participants receive 'advance warning' of the consequences of their actions, coded in terms of *emotion,* which allow them to avoid negative consequences (Bechara *et al.* 1994).

In practice, all participants start by choosing the risky decks, but neurologically normal participants (even those who regard themselves as 'gamblers') rapidly shift to decks where they will accrue the smaller amounts of money over longer periods. Neurological patients with lesions to the ventromesial frontal lobes also show a strong galvanic skin response *after* a bad choice has been made (showing that they still *feel* emotion), but have no ability to develop the 'advance warning' effect which would be provided by the advance warning of a potentially poor-outcome choice. As a result they do not develop an avoidance of bad-outcome choices, and consistently lose money (Bechara *et al.* 1994). This inability to predict the likely emotional outcome of their actions is probably the cause of their many difficulties in everyday life.

Intuition and subjective experience

Thus, participants on the Iowa Gambling Task seem to acquire normal performance by using an *implicit* learning system – relying on an (emotionally mediated) 'feeling', or 'hunch', about which decks are good or bad, in the absence of explicit (cognitive, conceptual) awareness of the way that the decks pay out (Bechara *et al.* 2000). This is a reasonable definition of reliance on 'intuition' or belief – i.e., confidence in something not immediately susceptible to proof. Participants cannot prove, or explicitly demonstrate, *why* they are choosing the decks that they do – but they are prepared to 'trust their feelings' in making the choices. In other words, participants are required to base their choices on a system that *appears* to be outside of rational control, because they are asked to 'feel' their way through performance on the task. In practice, their ability to perform well is far from mysterious – they are merely attending to the input from a second (affective) source of knowledge about the properties of objects: so that decisions are made based on two 'sources' of information – both affective and cognitive (see Solms 1997b, or Solms and Turnbull 2002, for more on this 'two sources' concept).

Clearly, as the evidence from patients with ventromesial frontal lesions demonstrates, the affective source of knowledge is *central* to learning and problem-solving processes – though it is clearly an under-researched aspect of decision making (Fridja *et al.* 2000). It is also, of course, a phenomenon of great interest to psychotherapists. The analytic situation regularly requires the analyst to make judgements on the basis of such affective knowledge – which might well be argued to form the basis for the counter-transference (in its modern usage). These findings offer, therefore, the possibility of that most unlikely of things: a neuro-biological explanation of intuition.

Memory in childhood

From the evidence that we have discussed thus far in this chapter, we can draw some further (hypothetical) conclusions about the nature of memory in young children (under 2 years). We have already suggested that their subjective experience of memory relies very little on veridical episodic retrieval – so that being faced with an object in the world (i.e., a feared dog or a loved parent) they are unlikely to consciously recall specific events in relation to that object (i.e., the dog barking or the parent being affectionate). This, we have argued, results from the fact that the 'hippocampal' memory system has not developed, in any viable sense, in the young child. We have also argued that affect-based learning systems *are* available to the young child, and we have been able to characterise the experi-ence of these systems as being the feeling of 'intuition' associated with incomplete confidence about the reliability of such memory. Thus, we have a feeling, a 'hunch', about the likelihood of an object behaving in a particular way.

In adults, such intuitions about the likely behaviour of objects are usually[25] backed by a set of episodic memories, which bolster our confidence about the likelihood of an event occurring. In the young child, the additional information provided by episodic memory will not be available – reducing the 'confidence' that an object will behave in a predictable way. In this way, therefore, the world of the young child must be a good deal more unreliable than the world of the adult – with the child constantly being forced to guess, or estimate, the way in which objects (people) will behave, all on the basis of the flimsy evidence of emotional learning systems. It is, therefore, a world of fleeting intuitive feelings and hunches – where objects appear to behave quite unpredictably.

The psychoanalytic implications are quite clear. A central tenet of much psychoanalytic thinking about the nature of early childhood emphasises the importance of the *reliability* of the mother's (or primary caregiver's) behaviour in relation to the child. The neurobiological evidence reviewed above suggests that the young child is so dependent on a *reliable* caregiver (or facilitating environment) for the reason that the infant is not equipped with the range of memory systems available to the adult, and therefore can rely internally only on 'intuitive' impressions about the behaviour of objects (people).

Conclusion

This concludes our brief review of the neuropsychology of memory. There is a great deal more that could have been said, as memory is one of the most popular research topics in modern neuroscience, and it bears on a number of questions of importance for psychoanalysis. We stand at the dawn of an exciting new era in mental science, where all sorts of possibilities are opening up. We appear, at last, to have within our grasp the possibility of studying in measurable, physical units, the inner life of the mind – the traditional preserve of psychoanalysis. This places the discipline in a very interesting situation with regard to the rest of science.

Despite a century of concerted effort, psychoanalysts have not been able to convince the scientific community at large that they have truly revealed the laws that govern this most interesting and mysterious piece of nature: our very own selves. A substantial body of neurobiological knowledge now exists which borders on many issues of traditional interest to psychoanalysts, making the present moment something of a crossroads for the field. Psychoanalysts can choose to remain aloof from neuroscience for another 100 years, but we have little doubt that that would be to the detriment of both psychoanalysis and neuroscience. There is only one mental apparatus. In the long term, a coherent neuroscience of *all* of memory (and the 'inner world' in general) will be developed, with or without psychoanalysis. The cooperation of psychoanalysts at this point will surely speed up the process, but science has a way of eventually finding a route through the darkest forests, and it will no doubt do the same with this one in the end.

The high road for psychoanalysis is to engage with the neuroscientific issues that should now directly interest it. This will not be an easy task. Most psychoanalysts are unfamiliar with the complexities of neuroscience, and (one must admit) they are often poorly equipped to design and implement systematic scientific investigations. An increasing number of psychoanalysts today are, however, keen to rise to the challenge, and this chapter is designed to aid those who wish to do so. If a critical mass of psychoanalysts choose this path, there is much to be gained in return for the effort that it will involve. A radically different psychoanalysis will emerge. It will be a psychoanalysis that retains its pride of place as the science of the human *subject* – the discipline through which we investigate the stuff of inner experience and the living of a life. But its claims will be far more securely grounded. We will better understand how mental disorders arise. We will be better able to target our therapies at those who can benefit most, and in the ways that work best. We may extend our clinical reaches in previously undreamt of directions. And in the end, we believe, we shall be able to say with confidence at last: this is how the mind *really* works.

Notes

1 A number of books provide accessible overviews of this literature: Larry Squire's (1987) *Memory and Brain* emphasises the neuroscience issues – although his book is starting to date now. Daniel Schacter's (1996) *Searching for Memory* emphasises the cognitive issues. Alan Baddeley's (1997) *Human Memory: Theory and Practice* also provides a comprehensive, but rather technical, review of the cognitive literature.

2 Box-and-arrow diagrams never reflect the *full* reality of a mental function, and nor are they meant to. We use boxes in order to *simplify* our metapsychological picture of the 'mental apparatus' and mainly for *didactic* purposes. In reality, the component functions of the mind fluidly interrelate with each other in far more complicated ways than any box-and-arrow diagram can convey.

3 Breuer and Freud noted (in 1895) that consciousness and memory are, in this sense, mutually exclusive.

4 See Anderson and Green (2001) for some recent findings in this domain.

5 For a more detailed account of these mechanisms, see Kandel *et al.* (2000).

6 What Freud actually said was this: 'Perhaps we ought to content ourselves with asserting that what is past in mental life *may* be preserved and is not *necessarily* destroyed. It is always possible that even in the mind some of what is old is effaced or absorbed . . . to such an extent that it cannot be restored or revived by any means; or that preservation in general is dependent on certain favourable conditions. It is possible, but we know nothing about it. We can only hold fast to the fact that it is rather the rule than the exception for the past to be preserved in mental life' (Freud 1930: 71–72).

7 Schacter (1996: 151, emphasis added).

8 'Modal' specificity refers to information that is confined to a concrete *perceptual* modality (e.g. vision or hearing). 'Material' specificity refers to information that is confined to a particular *abstract* category (e.g. verbal vs. visuospatial).

9 It is important to note that these regions do not *contain* the entire memory trace, for example of an individual face or name. Rather, critical *regions* (or *nodes*) of such circuits are to be found in the regions in question, which results in the psychological function becoming heavily degraded when these vulnerable regions are damaged.

10 See Mesulam (1998).

11 Together with his colleague Lev Vygotsky (see Luria, 1973: 74–75).

12 Schacter (1996: 135, emphasis added).

13 Positron emission tomography (abbreviation: *PET*) and functional magnetic resonance imaging (abbreviation: *fMRI*) are techniques that reveal the relative activation of different parts of the brain by scanning the level of metabolic activity (which reflects the rate at which cells are firing) in different regions of brain tissue. Using these techniques while someone performs a particular task, and comparing the results with those for a different task, reveals differences in the parts of the brain involved in the different tasks.

14 See Gallwey (1986).

15 Schacter (1996: 17, emphasis added).

16 Conscious *thoughts* are 'perceptual events' too, and can also be reactivated.

17 Claparede (1911).

18 See Ogden (1996) for an excellent case description of HM's world. Oliver Sacks' (1985) *Lost Mariner* offers a wonderfully clear description of another such amnesic patient, though there are several key differences between Sacks' patient and HM – mainly because the underlying cause of the amnesia (and hence also the precise lesion site) differs, as discussed in the text.

19 Our earliest childhood memories are often patched together retrospectively from photographs and parents' accounts of the events in question. The reconstructed quality of these memories is often given away by the fact that we actually *see* ourselves (from a third-person point of view) in the 'remembered' episodes.

20 See Solms (1997a) for some case examples.

21 Not his real name.

22 Freud (1915: 187).

23 See Kaplan-Solms and Solms (2000).

24 However, this analogy should not be pushed too far. For example, adults with Korsakoff's syndrome are able to compensate for their retrieval difficulties in other ways, because the rest of the mental apparatus is already developed, and remains (largely) intact.

25 We should note, however, that adults are not *immune* to making judgements on the basis of intuition alone. The 'Gambling Task' findings discussed above suggest that people are correct in relying on this source to a *reasonable* extent. However, excessive reliance on this class of knowledge may well result in false beliefs – again, an area in which we are currently collecting some data.

References

Anderson, M. C. and Green, C. (2001). Suppressing unwanted memories by executive control. *Nature 410*: 366–369.

Baddeley, A. (1997). *Human Memory: Theory and Practice*. Hove: Psychology Press.

Bechara, A., Damasio, A. R., Damasio, H. and Anderson, S. W. (1994). Insensitivity to future consequences following damage to human prefrontal cortex. *Cognition 50*: 7–15.

Bechara, A., Damasio, H. and Damasio, A. R. (2000). Emotion, decision making and the orbitofrontal cortex. *Cerebral Cortex*, *10*: 295–307.

Claparede, E. (1911) *Experimental Pedagogy and the Psychology of the Child*. Bristol: Thoemmes Press.

Crick, F. and Mitchison G. (1983). The function of dream sleep. *Nature 304*: 111–114.

Damasio, A. (1994). *Descartes' Error*. New York: Grosset/Putnam.

Damasio, A. R. (1996). The somatic marker hypothesis and the possible functions of the prefrontal cortex. *Philosophical Transactions of the Royal Society of London (Biology) 351*: 1413–1420.

Damasio, A. (1999). *The Feeling of What Happens*. London: Heinemann.

Edelman, G. (1989). *The Remembered Present*. New York: Basic Books.

Freud, S. (1915). The unconscious. *S.E. 14:* 161.

Freud, S. (1930). Civilisation and its Discontents. *S.E.21:* 59.

Fridja, N. H., Manstead, A. S. R. and Bem, S. (2000). *Emotions and Beliefs: How Feelings Influence Thoughts*. Cambridge: Cambridge University Press.

Gallwey, W. T. (1986) *The Inner Game of Golf*. Pan: London.

Kandel, E. R., Schwartz, J. H. and Jessell, T. M. (2000). *Principles of Neural Science*. Norwalk, CT: Appleton & Lange.

Kaplan-Solms, K. and Solms, M. (2000). *Clinical Studies in Neuro-Psychoanalysis*. London: Karnac.

LeDoux, J. (1996). *The Emotional Brain*. London: Weidenfeld & Nicolson.

Luria, A. R. (1973). *The Working Brain*. Harmondsworth: Penguin.

Mesulam, M-M. (1998) From sensation to cognition. *Brain 121*: 1013–1052.

Ogden, J. A. (1996). *Fractured Minds: A Case-Study Approach to Clinical Neuropsychology.* New York: Oxford University Press.

Panksepp, J. (1998) *Affective Neuroscience.* Oxford: Oxford University Press.

Sacks, O. (1985). *The Man Who Mistook his Wife for a Hat.* London: Picador.

Schacter, D. (1996). *Searching for Memory.* New York: Basic Books.

Solms, M. (1997a). *The Neuropsychology of Dreams.* Mahwah, NJ: Earlbaum.

Solms, M. (1997b). What is consciousness? *Journal of the American Psychoanalytic Association 45:* 681–778.

Solms, M. (2000). Dreaming and REM sleep are controlled by different brain mechanisms. *Behavioral and Brain Sciences 23*: 843–850.

Solms, M. and Turnbull. O. H. (2002). *The Brain and the Inner World: An Introduction to the Neuroscience of Subjective Experience.* London: Karnac.

Squire, L. R. (1987). *Memory and Brain.* New York: Oxford University Press.

Chapter 3

Attachment, actual experience and mental representation

Miriam Steele

Introduction

In this chapter I will delineate the ways in which the quality of early attachment relationships and actual experiences with the caregiver(s) form the building blocks for the representational world. I will begin by outlining the four basic assumptions of attachment theory, and then provide an overview of both past and more recent evidence that supports the theory. Development is looked at in the light of the attachment system. Developmental vicissitudes will be understood in the light of the manner in which basic attachments needs have been met by the caregiver(s). The concomitant effects of the maintenance or disruption of emotional bonds will be described.

Attachment theory is based on the original and enduring ideas of John Bowlby. It states that humans are biopsychologically motivated by the need for attachment to others. Attachment theory posits that our survival is inextricably linked to and dependent upon the capacity to establish and maintain emotional ties to others. Attachment theory together with core achievements in attachment research which have validated the theory has attracted a great range and depth of interest in recent years. The verifiable burgeoning interest in attachment research comes from a variety of disciplines including child psychotherapy, child psychiatry, clinical psychology and social work, and attachment theory has now assumed a position of central importance. The four basic assumptions of attachment theory have been robustly supported by observational research that helps us understand the fundamental and enduring influence parents, in one generation, have upon the next (and later) generations.

The four assumptions which convey the essence of Bowlby's attachment theory are as follows:

1 Intimate emotional bonds between individuals have a primary status and biological function.
2 The way a child is treated has a powerful influence on a child's development and later personality functioning.
3 Attachment behaviour is to be viewed as part of an organisational system

which utilises the notion of an 'internal working model' of self and other to guide expectation and the planning of behaviour.

4   Attachment behaviour is resistant to change, but there is a continuing potential for change so that at no time in a person's life are they impermeable to adversity or to favourable influence.

The primary status and biological function of intimate emotional ties

This idea, now widely assumed to be true, when first put forward by Bowlby in the late 1950s caused him to be branded a heretic by many of his psychoanalytic colleagues. For Bowlby, our survival as individuals and as the human species depends upon the ability to establish and maintain emotional ties to others. Operational from birth and evident across the life span (especially at times of crisis), the 'instincts' of crying, reaching out, and holding on are the functional expressions of a biological imperative with evolutionary origins. Bowlby anchored his ideas about the importance of relationships on a new model of human motivation, drawing on the latest advances in neurochemical, cognitive, ethological and evolutionary theory (see Cassidy and Shaver 1999; Schore, 2000 and this volume; Suomi, 1999).

Despite or because of John Bowlby's position, working in the immediate aftermath of World War II and the myriad of separation and grief issues that it brought, he transformed thinking about the parent–child attachment relationship into one of the most viable theoretical concepts to arise out of twentieth century psychiatry. This viability stems from his awareness that a full understanding of the parent–child relationship could not be arrived at by a single perspective from child psychiatry or child psychoanalysis. After establishing the Child and Family Department at the Tavistock Clinic, he invoked the help of leading clinical and developmental psychologists, child and adult psychiatrists and ethnologists – with a unifying interest in how to understand the ways parents influence their children.

Mary Ainsworth, who participated in those meetings for 4 years, was to play a critical role in the development of attachment theory, through her devotion to attachment research and the training of other researchers. Determined to collect evidence that might test the ideas discussed at the Tavistock meetings, Ainsworth set out to conduct field studies involving detailed observations of mothers and babies, first in Uganda (Ainsworth 1967), and later in repeated home observations of mothers and babies over the first year of life in America (Ainsworth et al. 1978). It is important to point out that some of the crucial elements of attachment theory arose from Ainsworth's careful observations of mothers and babies in the field in Uganda, which counter the criticism that attachment theory is a theory of parent–child relationships for white, middle-class Western families. It was the observations in Uganda which prompted her to see the attachment system as species, not culturally, specific. Mary Ainsworth was also convinced that the hundreds of hours of home observations across a range of settings in Baltimore taught her the most, including – centrally – the importance of tender bodily contact between mother and baby. Conceiving of the lab-based observation sequence known as the Strange Situation, the method which would be applied in thousands of developmental research studies across the globe, took her and a colleague about a half-hour, and was an afterthought (Ainsworth and Marvin 1995). That is, it was an attempt to see if observing mother and baby in a stressful situation, *outside the home*, would relate to maternal behaviour in the home setting.

Ainsworth *et al.* (1978) built on Bowlby's premises about the biological basis of attachment, and the importance of actual experiences with caregivers, highlighting the need to 'stress' or activate the attachment system in order to study and measure it. By introducing the 1-year-old, and his/her mother, into a brightly decorated toy-laden playroom, she aimed to activate the child's exploratory (or play/work) system. By minutes later engineering the separation of mother from child, she aimed to activate the attachment (love) system. With one system called into action, she anticipated, the other would (normally) recede. And so it was, for the normal or securely attached child who played joyfully in the presence of the mother, showed a diminishment of play and joy upon separation, and then bounced back upon reunion. For such children, home observations confirmed a history of sensitive responsiveness from the mother. But for other children, less than joyful and often ineffective exploratory play behaviours predominated, and appeared to be used defensively to mask inner distress upon reunion. For these children, home observations confirmed a history of insensitive (interfering) and/or unresponsive (rejecting) maternal behaviour. For still other children, exploration was ineffective, and distress prevailed across the lab observation and home observations confirmed an ineffective style of maternal behaviour, despite (as is always the case) good intentions.

Ainsworth and her colleagues observed that mothers of infants who would later be judged secure in the strange situation were able to manage feedings in a manner that responded to infant signals, e.g. adjusting the provision of bottled and solid foods in step with the infant's capacity to ingest. Feeding was in response to the infant's initiative and never forced by the mothers of secure infants (Ainsworth and Bell 1974). Thus, in face-to-face interactions, some mothers were able to skilfully regulate pacing to establish smooth turn taking and coordination with the children's initiatives (Blehar *et al.* 1977). Physical contact between secure infants and their mothers was marked by a gentle and tender style that made the contact pleasurable for both mothers and infants. By the end of infancy, infants who had experienced open communication marked by sensitive care were more effective in communicating with their mothers.

The neurochemical, biological, and evolutionary origins of the attachment behavioural system are well illustrated by the classic Strange Situation (Ainsworth *et al.* 1978) valid for infants aged 12–18 months. In the Strange Situation, infants are convincingly distressed at both a behavioural and biological level (Spangler and Grossmann 1993). The situation works as well as it does because of its ability to provoke into action the attachment system and evokes in the good-enough mothered child a search for the secure base. Quite simply, no newborn can survive *and* thrive without the provision of a secure base from the caregiving environment. For a 1-year-old child to behave as if this were not the case is a defensive manoeuvre of impressive proportions.

The way an infant is treated by caregivers has a profound influence on their development

A painstakingly detailed approach to measuring the qualities of the parent–child relationship, which follows directly from Bowlby and Ainsworth's observations and has been enabled by advances in video-film technology, was undertaken by the innovative work of the 'baby watchers', including Edward Tronick and Beatrice Beebe. Edward Tronick's impressive work on the timing and quality of mother–infant interactions highlighted how even the securely attached dyad doesn't get it right 100% of the time. In fact the rate of misattunement observed in lab-based interactions, when things are 'as good as they get', is more like 50%! (see Stern 1985). From this can be understood that 'normal' social interactions involve children in interactions with caregivers in the confident hope of being understood, and the understanding of how reparation may be achieved if one feels misunderstood. It may be that the working through of the mismatches provides an essential ingredient for becoming securely attached; i.e., the infant or child is provoked to find a strategy for bringing the caregiver back into a focused interaction and from this learns (consciously and mainly unconsciously) what works and what doesn't. This may be the essential ingredient for a sense of inner confidence, cohesion, and attachment security. For those parent–infant pairs for whom the mismatches are simply too frequent and/or too intense, the frustration may simply be too great and they are provoked to give up on the search for attunement. In these instances we can see that defensive manoeuvres get built up relatively quickly (i.e., by 9 months of age) that help protect against the pain of overwhelming and misattuned interactions.

Beatrice Beebe and her colleagues have been able to carefully calibrate the sophisticated minutiae of the pre-linguistic interactions between mothers and their infants. In a recent monograph Jaffe *et al.* (2001) highlight how they were able to predict infant–mother attachment classifications from assessments of 'rhythmic coupling' in 88 4-month-old infants. By looking at the features of these conversations in terms of such constructs as 'turn taking, joining, yielding and tracking' they were able to define mother–infant attunement in an empirically robust manner. That these observations at 4 months predict joyous responses to mother, following separation (in the Strange Situation), at 12 months is highly suggestive of how early mother–child interaction patterns contribute to the building up of the child's inner world (or internal working model), including representations of self and others. Jaffe and colleagues appear to have captured the actual experiences which contribute to the building up in the child's mind of an enduring sense of what it feels like to be in, what to bring to, and what to expect from, relationships. Increasingly, developmental research is able to distinguish between normative mother–infant interaction and mild to major disturbances in this core relationship system.

One of the most creative and clinically relevant discoveries in the world of attachment research emerged from a pre-eminent centre of attachment research, i.e. the Social Development Lab, run by Mary Main and Erik Hesse, in Berkeley, California. Main, a purveyor of ingenious methodological innovations, observed that some of the infants she was trying to classify in the original Strange Situation system simply did not fit. They appeared not to have an organised strategy for dealing with the stresses the paradigm engendered and so she described this group as having a disorganised classification (Main and Solomon 1990). The infant displaying a disorganised pattern appeared to view the parent as frightening (Main and Hesse 1990), suggesting the infant was uncertain of which behaviour would be appropriate in the presence of the parent – sometimes showing avoidance, other times resistance, perhaps attending more closely to the stranger than the parent upon reunion, and/or demonstrating extreme self-protective gestures such as covering the face, lying prostrate or maintaining a frozen posture. This bemused stance runs counter to the child's inner striving for integration and security and cannot long be maintained by the infant. As Main and Hesse describe, the attachment figure 'is at once the source of and the solution to its alarm', (Main and Hesse 1990: 163). The incidence of disorganisation in the population as a whole ranges from 10% to 15%, while in populations where levels of risk to the parent–child relationship, i.e. child maltreatment are high, parental psychopathology not surprisingly increases the risk to up to 90% (Lyons-Ruth and Jacobovitz 1999). The clue for this disorganised pattern was sought in home observations of maternal behaviour.

Careful home observations of mothers and their infant were coded along guidelines suggested by Main and Hesse (1995) for frightened or frightening behaviour. In the United States Jacobovitz pioneered this fieldwork (see Lyons-Ruth and Jacobovitz 1999), while Dutch colleagues Schuengel et al. (1999) also sought and found correlations between maternal frightening behaviour and disorganised infant–mother strategies. Notably, Karlen Lyons-Ruth and colleagues expanded the set of potentially frightening behaviours observed between mothers and babies to find that extreme parental misattunement to the specific content of an infant's attachment-related communication, and the display of competing caregiving strategies that both elicited and rejected infant attachment affects and behaviours, contributed to disorganised attachment (see Lyons-Ruth and Jacobovitz 1999). It is clear from these independent research endeavours that observable connections exist between parents' actual behaviour and attachment classification of disorganisation, but actually capturing the behaviour is not at all easy.

To say that the actual behaviour of parents toward children is important highlights what most of us, even the man in the street, might be able to tell you. However, historically many analysts have suggested that the focus of clinical energies must be upon fantasy. To this, Bowlby said 'No'. He refuted this point by saying as clinicians we need to know as far as is possible what *probably* happened to a particular child because we would intervene differently depending on what we know about the child's actual experience. For example, a child who ties up doll figures during a therapy session needs to be considered as someone who *may have* experienced being tied up. And, if this is the case, we need to respond differently from a situation where the idea of being physically constrained stems from a neurotic circumstance involving an intrusive mother who has helped provoke this kind of fantasy in her child.

In work with adoptive parents of children who faced severe adversity in the form of physical, sexual, and emotional abuse one can often hear the adoptive parent's disbelief when they report how when they have wished to provide an experience of fun or affection they have been met with rejection, spoiling or even fear. For some of these children, the enduring representations of caregivers who maltreat and abuse break through and the need to provoke the new caregiver into behaving in the familiar pattern is unrelenting. Other adopters of the newly placed older child comment on how shocked they have been when a body movement, such as reaching across the table for the salt, provokes cowering and discernible fear in the child. It takes adults some minutes to figure out how their seemingly benign behaviour may prompt a terrified response.

The powerful influence of actual behaviour by caregivers has been richly documented in the ethological literature to which Bowlby was greatly indebted. The work of primate researcher Stephen Suomi has offered stimulating data on the way in which variations in the early attachment histories of rhesus monkeys can have lifelong consequences. For example, when rhesus monkeys are reared for the first 6 months of life in the company of same-age peers, but not adults, strong bonds form amongst the peers. However, because the peers are not as effective as a secure base, in the way an adult mother would be, the attachment relationships with the peers are of an 'anxious' nature (Suomi 1991). While in familiar environments, these peer-reared monkeys cannot be distinguished from mother-reared ones; however, when faced with a novel situation they are much more timid, show more aggression and when followed into maturity are much less able to show adequate care to their own offspring.

Other innovative studies by Suomi have examined the consequences of foster-reared monkeys. Foster-reared monkeys with difficult temperaments but whose unrelated mothers were especially nurturant had positive long-term developmental outcomes where they were able to adeptly recruit support from their group members and even rose to the very top of their social group's dominance hierarchy. These were contrasted with the monkeys with difficult temperaments who, raised by punitive foster mothers, develop 'insecure' attachments and subsequently display extreme reactions to environmental novelty and stress and end up at the bottom of their group's dominance hierarchy. Interestingly, monkeys with an easy temperament seem less affected by the quality of mothering (Suomi 1995). A similar finding as to the importance of context was shown to be critical in a study by Werner and Smith (1982), who found that in their study of high- and low-risk families good parenting was unrelated to child outcome in the low-risk families but critical in the high-risk families.

To sum up on the documented importance of actual experiences with caregivers, there are fascinating interactions with the emotional characteristics or temperament of the infant. This has interesting implications for our understanding of the way in which resilience, and the related capacity to reflect on relationships, are facilitated. It might well be that the origins of healthy psychic development are to be found not simply in the count of attuned or misattuned interactions, but in the sequence of connection, misconnection or disconnection followed by repair and restoration of the interaction. The infant who experiences losing and regaining his balance is less likely to tumble badly in the future.

These suggestions about the immense value of compensatory experiences in the midst of or following adversity are consistent with clinical observational reports (Hopkins 1996), developmental research on temperament and attachment (Crockenberg, 1981; van den Boom 1994) and epidemiological findings (e.g. Rutter *et al*. 1990). Hopkins highlights the risks of too good as well as not good enough mothering, in addition to the potential for mothers to turn things around and embrace the joy, and tolerate the frustration, of being just good enough! Crockenberg's classic study demonstrated that highly irritable, easily overwhelmed, newborns may well be prone to develop insecure attachments (as earlier research suggested) *but only* if the mother has experienced a low level of social support over the first year. Relatedly, van den Boom's well-controlled study provided strong evidence that a brief therapeutic intervention in the middle of the first year of life can help a highly irritable newborn become a securely attached infant at 1 year. While Rutter *et al*. show that early severe relationship adversity is unlikely to lead to ongoing psychosocial problems for women who succeeded at school, developed effective planning strategies relating to work and life, and correspondingly established and maintained a satisfying marital relationship.

Internal working models

Psychoanalytic theorist Morris Eagle (1995: 136) points out that 'contemporary and classical psychoanalytic theory has paid remarkably little attention to what people actually *do* to perpetuate their pathology, particularly, their maladaptive relationship patterns'. He contrasts this with the almost exclusive focus upon actual behaviour, goals, and strategies in attachment theory and research, based on Bowlby's premise about the way the meaning of experiences is encoded in the internal working model thereafter guiding expectations and behaviour. That is, until new experiences that don't fit easily into an existing mental model accumulate to a point where, optimally, there is updating and revision of that inner model – the process of psychological development or 'accommodation' in Piaget's classic account of the presumed universal stages of cognitive development.

The idea of an internal working model of self and attachment figure(s) which organises thoughts and feelings regarding relationships and guides expectations arose out of a synthesis between classical psychoanalytic thinking and cognitive psychology. Bowlby points directly to the notion that we each carry within ourselves a representation of the self and other, and the self in metaphorical conversation with the other. Thus others are often unwittingly drawn into conversation with us, on the terms we attempt to dictate. But equally, as Sandler's theory of role responsiveness indicates, 'it takes two to tango' (see Sandler 1987). The challenge for adults interacting with children, whether they be natural parents, adoptive parents, teachers, or child care workers, is to recognise the tunes children wish for us to dance to, and help them achieve joyful, responsible and confidence-building movements that advance their development.

The ways in which the internal working model of attachment within the child not only influences beliefs and expectations about others, but equally may elicit behaviours and responses in others, has been illustrated by attachment research. For example, Eagle (1995) draws attention to Alan Sroufe's longitudinal study of early infant–mother attachment in a high-risk sample where nursery teachers expressed their feelings about children, whose early attachment patterns were unknown to them. The teachers reported that they felt warmly, uncontrolling and positive to the children who had been classified as securely attached at age 12 months. This contrasted with the teachers' self-reports of feeling and behaving in a more angry, controlling and negative manner to those children who had been avoidantly attached as infants. Further, the teachers report that the anxious/resistant children provoked unduly nurturant and tolerant behaviour but also expressed their expectations to be controlling with them. Importantly, for both the insecure groups the teachers did not have expectations that the children would behave in an age-appropriate manner with their peers. Sroufe makes the point that the behaviours the children expressed to their teachers, which in turn provoked a particular teacher response, was very akin to what the children had come to expect from their caregivers. As for the internal working models within caregivers, i.e. those processes which govern what caregivers expect of their infants, this is an area that has been vigorously researched for more than 15 years. This period in attachment research was initiated by the 'move to the level of representation' (Main *et al.* 1985) and involved the development of an interview technique which elicits the adult's internal representations of self, attachment figure(s), and implicit strategies for regulating emotional arousal. The interview is known as the Adult Attachment Interview or AAI. It is already well known in child psychotherapeutic, psychoanalytic, and increasingly social work circles. The AAI takes seriously the role of unconscious mental and emotional processes in the adult. Its stated aim is to 'surprise the unconscious' (George *et al.* 1985). Thus, psychoanalytic clinicians, traditionally and justifiably wary of the positivistic and otherwise limiting features of psychological research, were inclined to take notice. No doubt the political and economic climate demanding 'evidenced-based' treatments has contributed to the growing interest in the AAI, an instrument which may be said to have appeared at the right time, and in the right place. Because the AAI depends crucially upon listening to the adult tell a story, in his or her own words, of their family history, the clinician – trained to listen to the patient – can readily appreciate the method. Whereas the clinician tends to rely on intuition, however well grounded, in order to analyse the patient's material of necessity they deal with relatively small numbers of patients. The AAI researcher by contrast is able to collect information from relatively large groups of individuals and to apply a rigorous and detailed method of analysis, with a lengthy written set of guidelines (Main and Goldwyn 1998). In the hands of a trained rater, this leads to a highly reliable measurement of the interviewee's probable childhood experiences, and their current state of mind regarding attachment, as well as to classification of the adult's overall pattern of attachment. The now well-known patterns of attachment, expressions of the adult's internal working model of attachment and caregiving, are the patterns termed autonomous–secure, insecure–dismissing, insecure–preoccupied and/or unresolved with regard to past loss or trauma. In diverse cultural and linguistic settings, these adult patterns have been observed to map onto the infant–parent patterns of attachment (secure, avoidant, resistant, disorganised respectively), and thus intergenerational consistency has been widely reported (see Hesse 1999; van IJzendoorn 1995; Steele *et al*. 1996).

The AAI is structured entirely around the topic of attachment, principally the individual's relationship to mother and to father (and/or to alternative caregivers) during childhood. Subjects are asked to describe their relationship with their parents during childhood and to provide specific memories to support global evaluations. The interview's power rests in the systematic method of eliciting this attachment story. Notably, AAI questions may be seen to comprise three distinct challenging modes of inquiry into memories for, and current evaluations of, past experiences of attachment-related distress. First, there are questions that ask about negative experiences and related emotions which are part of *everyone's* childhood experiences, including emotional upset, physical hurt, illness and separations from parents. Second, there are questions about negative experiences and related emotions that are part of *some people's* childhood experiences, including loss and abuse. And, third, there are questions which demand that the speaker think about the possible meaning and influence upon adult personality of childhood attach-ment experiences, including requests that the speaker provide an account of why parents behaved as they did during childhood. Importantly, the trained rater first scores the narrative on a number of nine-point dimensions pertaining to probable past experience and current state of mind concerning attachment. The dimensions of probable past experience to which the rater pays immediate attention is how loving, rejecting, neglecting and role reversing each parent was during the inter-viewee's childhood, exemplifying Bowlby's notion of the importance of actual experiences with caregivers during childhood. The dimensions of current 'state of mind' concerning attachment which are rated include attention to the emotional quality of parent-specific mental representations, e.g. the extent to which each parent is spoken of with idealisation, anger or derogation. Additionally, state of mind of the interviewee is rated in terms of more global considerations including the extent to which the narrative is coherent, passive, and showing signs of metacognition (Main and Goldwyn 1998). Noteworthy, especially for its clinical relevance, is that we have been involved in a London-based effort to extend the scoring of metacognition (awareness of one's own thought processes) to include awareness of mental states as motivators of behaviour in oneself *and others* (Fonagy *et al.* 1991). This effort has led to the development of the concept of 'reflective functioning' which we see as normatively growing out of early child-hood experiences of having our inner worlds reflected upon more or less accurately by caregivers (e.g. Fonagy *et al.* 1995). Further, reflective functioning may be markedly inhibited or skewed as a result of deficient empathic responsiveness from caregivers in early childhood. In such circumstances, an elevated likelihood of psychopathological child and adult outcomes may be expected.

A further important consideration when rating and classifying attachment inter-views concerns past loss and trauma. When there is clear evidence of a significant loss or trauma (physical and/or sexual abuse) the judge follows a number of specified guidelines (Main and Goldwyn 1998) for assessing the extent to which the past trauma is resolved. In sum, this comes down to determining the extent to which the overwhelmingly negative experiences are (a) identified as such and (b) spoken about in such a way as to indicate that they have acquired the characteris-tics of belonging to the past. Unresolved mourning is most notable when there are lapses in the monitoring of reason or discourse when discussing the past loss and/or trauma (after Main and Goldwyn 1998). For example, where loss has occurred, it is important for the speaker to demonstrate full awareness of the permanence of this loss. And, where abuse has occurred in speakers' childhood experiences, it is important for speakers to at once acknowledge the abuse, and also show that they understand they are not responsible for the maltreatment they suffered. Important clues as to the extent of resolution in the speaker's mind fol-low from careful study of the narrative for a logical and temporally sequenced account of the trauma which is neither too brief, suggesting an attempt to minimise the significance of the trauma, nor too detailed, suggesting ongoing absorption.

Unresolved responses of mothers when asked about past loss and/or abuse in the AAI context have been linked, in multiple independent investigations, to dis-organised/disoriented attachments in the infant–mother attachment. Main and Hesse (1990) speculated, and subsequent research (Lyons-Ruth and Jacobvitz 1999; Schuengel *et al.* 1999) has confirmed, that frightening or frightened mater-nal behaviour is the likely intervening mechanism. Put simply, a woman who is still frequently haunted by ghosts from her past is likely to create, however un-wittingly, in her infant's experience an ongoing sense of potential terror in the relationship.

This phenomenon has recently been investigated in the Israeli context, where there is a substantial number of grandmothers who lost both parents in early child-hood during the Nazi Holocaust. Many of these child survivors of the Holocaust, bereft of family, settled in Israel and established new families. Sagi-Schwartz *et al.* (2003) have studied this population in order to observe the extent to which these traumatic Holocaust experiences may have been transmitted to the second generation (the daughters), and the third generation (the 1-year-old grandchildren). Sagi-Schwartz *et al.*'s investigation of this remarkable community-based sample (as compared to clinical reports) has revealed a phenomenal resilience in the way the first generation of traumatised parents, who had suffered inhuman atrocities during their childhood, managed to insulate their children (and grandchildren) from being adversely affected as well. The grandmothers did show an elevated (50%) level of unresolved mourning, in contrast to a matched comparison group (10% unresolved), but this was not transmitted to the daughters, who in turn were not observed to display frightening maternal behaviour to their infants. These grandmothers may have been able to keep the influence of their horrendous experiences in check because the Holocaust trauma did not entail the cruellest of all attachment experiences. That is, the infliction of trauma by one's parents or other trusted attachment figures, as is the case in victims of child abuse. Also, the pre-traumatic attachment experiences of these grandmothers, i.e. before the Nazis murdered their parents, would have been largely good enough and thus helped insulate the children against the trauma later perpetrated by an utterly 'other', almost anonymous inhuman social–political force (the Nazis). Finally, these child survivors/mothers/grandmothers would have gleaned considerable strength and forbearance from the post-Holocaust environment they found themselves in, i.e. the Israeli context where a large number of survivors contributed directly to building a nation not unrelated to a collective memory of the Holocaust.

Arguably, attachment experiences in early childhood never lead directly to the attachment emotions, beliefs, and behaviour in adult. Traumatic attachment experiences are only associated with unresolved mourning in an adult, and potentially frightening or frightened behaviour in a parent, if the adult has been unable to come to terms with their unfavourable past. The ability to 'work through' and come to terms with one's experience is reflected in the coherence of discourse in the interview context and this appears to be underpinned by a minimal reliance on defensive strategies. The result is an interview which can reveal difficult and painful experiences that are integrated into a present-day attitude towards attachments, which conveys a valuing of intimate relationships. Consider the following example of a 30-year-old woman recalling what it was like for her as a child to have a mother who was physically ill much of the time and prone to a highly controlling, occasionally abusive, style of parenting. When asked to think about the adjective she provided in describing her relationship with her mother as one in which she was 'scared' this mother said:

> One thing . . . which I've only realised since I've been an adult and which, once I realised, helped me to understand a lot of things, um, was that her way of keeping control was to be ill, so you, one was always scared if you did something wrong then she'd be ill and it was your fault, so that was the cycle that I remember very clearly, about five or six years old . . . you learn to live with that as you get older but at that age I remember being very upset and threatened.

This excerpt scores highly on our index of reflective functioning as this mother-to-be demonstrates a capacity for a developmental perspective, seeing how events in her childhood would be understood differently in adulthood. She is also able to connect her mother's physical illness with a psychological state of mind that led her to behave in a controlling way, and she demonstrates an impressive lexicon for describing affect and mental states. Clearly, in her relationship experiences, and inner world, there have been some marked discontinuities contributing to a resilient stance.

Continuity and potential for change in attachment patterns

This final section of the chapter highlights both continuity and change in attachment patterns. This is in line with Bowlby's comments that just because an internal working model reflecting early attachment experiences has been set up, life's adversities, if severe or cumulative enough, can topple a secure base. But, equally, an early insecure base can become more stable and hardy if a sufficiently positive set of relationship experiences follows early adversity. Bowlby repeatedly pointed out that at no time in life is positive change impossible.

Continuity has been observed within the life of the child, and across generations. Given reasonable stability in the caregiving environment, these patterns of response to the Strange Situation are reasonably stable over time (Lyons-Ruth et al. 1991; Waters 1979; Vaughn et al. 1979). Additionally, these four main patterns of infant–parent attachment are unlikely be directly determined to any significant extent by a property of the child such as temperament (Crockenberg 1981; van den Boom 1994). The majority of studies which have compared infant–mother attachment quality with infant–father attachment quality report that each infant–parent relationship is statistically independent of the other (e.g. Main and Weston 1981; Steele et al. 1996). The child's behaviour upon reunion in the Strange Situation with the mother largely reflects the unique history of interactions *with* the mother, how she responded to her infant's bids for contact and comfort and how these were interpreted by the infant. A different history of interactions is likely to underpin the child's attachment to the father. Thus, attachment quality during infancy is best understood as a characteristic of the child–caregiver relationship most readily observable in the Strange Situation procedure. The Strange Situation may thus be said to provide a reliable index of infant behaviour in response to stress-inducing circumstances, and in doing so provides a window upon young children's internal working models of their relationships to caregivers. That caregivers' own unique internal working models of relationships, assessed via the AAI, is the most powerful predictor of the infant–caregiver relationship quality further underlines the relationship-specific nature of the attachment construct (see Steele et al. 1996; van IJzendoorn 1995).

There have been an enormous number of studies charting the developmental sequelae from Strange Situation assessments in infancy to a variety of social and cognitive developments in toddlerhood, in the nursery years, in latency, in adolescence and most recently into adulthood. The following provides a selected overview of this vast literature on how attachment needs, and resulting actual experience, lead to mental representations (or internal working models) that, in turn, influence subsequent experiences.

The longitudinal work of Klaus and Karin Grossmann in Germany has identified long-term implications of early attachment to the mother. One of their many impressive studies showed that securely attached 3-year-old children were able to openly communicate their sadness (looking into the face of their competitor) upon losing a competitive game with an adult examiner. In contrast, those children with an insecure–avoidant history revealed distress when losing but were unable to directly show their sad faces and instead presented a 'social smile'. These findings map meaningfully onto their independent observation that avoidantly attached 1-year-olds hide their negative feelings while internal indicators as measured by physiological responses in the form of salivary cortisol measurements show intense and prolonged stressful arousal (Spangler and Grossmann 1993). It would be a mistake to think of these findings as residing in the child alone, as there is evidence that mothers of the avoidantly attached children have powerfully conveyed to them a willingness to respond favourably, but only when they display positive affect. Their display of negative affect is likely to be ignored or rejected, and thus such children learn *by 1 year of age* to disguise their feelings (Grossmann et al. 1986).

Mary Main and her colleagues found impressive continuity in a range of assessments of 6-year-olds who had participated in earlier Strange Situation assessments collected 5 years previously. This longitudinal study used a range of distinct and innovative tasks to assess the current attachment relationship of the 6-year-olds which included careful observations of reunion behaviour between parent and child following an hour-long separation, as well as narrative assessments provided by the child in response to attachment-themed prompts. For example, when the children were asked, 'What would the child do during a 2-week separation from parents?' the children who had been securely attached at age 1 year were now at age 6 more likely to imagine ways of dealing with the separation, i.e. asking the parents not to go, expressing disappointment or anger, finding ways of keeping in touch. The children who had been assessed at age 12 months to be insecurely attached, at age 6 had a tendency not to know what the child could do, or to remove themselves further from the attachment figures by locking themselves away or even killing themselves (Main et al. 1985). These findings provide support for the notion that the internal working model is resistant to change and that it is possible to track the way in which early versions evolve as development progresses so that an assessment of behaviour at one age can be strongly correlated ($r = 0.59$) to narrative indices later in childhood.

In our own longitudinal research into patterns of attachment across generations, we have found that children who were rated as insecurely attached to mother at 12 months, and whose mothers' AAIs were either dismissing or preoccupied, were advanced in their recognition and understanding of emotion, including ambivalent or mixed feelings at 6 years of age (Steele *et al.* 1999). Further follow-ups of these children as they reach early adolescence has revealed social cognitive capacities that have again been predicted from attachment classifications collected 10 years previously. Early security with the mother is linked to the capacity at 11 years to acknowledge distress in response to cartoon depiction of affect-laden dilemmas and to elaborate thoughtful resolutions (Steele *et al.* 2002). Emotional literacy and the often-cited goal of most psychotherapeutic interventions to put 'feelings into words' can easily be conceptualised as the important underpinning to mental health.

AAI research involving non-clinical samples suggests that by 17 or 18 years of age, if not sooner, individuals have developed a well-functioning capacity to report, monitor and evaluate their possibly very different types of early attachment experiences, i.e. with mother, father and others (e.g. Kobak and Sceery 1988). Further, Main (1991) has suggested that by 10 years of age children who have benefited from a secure early attachment to mother are more likely to demonstrate metacognitive awareness in response to probing questions exploring the nature of mind and knowledge. But how far into the future has continuity from early infant–mother patterns of attachment been observed?

Notably, the year 2000 saw the appearance of three longitudinal studies comparing the assessment of infant–mother attachment in the Strange Situation at 12 months with AAIs obtained circa 20 years later (Waters *et al.* 2000; Hamilton 2000; Weinfeld *et al.* 2000). The three studies revealed continuity where there was continuity of experience, marked discontinuity where there were indications of severe life events and difficulties, and weak to moderate continuity where there were the usual ups and downs of family life over the intervening years. Hardly surprising, one might say. Other research is needed to reveal what from earliest experience is carried over into later life, and what is most likely to be reworked, updated or otherwise changed as a function of later experiences. Clearly, the language we use, the story we tell, and the meaning we derive from our lives must be open to revision across the life cycle. At the same time, there may be spontaneous modes of responding to the world, and automatic interpretations of emotional and social stimuli that remain, even as we may learn not to trust these 'first impressions' or prejudices.

It is certainly a hopeful and positive sign when a speaker demonstrates that past trauma has been resolved. Indeed, in the non-clinical population, where childhood experiences have involved trauma it is not uncommonly the case that the speaker conveys a sense of moving beyond the fear they felt so often as a child. Additionally, such speakers are capable of going some way toward understanding, though not necessarily forgiving, *caregiving* figure(s) who perpetrated abuse against them as children. In these circumstances, the AAI often reveals a robust sense of self, interpersonal awareness and valuing of attachment so that one can say the adult who was abused is not likely to become an abuser. Such resilience invariably emerges out of the individual discovering one or more secure bases or refuges beyond the abusive relationship, such as may be provided by an extended family member, spouse or therapist. In this respect, the AAI offers a uniquely powerful clinical and legal tool insofar as it may be seen to provide a reliable indication as to whether or not abused adults are likely to repeat the pattern with their children.

We have explored one area of overlap between AAI research and the clinical process in London, at the Anna Freud Centre, stemming from our work on the dimensional concept of reflective functioning. Notably, ratings of this capacity in the AAIs from pregnant women we have studied in London (Steele *et al.* 1996) have revealed that reflective functioning is a more powerful predictor of infant–mother attachment security than any other single AAI rating scale (see Fonagy *et al.* 1995). The capacity to reflect on one's own internal world and to appreciate the perspective of another individual is a crucial question in the mind of the clinician when they are assessing a patient for 'treatability'. Often there are limited resources with which to offer psychotherapy services to those that seek it and could benefit from it. The question of how to assess whether an individual might make use of treatment is a critical one for the clinician, whether in public or private practice. A familiarity with the concept of reflective functioning might have a very important role to play in this challenging area of clinical practice. An example of an adolescent boy who sought help at the Anna Freud Centre exemplifies a situation in which a capacity to reflect upon his painful situation was predictive of a good therapeutic outcome. Steven, at age 16 years, suffered from intense bullying by his schoolmates. This included being locked in a locker at school for a full hour, and having a cigarette lighter held to his cheek. He was engaging in some self-harming behaviour and was involved in a sado-masochistic relationship with his father, with whom he battled on a daily basis. However, he was also able to comment at the diagnostic stage of potential treatment, 'My father will never be satisfied . . . even if I was the type of boy my father thinks he'd be happy with, he still wouldn't be happy with me.' Indeed, over the course of intensive psychotherapy that followed, Steven was able to explore both his own role in the difficult relationship with his father but also to see his father's contribution to the pathological situation.

Some of the most provocative findings in the literature around continuities, discontinuities and the importance of being able to reflect, upon oneself and others, have arisen in studies of clinical populations where somewhat counter-intuitive results have emerged. The work of Marian Radke-Yarrow on families where the primary caregiver suffers from psychopathology is relevant to a discussion on continuities and discontinuities in attachment. Radke-Yarrow's pioneering study is one of the only prospective longitudinal studies with a strong emphasis on the developmental processes and the transmission of psychopathology and adaptation from parent to child (Radke-Yarrow 1998). This carefully designed study compared children of mothers who were clinically depressed, those with bipolar illness and those without any psychiatric diagnosis at successive stages of development, in terms of their psychiatric and psychosocial development. This study has yielded many interesting findings. However, from an attachment point of view the discovery that the children who were classified as securely attached to their mothers with psychiatric symptoms *more* often developed later problems than did the children who were insecurely attached to symptomatic mothers. This of course is counter-intuitive to what attachment theory and research might have predicted. However, if we think for a moment what it might mean for a child to be securely attached to a mother with psychiatric illness this finding might not be so very surprising. If security is linked to interactions characterised by being in tune with, and reflecting on the mind, thoughts, feelings and intentions of the other, one can quickly detect the risks for the child of being 'too close' to the mentally disturbed parent. For if the mind of the parent is at times chaotic, or non-responsive alternating with islands of appropriateness, security may become more of a risk than a resilient factor. In this situation of being cared for by a disturbed parent, children who are able to distance themselves, both psychically and even physically, might be free to explore other relationships and thus be better off.

Another set of findings that at first glance seem counter-intuitive arises out of study of adoptive parents who chose to adopt children with severe disabilities (Steele *et al.* 2000). These families were especially selected by the adoption agency as examples of successful placements where the children were considered to be doing very well by all those concerned. We administered the AAI to a group of 30 of these parents, as we were interested in whether their attachment histories and what they made of them, might have predicted the successful outcomes. One of the interesting features of the study was that 96% of the sample reported having faced severe adversity in the form of having endured the loss of an important attachment figure. The families also reported to especially seeking out a child who was disabled because, as one parent put it, 'I wanted to have a child for life.' Surprisingly, the majority of the interviews were classified as insecure–dismissing. To begin with we were puzzled by this result. However, we soon began to understand that the adults were probably using a similar strategy in thinking and feeling about their children. Just as they evaluated their own attachment histories in an idealising way, where the negative or deleterious aspects were defensively kept out of consciousness by failing to recall them, they could successfully use a similar strategy when thinking about their relationship with their adopted disabled child. These were parents who were devoted to the care and nurturance of the children, but were not particularly interested in thinking about feelings or being reflective. From the children's point of view it seemed this is perhaps just what they needed, that is, a parent who would idealise them and see every small increment of development as a huge step forward. At some level, it seems that these parents were aware that their own childhood histories were not optimal in providing a loving relationship, and so they could embark on a new relationship perhaps as a way of redressing the balance.

These studies (Radke-Yarrow 1998; Steele *et al.* 2000), which highlight some interesting counter-intuitive findings, alert one to the importance of being open to new evidence, and being prepared to refine and extend our thinking, a central and enduring characteristic of John Bowlby's approach to psychoanalytic work. It was an approach devoted to charting and understanding developmental trajectories in methodologically robust ways at the crossroads of developmental research and psychoanalytic interests.

Conclusion

Bowlby set himself upon a therapeutic path which led him, over some 50 years, to direct his efforts at understanding attachment relationships and facilitating research and clinical work universally. Attachment theory – with its psycho-analytic core – has established itself as a leading theory. But why? I think there are two main reasons. Firstly, the biological, social and psychological foundation of attachment relationships, and the violation as well as restoration of them, has been extensively studied by an increasing available, creative, user-friendly and scienti-fically sound set of methods. Secondly, the theory and research do actually speak, plainly and directly, to some of the most salient social issues facing us. These pressing social issues include a variety of urgent questions, including the follow-ing. How can we best understand, *measure*, and ultimately improve the quality of parent–child relationships? How can we deliver successful and cost-effective parent–infant and child psychotherapy? How can we improve the quality and availability of childcare? How can we facilitate the making of 'right' choices in the fields of adoption and foster care?

I think John Bowlby would be pleasantly surprised to learn of the way in which his theoretical writings from some half-century ago have given rise to the attach-ment industry. In fact in his highly readable *A Secure Base* (Bowlby 1988), based on lectures he delivered in the late 1970s and early 1980s, he showed his conster-nation with the way that clinicians so long ignored his work. 'I find it somewhat unexpected that whereas attachment theory was formulated by a clinician for use in the diagnosis and treatment of emotionally disturbed patients and families, its usage has been mainly to promote research in Developmental Psychology' (Bowlby 1988: xii). This quote is of interest for several reasons. One is that Bowlby defined himself as a clinician, not just a researcher. He often commented on his interest in attachment theory to rest firmly on therapeutic work. He also mentions not just 'disturbed patients' but also points us to think of families and can be credited with being one of the first family therapists (see Bowlby, 1947). The current applications of his seminal contribution re-echo a sentiment Bowlby expressed in 1951, and frequently included in his later writings: 'if a society values its children, it must cherish their parents'.

References

Ainsworth, M. D. S. (1967). *Infancy in Uganda: Infant Care and the Growth of Love.* Baltimore, MD: Johns Hopkins University Press.

Ainsworth, M. D. S. and Bell, S. M. (1974). Mother–infant interaction and the development of competence. In Connolly, K. and Bruner, J. (eds) *The Growth of Competence*, 97–118. New York: Academic Press.

Ainsworth, M. D. S. and Marvin, R. S. (1995). On the shaping of attachment theory and research: an interview with Mary D. S. Ainsworth (Fall, 1994). In Waters, E., Vaughn, B. E., Posada, G. and Kondo-Ikemura, K. (eds), *Caregiving, Cultural, and Cognitive Perspectives on Secure-Base Behavior and Working Models: New Growing Points of Attachment Theory and Research.* Monographs of the Society for Research in Child Development, vol. 60, Serial No. 244 (2–3), 3–21.

Ainsworth, M. D. S., Blehar, M. C., Waters, E. and Wall, S. (1978). *Patterns of Attachment: A Psychological Study of the Strange Situation.* Hillsdale, NJ: Erlbaum.

Blehar, M., Lieberman, A. and Ainsworth, M. (1977). Early face-to-face interaction and its relation to later infant–mother attachment. *Child Development*, 48, 182–194.

Bowlby, J. (1944). Forty four juvenile thieves: Their characters and home life. *International Journal of Pscyhoanalysis* 25:19–52.

Bowlby, J. (1949) The study of group tensions in the family. *Journal of Human Relations* 2: 123–128.

Bowlby, J. (1951). *Maternal Care and Mental Health.* Geneva: World Health Organization.

Bowlby, J. (1988). *A Secure Base. Clinical Application of Attachment Theory.* London: Routledge.

Cassidy, J. and Shaver, P. (eds) (1999). *Handbook of Attachment.* New York: Guilford Press.

Crockenberg, S. (1981). Infant irritability, mother responsiveness, and social support influences on the security of infant-mother attachment. *Child Development 52*: 857–965.

Eagle, M. (1995). The developmental perspectives of attachment theory and psychoanalytic theory. In Goldberg, S., Muir, R. and Kerr J. (eds), *Attachment Theory: Social, Developmental and Clinical Perspectives*, 123–150. New York: Analytic Press.

Fonagy, P., Moran, G. S., Steele, M., Steele, H., and Higgitt, A. C. (1991). The capacity for understanding mental states: the reflective self in parent and child and its significance for security of attachment. *Infant Mental Health Journal 13*: 200–216.

Fonagy, P., Steele, M., Steele, H., Leigh, T., Kennedy, R., Mattoon, G. and Target, M. (1995). Attachment, the reflective self, and borderline states: the predictive specificity of the Adult Attachment Interview and pathological emotional development. In Goldberg, S., Muir, R. and Kerr, J. (eds), *Attachment Theory: Social, Developmental and Clinical Perspectives*, 233–278. New York: Analytic Press.

George, C., Kaplan, N. and Main, M. (1985). *The Adult Attachment Interview.* Unpublished manuscript, Department of Psychology, University of California, Berkeley.

Grossmann, K. E., Grossmann, K. and Schwan, A. (1986). Capturing the wider view of attachment: A reanalysis of Ainsworth's Strange Situation. In Izard, C. E. and Read, P. (eds), *Measuring Emotions in Infants and Children,* Vol. 2, 124–171. Cambridge: Cambridge University Press.

Hamilton, C. (2000). Continuity and discontinuity of attachment from infancy through adolescence. *Child Development 71*: 690–693.

Hesse, E. (1999). The Adult Attachment Interview: historical and current perspectives. In Cassidy, J. and Shaver, P. (eds), *Handbook of Attachment*, 395–433. New York: Guilford Press.

Hopkins, J. (1996). The dangers and deprivations of too-good mothering. *Journal of Child Psychotherapy 22* (3): 407–422.

Kobak, R. R. and Sceery, A. (1988). Attachment in later adolescence: working models, affect regulation, and representations of self and others. *Child Development 59*, 135–146.

Jaffe, J., Beebe, B., Feldstein, S., Crown, C. and Jasnow, M. (2001). Rhythms of Dialogue in Infancy. *Monographs of the Society for Research in Child Development*, 265 (66) Serial No. 265.

Lyons-Ruth, K. and Jacobvitz, D. (1999). Attachment disorganization: unresolved loss, relational violence, and lapses in behavioural and attentional strategies. In Cassidy, J. and Shaver, P. (eds), *Handbook of Attachment*, 520–555. New York: Guilford Press.

Lyons-Ruth, K., Repacholi, B., McLeod, S. and Silva, E. (1991). Disorganized attachment behavior in infancy: short-term stability, maternal and infant correlates, and risk-related subtypes. *Development and Psychopathology 3*: 397–412.

Main, M. (1991). Metacognitive knowledge, metacognitive monitoring, and singular (coherent) vs. multiple (incoherent) models of attachment: findings and directions for future research. In Parkes, C. M., Stevenson-Hinde, J. and Marris, P. (eds), *Attachment Across the Lifecycle*, 127–159. New York: Routledge–Kegan Paul.

Main, M. and Goldwyn, R. (1998). Adult attachment scoring and classification system. Unpublished manuscript, University of California at Berkeley.

Main, M. and Hesse, E. (1990). Parents' unresolved traumatic experiences are related to infant disorganized attachment status: is frightened and/or frightening parental behaviour the linking mechanism? In Greenberg, M. T., Cicchetti, D. and Cummings, E. M. (eds), *Attachment in the Preschool Years: Theory, Research and Intervention*, 161–182. Chicago: University of Chicago Press.

Main, M. and Hesse, E. (1995). Frightening, frightened, dissociated, or disorganized behavior on the part of the parent: a coding system for parent–infant interactions, 5th edn. Unpublished manuscript, University of California at Berkeley.

Main, M. and Solomon, J. (1990). Procedures for identifying infants as disorganized–disoriented during the Strange Situation. In Greenberg, M., Cicchetti, D. and Cummings, E. M. (eds), *Attachment in the Preschool Years: Theory, Research and Intervention*, 121–160. Chicago: University of Chicago Press.

Main, M. and Weston, D. (1981). The quality of the toddler's relationship to mother and to father: related to conflict behavior and the readiness to establish new relationships. *Child Development*, 52, 932–940.

Main, M., Kaplan, K. and Cassidy, J. (1985). Security in infancy, childhood and adulthood: a move to the level of representation. In Bretherton, I. and Waters, E. (eds), *Growing Points of Attachment Theory and Research. Monographs of the Society for Research in Child Development*, Vol. 50, Serial No. 209 (1–2), 66–104.

Radke-Yarrow, M. (1998). *Children of Depressed Mothers: From Early Childhood to Maturity*. Cambridge: Cambridge University Press.

Rutter, M., Quinton, D., and Hill, J. (1990). Adult outcome of institution-reared children: males and females compared. In Robbins, L. and Rutter, M. (eds), *Straight and Devious Pathways from Childhood to Adulthood*, 135–157. Cambridge: Cambridge University Press.

Sagi-Schwartz A., van IJzendoorn, M. H., Grossmann, K. E., Joels, T., Grossmann, K., Scharf, M., Koren-Karie, N. and Alkalay, S. (2003). Child survivors – but not their children – suffer from traumatic holocaust experiences. *The American Journal of Psychiatry* 160: 1086–1092.

Sandler, J. (1987). The concept of projective indentification. In Sandler, J. (ed.), *Projection, Identification, Projective Identification*, 13–26. London: Karnac.

Schore, A. N. (2000). Attachment and the regulation of the right brain. *Attachment and Human Development 2* (1): 23–47.

Schuengel, C., Bakermans-Kranenburg, M. J. and van IJzendoorn, M. H. (1999). Attachment and loss: Frightening maternal behavior linking unresolved loss and disorganized infant attachment. *Journal of Consulting and Clinical Psychology 67*: 54–63.

Spangler, G. and Grossmann, K. E. (1993). Biobehavioural organization in securely and insecurely attached infants. *Child Development 64:* 1439–1450.

Steele, H., Steele, M. and Fonagy, P. (1996). Associations among attachment classifications of mothers, fathers and their infants. *Child Development 67*: 541–555.

Steele, H., Steele, M., Croft, C. and Fonagy, P. (1999). Infant-mother attachment at one-year predicts children's understanding of mixed-emotions at six years. *Social Development 8*: 161–178.

Steele, M., Steele, H. and Johansson, M. (2002). Maternal predictors of children's social cognition: an attachment perspective. *Journal of Child Psychology and Psychiatry* 43(7): 189–198.

Steele, M., Kaniuk, J., Hodges, J., Haworth C. and Huss, S. (2000). The use of the Adult Attachment Interview: implications of adoption and foster care. In *Assessment, Preparation and Support: Implications from Research*. London: British Agencies for Adoption and Fostering Press.

Stern, D. N. (1985). *The Interpersonal World of the Infant: A View from Psychoanalysis and Developmental Psychology*. New York: Basic Books.

Suomi, S. J. (1991). Early stress and adult emotional reactivity in rehesus monkeys. In Barker, D. (ed.), *The Childhood Environment and Adult Disease*, 171–188. Wiley: Chichester.

Suomi, S. J. (1995). Influence of attachment theory on ethological studies of biobehavioral development in nonhuman primates. In Goldberg, S., Muir, R. and Kerr J. (eds), *Attachment Theory: Social, Developmental and Clinical Perspectives*, 185–201. New York: Analytic Press.

Suomi, S. J. (1999). Attachment in rhesus monkeys. In Cassidy, J. and Shaver, P. (eds), *Handbook of Attachment*, 181–197. New York: Guilford Press.

van den Boom, D. C. (1994). The influence of temperament and mothering on attachment and exploration: an experimental manipulation of sensitive responsiveness among lower-class mothers with irritable infants. *Child Development 65*: 1457–1477.

Vaughn, B. E., Egeland, B., Sroufe, L. A. and Waters, E. (1979). Individual differences in infant–mother attachment at twelve and eighteen months: stability and change in families under stress. *Child Development 50*: 971–975.

van Ijzendoorn, M. (1995). Adult attachment representations, parental responsiveness, and infant attachment: a meta-analysis of the predictive validity of the Adult Attachment Interview. *Psychological Bulletin 117*: 387–403.

Waters, E. (1979). The reliability and stability of individual differences in infant–mother attachment. *Child Development 49*: 483–494.

Waters, E., Merrick, S., Treboux, D., Crowell, J. and Albersheim, L. (2000). Attachment security in infancy and early adulthood: a twenty-year longitudinal study. *Child Development 71*: 684–689.

Weinfeld, N., Sroufe, A. and Egeland, B. (2000). Attachment from infancy to early adulthood in a high risk sample: continuity, discontinuity, and their correlates. *Child Development 71*: 695–702.

Werner, E. and Smith, R. (1982). Vulnerable but invincible: a longitudinal study of resilient children and youth. New York: McGraw-Hill.

Chapter 4

The interpersonal interpretive mechanism: the confluence of genetics and attachment theory in development

Peter Fonagy

The demise of socialization: parenting versus genetics

Our understanding of the interrelationship of genetic predisposition, experiences in the first 3 years of life and psychological disturbance in later development is currently in something of a flux. We are all mesmerized by the rapid unfolding of scientific understanding concerning the genetic transmission of disease. This has raised the welcome possibility of a cure – gene therapy – for many deadly and painful illnesses and disabilities. 'Genomics', the process of identifying the specific function of individual genes, has become the best-funded and most aggressively pursued subject in the field of biology and medicine. In the behavioural and social sciences the influence is also beginning to be felt; unfortunately principally detracting from its standing in models of disease causation. The discovery of genetic influences appears to have profoundly undermined interest in the psychological and the social and strengthened an already powerful move towards biological reductionism. The shifts in implicit and explicit scientific understanding to favour genetic determination of psychological problems and characteristics has begun to impact on all our attitudes towards the psychological as a pivotal causal influence and an appropriate level of analysis for the understanding of mental disorder.

Nowhere has this shift been more acutely felt than in the area of the social determinants of childhood psychological disorder (Rutter 2000). Never, since the illuminating contribution of Jean-Jacques Rousseau, has there been so much scepticism expressed about the role of early socialization, particularly the role of the child's parents in shaping, for better or worse, the child's destiny. It is self-evident that if the key influences on the child's unfolding personality are genetic then previous conclusions concerning parental influence were due to an understandable misapprehension: the confusion of correlate with cause. Indeed, it is possible that the parent who carries the gene has expressed his total influence on the child at the time of conception. Any further apparent associations between the behaviour of the caregiver and the child's characteristics, it could be said, is without causal significance, and is better understood in terms of a misattribution of causality. Psychoanalysis, along with learning theory and other social science approaches, perhaps fell victim to confusing correlation with causation. There is some substance to these critiques. But the pendulum has swung too far.

In this chapter I will try to argue that the case for reducing the emphasis on parenting, particularly the emphasis on early attachment relationships, is based on false evaluations of behaviour genetics data. However, I will also argue that perhaps in the past our emphasis on the role of parenting was somewhat naïve in trying to see the parents' influence simply in terms of relationship quality, internalization, introjection, identification or what have you. Whether or not specific environmental factors trigger the expression of a gene may depend not only on the nature of those factors, but also on the way the infant or child experiences them, which will be a function of attachment and other intrapsychic experiences in many instances. The quality of the experiential filter which attachment provides may in turn be a function of either genetic or environmental influences, or their interaction (Kandel 1998). *Thus intrapsychic representational processes are not just consequences of environmental and genetic effects – they may be critical moderators.* I will try to show that the primary evolutionary function of attachment may be the contribution it makes to the creation in the individual of a mental mechanism that could serve to moderate psychosocial experiences relevant for gene expression.

There are three primary agents of socialization of children in Western society: families, peer group and day-care centres or schools (Maccoby 2000). For the best part of the past century, the emphasis, both professional and cultural, has been on the family as the primary agent of socialization. Both psychological theories (such as learning theory and psychoanalysis) (e.g. Alexander and Parsons 1982; Bowlby 1958; Patterson 1976; Winnicott 1963) and common-sense psychological views (Leach 1997; Spock and Rotherberg 1985) have maintained that experience with parents is pivotal in shaping an individual's values, beliefs, character and, naturally, dysfunctions in adaptation.

In the last quarter of the twentieth century cognitive mental science provided a different perspective on individual development (e.g. Barasalou 1991; Johnson-Laird 1983). The views of socialization that emerged from cognitive social learning theory have underscored that the child also plays a role in determining their socialization experience. Clearly, mothering an infant high in emotionality must elicit quite a different set of maternal behaviours from the mothering of a sociable, unemotional infant. This realization radically moderated the parent-blaming tendency of early psychopathologists. Although these transactional models of child-to-parent effects were later used to support the argument of those proposing a nativist revival, cognitive social learning theory for the most part maintained the environmentalist tradition of psychoanalytic and learning theories.

Partly in consequence of social learning theory's influence, the key research question of developmental psychopathology became the interaction of person and environmental characteristics in the generation of psychological disturbance through individual development. Attachment theory became one of the guiding frameworks of the approach (e.g. Cicchetti and Cohen 1995; Sroufe and Rutter 1984), and John Bowlby was, to some degree posthumously, recognized by many as one its pioneers (Sroufe 1986). Thus, despite the dominance of cognitive psychology and social learning theory, developmental psychopathology remained a broad church retaining many psychodynamic concerns, particularly a focus on early relationships (e.g. Cicchetti 1987), on relationship representations (e.g. Dodge 1990), on affect regulation (e.g. Sroufe 1996) and on processes of identification (e.g. Crittenden 1994), internalization (e.g. Fonagy *et al.* 1995) and self organization (e.g. Fischer and Ayoub 1994). In the last quarter of the twentieth century developmental psychopathologists were mostly concerned with risk factors, those associated with the family occupying a most important role (e.g. Masten and Garmezy 1985). The characteristics of the family were seen as crucial to the child's developmental choices; the family environment was viewed as critical to both treatment and prevention. But alas, all this was too good to continue.

Over the last decade of the twentieth century, partly triggered by the excitement of the human genome project, and partly by research designs of increasing statistical sophistication, quantitative behaviour genetics was unleashed on early development research and threatened to all but eliminate the place for classical socialization theories with an emphasis on parenting, such as attachment theory, and refute all theories advocating the key role of early family experience (see Scarr 1992). Behaviour geneticists such as Rowe (1994) expressed doubt about whether any undesirable trait displayed by a child could be significantly modified by anything a parent does.

The genetic movement of the 1990s highlighted a number of important issues for early preventionists:

1   The overall connection between early parenting and socialization outcomes turns out to be quite weak. There is very limited evidence to link early relationship experiences with the development of personality and psychopathology.
2   Correlations between characteristics of early parenting and later child behaviour can be reinterpreted so that the child's genetic characteristics are seen as *determining* the parent's response, rather than assuming that parenting influences the child (the so-called child-to-parent effects).
3   Behaviour genetic models of twin and adoption studies partition variability into genetic and environmental components by subtracting the proportion of variability on a specific trait accounted for by genes (h^2) from 100 ($E = 100 - h^2$). In most domains h^2 is 50–60%, with less than half left to E.
4   Behaviour genetics research revealed that influences which had previously been considered environmental (such as children whose parents read to them learning to read sooner than those who are not read to) were actually genetically mediated (Kendler *et al.* 1996). Apparently environmentally mediated family influences can in fact be explained by the shared genetic predisposition of caregiver and offspring, and therefore are possibly in themselves unimportant (Harris 1998; Rowe 1994). In support of this, a recent analysis of

the Colorado adoption project showed that children adopted away from parents who later get divorced develop adjustment problems even if they are adopted into non-divorcing families (O'Connor *et al*. 2000).

5   In so far as behaviour genetic studies showed family environment to matter, it was environment specific to each child within the same family (non-shared environment) that mattered (Plomin and Daniels 1987). Environment may be partitioned into that shared by siblings and a non-shared component that is specific to each child. If shared aspects of the environment such as parenting are formative, then adopted siblings living in the same home should be significantly more alike than unrelated children in different households. However, the non-shared environment appears to be the bulk of the environmental component – shared environment, for example parenting skills, accounts for almost no variance (Plomin 1994). Adopted children, it seems, are no more like their adopted siblings than unrelated children growing up in a different household (Plomin and Bergeman 1991). The relatively weak observed effects of the shared environment have been used to suggest that environments generally assumed to affect children adversely (such as parental conflict, parental psychiatric disturbance or even relative social disadvantage) are either less important than previously thought, or, more likely, are actually genetically mediated (Plomin *et al*. 1994).

6   Even non-shared environmental effects may be better understood as genetic. Genetically influenced aspects of children's behaviour may provoke specific observed responses in parents and other people. Thus, the child's non-shared (specific) environment may have sometimes been erroneously attributed to parental behaviour rather than to his/her genes (O'Connor *et al*. 1998). Some studies of adopted children suggest that rather than accounting for oppositional behaviour in children, authoritarian parenting may actually be elicited by the child's genetically determined resistive or distractible behaviour (Ge *et al*. 1996).

Thus, it seems that over the past 10 years a genetic–biological frame of reference, which often *a priori* excludes consideration of child–parent relationships, has replaced the previous primarily psychosocial model of development. In an informal study, 20 consecutive parents referred to an outpatient child community mental health clinic who were asked about the likely cause of their child's problems all put brain chemistry at the top of the list. 'Bad genes' came second, peers third and early life experiences a poor fifth. The reduction of the mind to chemicals was appealing even to Freud. While our consciousness, our free will, our mind is undoubtedly our most treasured possession, it is also the source of all our sadness, conflict, pain, suffering and misery. The reduction of models of pathology to a principally genetic mode of causation is undoubtedly a relatively comfortable solution for all of us. But like all comforts, it comes at a price.

Scrutinizing the case for genetics

The apparent strength of genetic findings, the massive proportion of variability accounted for, no matter how specific the trait, leaves little room for socialization, for the mysteries and uncertainty of development. But are the genetic findings as unequivocal as they seem?

The evidence from behaviour genetics should be interpreted with caution for many reasons. We may question the notion of non-shared environment, since it merely refers to differences between siblings, not to their environment. In fact, shared environments could as easily serve to make children in the family different from one another as to increase intra-familial similarity, since two children may experience the same environment very differently. Furthermore, heritability estimates based solely on individual differences remove shared environmental effects such as historical trends. Height, IQ, as well as the prevalence of a number of psychological disorders (such as delinquency and eating disorder) have increased markedly over the last century, undoubtedly in consequence of environmental changes. Yet current behavioural genetic methods of estimating environmental effects preclude consideration of these.

There are studies where environmental determinants revealed substantial effects *after* genetic influences had been excluded (Johnson *et al.* 1999). Moreover, evidence on just how differently siblings are treated is actually quite mixed. Judy Dunn's naturalistic observational studies of siblings suggest that while cross-sectionally parents may appear to be treating siblings differently, this may be an artefact of how a parent treats children in a specific age group in particular ways; looked at longitudinally children at various ages receive comparable treatment (Dunn and McGuire 1994). But regardless of the ultimate conclusion concerning the differential treatment of siblings, the fact that studies of social development have tended to look at single children implies that they have on the whole underestimated the impact of parenting and other shared environmental influences. There may be specific pressures in family systems for differential responses of siblings as part of the need for each person within the system to have a unique role. Interestingly, the pressure for difference may be greatest when genetic differentiation is least.

Experimental manipulation of the environment as part of treatment and prevention interventions has sometimes yielded relatively large effects. The average effect size of parent training for children with ODD is around 1 (Serketich and Dumas 1996), yet neither of the two major attacks on the importance of family in socialization (Harris 1998; Rowe 1994) cover parent training. Accumulating evidence supports the usefulness of experimental interventions with parents such as home visitation (e.g. Olds *et al.* 1998) with long-term beneficial effects in reducing risk of criminality and delinquency. Of course, the impact of environmental manipulation is often not as large as one would hope. Many current prevention programmes are not evidence based and have quite inadequate evaluation components. Moreover, long-term follow-ups in prevention studies are still relatively rare, and even quite impressive changes initiated by experimental interventions dissipate (Fonagy *et al.* 2000).

As clinicians, our main objection to behaviour genetics data is that even a high genetic loading for a certain environmental hazard does not mean that the consequences associated with that risk factor would necessarily be genetically rather than environmentally mediated. For example, if child abuse were found to have a large genetic component, its toxic effect would still be via the destruction of trust in the world for the abused child, rather than via a purely genetic process. The implications of behaviour genetic data for prevention intervention are thus quite limited.

The role of genetics in personality development and psychopathology has been exaggerated. There are few examples where the conceptual journey between gene and behaviour is simple enough to be tracked. The assumptions of behaviour genetics are very substantial, and the interactions between genes and the polygenic nature of most attributes which are genetically determined makes simple extrapolations from genomics to psychology risky and improbable.

The role of experience in the expression of the genotype

All agree that development involves a gene–environment interaction. Some quantitative behaviour genetic studies strongly suggest interactive processes whereby environmental exposure triggers genetic vulnerability. For example, the classic Finnish adoptive family study of schizophrenia suggests that children with a schizophrenic biological parent were more likely to develop a range of psychiatric problems if, and only if, they were adopted into dysfunctional families (Tienari *et al.* 1994). Bohman (1996) reported that criminality appeared to be associated with a genetic risk only if children whose biological parents were criminals were adopted into dysfunctional homes. Genetic risk may or may not become manifest depending on the quality of the family environment to which a child is exposed. But if this is such a pervasive process, why is the quantitative behaviour genetic evidence for gene–environment interaction so sparse?

I think the answer is obvious: behaviour genetics studies the 'wrong' environment. The environment that triggers the expression of a gene is not the observable, objective environment. The child's experience of the environment is what counts. The manner in which environment is experienced will act as a filter in the expression of genotype into phenotype. And here we touch on the pivotal role of parenting for genetic research, particularly attachment theory. The primary concern of attachment theory is with the interaction of multiple layers of representations in generating developmental outcomes. Data from genetics call for exactly such sophistication in understanding the way genes may or may not be expressed in particular individuals.

The pathway from genes to phenotypes is a tortuous one, along which genetics and environment constantly interact (Elman *et al.* 1996). Internal and external stimuli, steps in the development of the brain, hormones, stress, learning and social interaction, all have a role to play (Kandel 1998). There is substantial individual variability in response to the risk factors of stress and adversity. Much of this variability is poorly understood (Rutter 1999), but it underscores the potential importance of intrapsychic variables. Increased knowledge of genetics has high-lighted that experience is often critical in determining whether a gene will be expressed, whether genotype is transformed into phenotype. In human beings, but possibly also in other primates, subjective experience defines the environment rather than the actual physical context. Thus, for example, social support has beneficial effects on homeostatic regulation even when it is only subjectively present. The belief that a friend is nearby reduces cardiovascular responsivity to stress even when the friend is not present, just assumed by the subject to be there. Similarly if experience is going to moderate the unfolding of genetic predisposi-tion then it will be felt experience, subjective experience, that is likely to be responsible for this influence in humans rather than objectively measurable aspects of the social context.

This has substantial significance for prevention, since the child's understanding of his environment is more readily modifiable than the environment itself, or the genes with which the environment interacts (Emde 1988). An attachment theory, intrapsychic perspective, may be helpful in considering not just what precipitates a disorder but also which processes influence the course of the disorder for better or worse. Before the last 5 years this was theory, but now the collaboration of molecular geneticists and attachment theory is making it a reality. Let me give an example of this powerful paradigm.

There is excellent evidence from rhesus monkeys (Suomi 2000) that individuals who carry the 'short' allele of a particular gene (the 5-HTT) associated with impaired serotonergic function are significantly more severely affected by maternal deprivation than individuals with the 'long' allele, which does not have this association (Bennett et al. 2002). But this is not the full story. The work of Suomi's laboratory over the last decade demonstrated that monkeys with the 'short' allele only grow up to be socially anxious in nature, to have a reactive temperament (a tendency to become emotionally aroused, aggressive, impulsive and fearful) and to drop to the bottom of dominance hierarchies (Higley et al. 1996; Suomi 1997) if they are deprived of normal maternal care. Expression of the gene associated with decreased serotonergic functioning and the psychological and social consequences of this is *only* triggered in peer-reared monkeys whose early environment was inadequate.

Studies where the foster mothering of specially bred high-reactive monkey infants was experimentally manipulated have indicated that genetic vulnerability does not constitute inevitability. Reactive infants assigned to particularly nurturant foster (super-)mothers appeared to be behaviourally precocious, unusually secure and when moved into larger social groups were particularly adept at recruiting and retaining other group members as allies and rose to and maintained high positions in the dominance hierarchy (Suomi 1991). The maternal style of high-reactive females raised by nurturant mothers reflected the style of their nurturant foster mothers rather than their own temperament. Thus the benefits of nurturant foster mothering can evidently be transmitted to the next generation, even though the mode of transmission is non-genetic in nature (Suomi and Levine 1998). As the example of the monkeys illustrates, early experience with the caregiver may trigger gene expression. Therefore, data from molecular biology might be illuminated by study of the early family environment, particularly parenting and attachment.

The genesis of an appraisal mechanism

I have tried to persuade you that the importance of family environment may have been underestimated in behavioural genetics research. I have also suggested that the child's representational system may be the filter that determines whether the genotype is expressed in the phenotype. If the mental processing of experience is critical for the expression of genetic material, the interaction between gene and environment is substantial. In the concluding section of my presentation I would like to persuade you that human attachment is key to the genesis of this all-important representational mechanism. There is scant evidence that the early relationship environment shapes the quality of subsequent relationships, but considerable data suggest that attachment serves to equip the individual with a mental representational system. The creation of this system is arguably a most important evolutionary function for attachment to a caregiver.

John Bowlby originally thought that the evolutionary function of attachment behaviours such as smiling or crying was to establish and maintain proximity with the caregiver so that the helpless infant would be less subject to environmental hazards endangering its survival. But another component of the package of attachment behaviours Bowlby outlined provides a better evolutionary rationale for human attachment, which goes beyond the issue of physical protection: the development of a representational system for mental states.

Four representational systems compose the internal working models: (1) expectations of interactive attributes of early caregivers created in the first year of life and subsequently elaborated; (2) event representations by which general and specific memories of attachment-related experiences are encoded and retrieved; (3) autobiographical memories by which specific events are conceptually connected because of their relation to a continuing personal narrative and developing self-understanding; (4) understanding of the psychological character-istics of other people (inferring and attributing causal motivational mind states such as desires and emotions and epistemic mind states such as intentions and beliefs) *and differentiating these from those of the self.* Thus a key developmental attainment of the Internal Working Model is that it enables the child to interpret its experience of self and significant others in terms of a set of stable and generalized intentional attributes, such as desires, emotions, intentions, and beliefs inferred from recurring invariant patterns in the history of previous interactions. The child comes to be able to use this representational system to predict the other's or the self's behaviour in conjunction with local, more transient intentional states inferred from a given situation.

Classical attachment theory argues that cognitive development propels the change in the attachment system from behaviour to representation, from proximity seeking to, for example, verbal reassurance (Marvin and Britner 1999). Our contention is the reverse: the attachment mechanism propels cognitive development. We propose that a major selective advantage conferred by attachment to humans was the opportunity it afforded for the development of social intelligence and meaning creation. The capacity for 'interpretation', which Bogdan (1997) defined as 'organisms making sense of each other in contexts where this matters biologically' (p. 10), becomes uniquely human when others are engaged 'psychologically in sharing experiences, information and affects' (p. 94). The capacity to interpret human behaviour – to make sense of each other – requires the intentional stance: 'treating the object whose behaviour you want to predict as a rational agent with beliefs and desires' (Dennett 1987: 15).

The capacity for interpretation in psychological terms – let's call this the Interpersonal Interpretive Mechanism – does not just generate or mediate attachment experience, it is also a product of the complex psychological processes engendered by close proximity in infancy to another human being, the attachment figure. The Interpersonal Interpretive Mechanism is not a memory bank of personal encounters with the caregiver but rather a mechanism for processing *new* experiences. How is it created?

The ontogenesis of the Interpersonal Interpretive Mechanism

In answering this question we are drawing upon George Gergely's and John Watson's model (Gergely and Watson 1996, 1999). Our core idea is that the attachment context enables the infant to develop sensitivity to self states, through what Gergely termed 'psycho-feedback'. The child acquires this capacity for sensitivity by developing a second-order symbolic representational system for motivational (desires) and epistemic (beliefs) mind states. What initiates the development of this representational system is the infant's internalization of the mother's mirroring response to his distress. The mother's empathic emotion provides the infant with feedback on his emotional state. Thus the infant develops a secondary representation of his emotional state, with the mother's empathic face as the signifier and his own emotional arousal as the signified. The mother's expression tempers emotion to the extent that it is separate and different from the primary experience, although crucially it is not recognized as the mother's experience, but as an organizer of a self state. This 'inter-subjectivity' is the bedrock of the intimate connection between attachment and self-regulation. At this level of human proximity the other's subjective state is automatically referred to the self. In infancy the contingent responding of the attachment figure is thus far more than the provision of reassurance about a protective presence. It is the principal means by which we acquire understanding of our own internal states, which is an intermediate step in the acquisition of an understanding of others as psychological entities.

In the first year, the infant only has primary awareness of being in a particular, internal, emotional state. This awareness is not put to any functional use by the system. It is in the process of psycho-feedback that these internal experiences are more closely attended to and evolve a functional role (a signal value) and a function in modulating or inhibiting action. Thus it is attachment processes that ensure the move from primary awareness of internal states to functional awareness. In functional awareness a feeling of anger may be used to simulate and so to infer the other's corresponding mental state or may be used to serve a signal value to direct action. The next level of awareness is reflective awareness, where the individual can make a causal mind state become the object of attention without it necessarily causing action. Whereas functional awareness is coupled with action, reflective awareness is separate from it. It has the capacity to move away from physical reality and may be felt to be not for real. A final level is autobiographical, where the child is able to place records of experiences imbued with psychological states into a sequence that represents his or her history as an individual.

Many studies provide evidence consistent with Gergely's intersubjective model for the development of internal state representations. For example, a study carried out by us showed that the rapidity with which distressed 6-month-olds could be soothed could be predicted by rating the emotional content of the mother's facial expression during the process of soothing; mothers of children who were soothed rapidly showed somewhat more fear, somewhat less joy but most typically a range of other affects in addition to fear and sadness. Mothers of rapid responders were far more likely to manifest multiple affect states (complex affects). These results support Gergely and Watson's idea that the mother's face is a secondary representation of the infant's experience – the same and yet not the same. This is functional awareness with the capacity to modulate affect states.

Evidence for the Interpersonal Interpretive Mechanism

Is there any evidence for an Interpersonal Interpretive Mechanism that evolves out of the attachment relationship, with its efficiency conditioned by attachment security? First, there is unequivocal evidence from two decades of longitudinal research that secure attachment in infancy is strongly associated with the precocious development of a range of capacities that depend on interpretive or symbolic skills, such as exploration and play, intelligence and language ability, ego resilience and ego control, frustration tolerance, curiosity, self recognition, social cognitive capacities and so on. Attachment security foreshadows cognitive competence, exploratory skill, emotion regulation, communication style and other outcomes. In our view this is not because of the general impact of attachment security on the child's self-confidence, initiative or ego functioning, or other broader personality processes, but rather because attachment processes provide the key evolutionarily prepared paths for an interpersonal interpretive capacity to develop.

Thus it is not the first attachments that are formative, it is not attachment security per se that predicts good outcome on this dazzling array of measures, but rather the features of the inter-personal environment which generate attachment security during the first year of life also prepare the ground for the rapid and competent ontogenetic evolution of interpersonal interpretation.

Second, there are a number of specific findings in the literature that link attachment to the development of an Interpersonal Interpretive Mechanism. Laible and Thompson (1998) reported securely attached children to have higher competence in understanding negative emotion. A unique study by Jude Cassidy *et al.* (1996) found that securely attached kindergarteners were less likely to infer hostile intent in stories with ambiguous content and this bias appeared to mediate their superiority in sociometric status. In the London Parent–Child Project Miriam and Howard Steele and Juliet Holder and I reported precocious performance on theory of mind tasks amongst 5-year-olds with a history of secure attachment in infancy. Since then, this finding has also been reported by other investigators (Meins *et al.* 1998). By contrast, harsh or abusive parenting is known to create enduring cognitive biases in the interpretation of human behaviour; children of such parents have great social problem-solving deficits, which can eventually lead to serious clinical disorders of conduct (Dodge *et al.* 1994; Kazdin 1996; Shure 1993).

Third, in a relatively full exploration of findings linking early attachment and later development, Ross Thompson (1999) concludes that 'the strength of the relationship between infant security and later socio-personality functioning is modest' (p.280). The associations are stronger contemporaneously than they are predictively. Within the context of the present theory, it is not the content of internal working models that are likely to be determined by early experience but rather the presence of a model or the quality or robustness of the model that is so determining. Thus, attachment classification might or might not be stable from infancy through middle childhood to adolescence. As prediction comes from the Interpersonal Interpretive Mechanism, not from attachment security per se, this is of no great concern.

The focus of study should not be attachment security, which achieved significance as a correlate of the Interpersonal Interpretive Mechanism, but has little stability, and possibly little predictive value. Rather, the Interpersonal Interpretive Mechanism, which is a genetically defined capacity, probably localized in the medial pre-frontal cortex, is the mechanism of predictive significance. Both PET and fMRI studies where subjects were asked to make inferences about the mental states of others found activity associated with mentalizing in the medial pre-frontal cortex. In addition, activity was elicited in the temporoparietal junction (Gallagher *et al.* 2000; Goel *et al.* 1995).

There is independent evidence for the developmental vulnerability of this structure from PET scan studies of Romanian adoptees who were deprived of the interpersonal experiences which we think might generate the Interpersonal

Interpretive Mechanism. Independently, we of course know that the attachment classification of these adoptees remains disorganized at age 3 and their social behaviour is abnormal at age 8. We also have evidence that the mentalizing capacity of individuals maltreated in early childhood continues to have significant limitations.

Fourth, Myron Hofer's work with rodent pups identified regulatory interactions within the mother–infant relationship which have clear analogies to what is proposed here (Hofer 1995; Polan and Hofer 1999). Hofer's work over three decades has revealed that the evolutionary survival value of staying close to and interacting with the mother goes way beyond protection and may be expanded to many pathways available for regulation of the infant's physiological and behavioural system. Hofer's view is analogous to ours in that he proposes that the attachment 'relationship provides an opportunity for the mother to shape both the developing physiology and the behaviour of her offspring through her patterned interactions with her infant' (Polan and Hofer 1999: 177). Attachment is not an end in itself – it is a system adapted by evolution to fulfil key ontogenetic physiological and psychological tasks.[1]

Hofer's reformulation of attachment in terms of regulatory processes, hidden but observable within the parent–infant interaction, provides a very different way of explaining the range of phenomena usually discussed under the heading of attachment. The traditional attachment model is clearly circular. The response to separation is attributed to the disruption of a social bond, the existence of which is inferred from the presence of the separation response. What is lost in 'loss' is not the bond but the opportunity to generate a higher-order regulatory mechanism: the mechanism for appraisal and reorganization of mental contents. We conceptualize attachment as a process which brings into being complex mental life from a complex and adaptable behavioural system. Some, but by no means all, of such mental function is unique to humans. The mechanisms which generate these (the attachment relationship) has evolutionary continuity across non-human species. Just as in rat pups the ontogenetic development of biological regulators crucially depends on the mother–infant unit, so in human development psychological interpretive capacity evolves in the context of the repetitive interactions with the mother.

Fifth, in a series of studies at the Menninger Clinic we explored the factor structure of a number of self-report measures of adult attachment. I do not have time to go into the detail of these studies but on both community and clinical samples we found very similar results across three investigations. We tend to find two factors: a secure–fearful axis and a dismissive–preoccupied axis (Allen *et al.* 2000). When we plotted the subjects in the sample, both patients and community controls, on the same two principal components it was clear that while the secure–fearful axis was excellent at distinguishing the community sample from the patient group, the preoccupied–dismissive axis did not distinguish the groups well. What was also clear was a somewhat unexpected relationship between component scores. Although the overall correlation between the two scales was negligible, as you would expect, the discrimination between preoccupied and dismissive was somewhat greater towards the middle point of the secure–fearful dimension.

One way of interpreting these data is to assume that security represents an experience of safety in closeness, while fearfulness relates to a disorganization of attachment. The fearfulness appears to be specific to attachment relationships, as non-attachment relationships rarely score highly on this dimension. The dismissing attachment style appears to offer protection to the self by isolation, whereas in enmeshed preoccupation self-protection is perhaps afforded by an amplification of the other, by a denial or subjugation of the self.

We would argue that the safety to fearfulness dimension corresponds to the quality of functioning of the Interpersonal Interpretative Mechanism. At the high end, the individual is well able to represent complex internal states of the other and of the self. With a well-established higher-order capacity for distinguishing psychological states of the other and the self they need no additional strategies for conducting productive interpersonal relationships. When the psychological mechanism crucially underpinning attachment is somewhat weaker (as a function of attachment history or biology), the capacity for sustaining a clear distinction between self and other also becomes weaker. In such a situation the individual will require specific strategies to accommodate to interpersonal encounters. The two prototypical strategies are the avoidant and resistant strategies.

But why are such strategies necessary? Both serve to protect the self in the context of intense interpersonal relations. We assume that these strategies may be necessary because the self, which is as we have seen the product of the other, for ever remains vulnerable to social influence. To avoid such instability, against a background of a relatively insecure internal working model, the individual can either deliberately withdraw and enhance the self representation relative to the other representations (dismissing), or protectively over-amplify and exaggerate the other representation (preoccupied). In either case, the strategies in representational terms are about deliberately separating the other from the self representation.

Neither of these strategies is inherently pathological, although both signal a certain degree of weakness. At the extreme end of the safety to fearfulness dimension, there can be no strategy because the attachment system is not there to sustain a consistent set of defences. In these cases the lack of the interpretive mechanism that sustains social relations functions so poorly that the capacity to arrive at representations of the motivational or epistemic mind states of the other independent of those of the self are profoundly compromised. This is attachment disorganization, or rather the absence of the mental function that sustains attachment. Thus we conceive of attachment disorganization as at the opposite end of attachment security and as an indicator of the regular failure of the Interpersonal Interpretive Mechanism.

To summarize, we feel that there are at least five strands of converging evidence to suggest that a key selective advantage of attachment might be the development of an understanding of internal states: (1) that secure attachment is associated with favourable outcomes across a wide range of relevant tasks; (2) that secure attachment predicts precocious performance in tasks specifically calling for symbolic capacity; (3) that the class of early attachment classification has less predictive weight than whether attachment experiences occurred; (4) that attachment has been demonstrated to have other ontogenetic biological functions in mammalian species which have analogies or which may parallel the evolutionary function for attachment proposed here; (5) that analysing the components of adult attachment scales identifies a factor to do with type of attachment (perhaps the Internal Working Model) and the quality of attachment (perhaps the Interpersonal Interpretive Mechanism).

Implications for clinical work

The twentieth century brought a culture where, perhaps for the first time in the history of humanity, a profession emerged with the unique role of listening to more or less psychologically troubled individuals reflecting on their narratives and directing them towards greater coherence of narration (Holmes 1998). Of course, the profession was not new and perhaps only had to be invented because of the increasingly secular character of human society. But what is the function of the individual, most recently paid, to listen to another person's understanding of their life and circumstances and reflect on this understanding in a more or less active way? Human consciousness cannot evolve in isolation (Hegel 1807). The Interpersonal Interpretive Mechanism is clearly a capacity prepared or 'canalized' (Waddington 1966) by evolution, as language is. We are destined to represent each other's actions symbolically. We could not work together in groups, or at least work effectively, without being able to interpret the actions of those around us in terms of units of explanation that make sense to us. These aliquots of meaning are subjective states. They are not necessarily mental states that we have access to – they may be non-conscious but they are experiential in the sense that they share a prepositional structure with conscious mind states. The beliefs and desires that lie behind behaviour can suddenly make sense of action that is otherwise experienced as arbitrary and random. The impulse to identify such belief is so strong that the mind feels obliged to attribute meaning to animals and may even understand moving geometric figures in the same frame of reference as human behaviour, imputing desires and beliefs to them (Heider and Simmel 1944). The same searchlight (the same interpretive mechanism) can be fixed on one's own behaviour where genetic vulnerability and social hardship have combined to create turbulence and disturbance sufficient to generate a discontinuity in subjective experience. To be able to remain close to another mind, to feel protected from the experience of having one's mind overtaken by the social context, the Interpersonal Interpretive Mechanism must function efficiently and effectively in relation to one's own subjective experience. To know one's own mind is a precondition of mature social interaction. The deviant interpersonal strategies of insecure attachment may be prototypical ways of protecting the self from being overwhelmed by the other's view of the self. These strategies, however, disrupt interpersonal relationships and can be the cause of deep unhappiness and painful disappointment. No wonder then that we turn to 'professionals' who lend us their subjectivity to regenerate our interpretive capacities. They are professionals (priests, counsellors, psychotherapists) in the sense that they implicitly undertake not to overwhelm our subjectivity with theirs, not to undermine our sense of our own mental states by creating alternative versions out of line with our inner experience. Rather, they cherish a vulnerable and deviant or deficient interpretive capacity, protecting it from itself in the sense of aiming not to allow it to adopt past deviant strategies of distancing or preoccupation. They may use an almost infinite range of techniques, from deep interpretation of unconscious processes to simple emotional resonance, from silent but accepting listening to active restructuring of the other's way of thinking, from an almost ascetic renouncing of direct instruction to the explicit re-programming of inadequate behaviour. All these interventions serve to re-engage the Interpersonal Interpretive Mechanism in a context that is sufficiently protected for the mentalization of life experience to grow.

The understanding of psychological states, acquired prototypically in the emotional cauldron of the earliest relationships, normally serves as an organizer and protector, and may account for much we assign to the rag-bag category of resilience and invulnerability. As the laborious move from genotype to phenotype is conditioned this way, the Interpersonal Interpretive Mechanism is a function of immense importance. Its efficient functioning underpins adaptation at all stages of development. As genes affecting brain function are activated throughout the life span, including the onset of old age, senility and death, the role of the Interpersonal Interpretive Mechanism remains critical as the mediator between biological destiny, internal and external circumstances and the functioning and contents of the mind. A full understanding of the interaction between individual mentalized representations of life experience and the expression of genetic dispositions is the task of developmental research and psychological therapy of the next decades. As Francois Jacob (1998, cited in Kandel, 1999: 508) in *Of Flies, Mice and Men* wrote: 'the century that is ending has been preoccupied with nucleic acids and proteins. The next one will concentrate on *memory and desire*. Will it be able to answer the questions they pose?'

Acknowledgements

The author would like to acknowledge the contribution of his colleagues at the Child and Family Center, Menninger Clinic Topeka. This paper is in large part based on data gathered by them. In particular the author is indebted to Drs Helen Stein, Jon Allen, Martin Maldonado and Jim Fultz. The author would also like to acknowledge Dr Anna Higgitt's guidance in the writing of the chapter. This chapter is part of an ongoing collaboration with Drs Mary Target, George Gergely, and Eliot Jurist. A co-authored book covering these themes is forthcoming with Other Press.

Notes

1 These ideas have a great deal in common with recent suggestions from Edward Tronick concerning a self-organizing affective control process which induces and stabilizes changes in emotional control. Tronick also assumes that a mutual regulation model, which takes its input from the caregiver's affects, as well as internally, creates an infant's mood as part of an intersubjective process. (Tronick submitted, 2001)

References

Alexander, J. F. and Parsons, B. V. (1982). *Functional Family Therapy*. Monterey, CA: Brooks/Cole.

Allen, J. G., Huntoon, J., Fultz, J., Stein, H. B., Fonagy, P. and Evans, R. B. (2000). *Adult Attachment Styles and Current Attachment Figures: Assessment of Women in Inpatient Treatment for Trauma Related Psychiatric Disorders*. Topeka, KS: Menninger Clinic.

Barasalou, L. W. (1991). *Cognitive Psychology: An Overview for Cognitive Scientists*. Hillsdale, NJ: Erlbaum.

Bennett, A. J., Lesch, K. P., Heils, A., Long, J. C., Lorenz, J. G., Shoaf, S. E., Champoux, M., Suomi, S. J., Linnoila, M. V. and Higley, J. D. (2002). Early experience and serotonin transporter gene variation interact to influence primate CNS function. *Molecular Psychiatry 7*(1): 118–122.

Bogdan, R. J. (1997). *Interpreting Minds*. Cambridge, MA: MIT Press.

Bohman, M. (1996). Predisposition to criminality: Swedish adoption studies in retrospect. In Rutter, M. (ed.), *Genetics of Criminal and Antisocial Behaviour*. Chichester: Wiley.

Bowlby, J. (1958). The nature of the child's tie to his mother. *International Journal of Psycho-Analysis 39*: 350–373.

Cassidy, J., Kirsh, S. J., Scolton, K. L. and Parke, R. D. (1996). Attachment and representations of peer relationships. *Developmental Psychology 32*: 892–904.

Cicchetti, D. (1987). Developmental psychopathology in infancy: illustration from the study of maltreated youngsters. *Journal of Consulting and Clincal Psychology 55*: 837–845.

Cicchetti, D. and Cohen, D. J. (1995). Perspectives on developmental psychopathology. In Cicchetti, D. and Cohen, D. J. (eds), *Developmental Psychopathology, Vol. 1: Theory and Methods*, 3–23. New York: Wiley.

Crittenden, P. M. (1994). Peering into the black box: an exploratory treatise on the development of self in young children. In Cicchetti, D. and Toth, S. L. (eds), *Disorders and Dysfunctions of the Self: Rochester Symposium on Developmental Psychopathology, Vol. 5*, 79–148. Rochester, NY: University of Rochester Press.

Dennett, D. (1987). *The Intentional Stance*. Cambridge, MA: MIT Press.

Dodge, K. (1990). Developmental psychopathology in children of depressed mothers. *Developmental Psychology 26*: 3–6.

Dodge, K. A., Pettit, G. S., and Bates, J. E. (1994). Effects of physical maltreatment on the development of peer relations. *Development and Psychopathology 6*: 43–55.

Dunn, J. and McGuire, S. (1994). Young children's non-shared experiences: a summary of studies in Cambridge and Colorado. In Hetherington, E. M., Reiss, D. and Plomin, R. (eds), *Separate Social Worlds of Siblings*. Hillsdale, NJ: Erlbaum.

Elman, J. L., Bates, A. E., Johnson, M. H., Karmiloff-Smith, A., Parisi, D. and Plunkett, K. (1996). *Rethinking Innateness: A Connectionist Perspective on Development*. Cambridge, MA: MIT Press.

Emde, R. N. (1988). Development terminable and interminable. I. Innate and motivational factors from infancy. *International Journal of Psycho-Analysis 69*: 23–42.

Fischer, K. W. and Ayoub, C. (1994). Affective splitting and dissociation in normal and maltreated children: developmental pathways for self in relationships. In Cicchetti, D. and Toth, S. L. (eds), *Rochester Symposium on Developmental Psychopathology: Vol. 5. Disorders and Dysfunctions of the Self*, 149–222. Rochester, NY: University of Rochester Press.

Fonagy, P., Leigh, T., Kennedy, R., Mattoon, G., Steele, H., Target, M., Steele, M. and Higgitt, A. (1995). Attachment, borderline states and the representation of emotions and cognitions in self and other. In Cicchetti, D. and Toth, S. S. (eds), *Rochester Symposium on Developmental Psychopathology: Cognition and Emotion, Vol. 6*, 371–414. Rochester, NY: University of Rochester Press.

Fonagy, P., Target, M., Cottrell, D., Phillips, J. and Kurtz, Z. (2000). *A review of the Outcomes of all Treatments of Psychiatric Disorder in Childhood* (MCH 17–33). London: National Health Service Executive.

Gallagher, H. L., Happe, F., Brunswick, N., Fletcher, P. C., Frith, U. and Frith, C. D. (2000). Reading the mind in cartoons and stories: an fMRI study of 'theory of mind' in verbal and nonverbal tasks. *Neuropsychologia 38*(1): 11–21.

Ge, X., Conger, R. D., Cadoret, R., Neiderhiser, J. and Yates, W. (1996). The developmental interface between nature and nurture: a mutual influence model of child antisocial behavior and parent behavior. *Developmental Psychology 32*: 574–589.

Gergely, G. and Watson, J. (1996). The social biofeedback model of parental affect-mirroring. *International Journal of Psycho-Analysis 77*: 1181–1212.

Gergely, G. and Watson, J. (1999). Early social–emotional development: contingency perception and the social biofeedback model. In Rochat, P. (ed.), *Early Social Cognition: Understanding Others in the First Months of Life*, 101–137. Hillsdale, NJ: Erlbaum.

Goel, V., Grafman, N., Sadato, M. and Hallett, M. (1995). Modeling other minds. *Neuroreport 6*: 1741–1746.

Harris, J. R. (1998). *The Nurture Assumption: Why Children Turn Out the Way They Do. Parents Matter Less than you Think and Peers Matter More.* New York: Free Press.

Hegel, G. (1807). *The Phenomenology of Spirit.* Oxford: Oxford University Press.

Heider, F. and Simmel, M. (1944). An experimental study of apparent behavior. *American Journal of Psychology 57*: 243–259.

Higley, J. D., King, S. T., Hasert, M. F., Champoux, M., Suomi, S. J. and Linnoila, M. (1996). Stability of individual differences in serotonin function and its relationship to severe aggression and competent social behavior in rhesus macaque females. *Neuropsychopharmacology 14*: 67–76.

Hofer, M. A. (1995). Hidden regulators: implications for a new understanding of attachment, separation and loss. In Goldberg, S., Muir, R. and Kerr J. (eds), *Attachment Theory: Social, Developmental, and Clinical Perspectives*, 203–230. Hillsdale, NJ: Analytic Press.

Holmes, J. (1998). Defensive and creative uses of narrative in psychotherapy: an attachment perspective. In Roberts, G. and Holmes, J. (eds), *Narrative and Psychotherapy and Psychiatry*, 49–68. Oxford: Oxford University Press.

Johnson, J. G., Cohen, P., Brown, J., Smailes, E. M. and Bernstein, D. P. (1999). Childhood maltreatment increases risk for personality disorders during early adulthood. *Archives of General Psychiatry 56*: 600–605.

Johnson-Laird, P. N. (1983). *Mental Models: Towards a Cognitive Science of Language, Inference and Consciousness*. Cambridge: Cambridge University Press.

Kandel, E. R. (1998). A new intellectual framework for psychiatry. *American Journal of Psychiatry 155*: 457–469.

Kandel, E. R. (1999). Biology and the future of psychoanalysis: a new intellectual framework for psychiatry revisited. *American Journal of Psychiatry 156*: 505–524.

Kazdin, A. E. (1996). Problem solving and parent management in treating aggressive and antisocial behaviour. In Hibbs, E. S. and Jensen, P. S. (eds), *Psychosocial Treatments for Child and Adolescent Disorders: Empirically Based Strategies for Clinical Practice*, 377–408. Washington, DC: American Psychological Association.

Kendler, K. S., Neale, M. C., Prescott, C. A., Kessler, R. C., Heath, A. C., Corey, L. A. and Eaves, L. J. (1996). Childhood parental loss and alcoholism in women: a causal analysis using a twin-family design. *Psychological Medicine 26*: 79–95.

Laible, D. J. and Thompson, R. A. (1998). Attachment and emotional understanding in pre-school children. *Developmental Psychology 34*: 1038–1045.

Leach, P. (1997). *Your Baby and Child: New Version for a New Generation*. London: Penguin.

Maccoby, E. E. (2000). Parenting and its effects on children: on reading and misreading behaviour genetics. *Annual Review of Psychology 51*: 1–27.

Marvin, R. S. and Britner, P. A. (1999). Normative development: the ontogeny of attachment. In Cassidy, J. and Shaver, P. R. (eds), *Handbook of Attachment: Theory, Research and Clinical Applications*, 44–67. New York: Guilford.

Masten, A. S. and Garmezy, M. (1985). Risk, vulnerability and protective factors in developmental psychopathology. In Lahey, B. B. and Kazdin, A. E. (eds), *Advances in Clinical Child Psychology*, 1–52. New York: Plenum.

Meins, E., Fernyhough, C., Russel, J. and Clark-Carter, D. (1998). Security of attachment as a predictor of symbolic and mentalising abilities: a longitudinal study. *Social Development 7*: 1–24.

O'Connor, T. G., Caspi, A., DeFries, J. C. and Plomin, R. (2000). Are associations between parental divorce and children's adjustment genetically mediated? An adoption study. *Developmental Psychology 36*: 419–428.

O'Connor, T. G., Deater-Deckard, K., Fulker, D., Rutter, M. and Plomin, R. (1998). Genotype–environment correlations in late childhood and early adolescence: antisocial behavioral problems and coercive parenting. *Developmental Psychology 34*: 970–981.

Olds, D., Henderson Jr, C. R., Cole, R., Eckenrode, J., Kitzman, H., Luckey, D., Pettitt, L., Sidora, K., Morris, P. and Powers, J. (1998). Long-term effects of nurse home visitation on children's criminal and antisocial behaviour: 15 year follow-up of a randomized controlled trial. *Journal of the American Medical Association 280*: 1238–1244.

Patterson, G. R. (1976). *Living with Children: New Methods for Parents and Teachers*, rev. edn. Champaign, IL: Research Press.

Plomin, R. (1994). *Genetics and Experience: The Interplay Between Nature and Nurture*. Thousand Oaks, CA: Sage.

Plomin, R. and Bergeman, C. S. (1991). The nature of nurture: genetic influences on 'environmental' measures. *Behavior and Brain Sciences 14*: 373–386.

Plomin, R., Chipuer, H. M. and Neiderhiser, J. M. (1994). Behavioral genetic evidence for the importance of non-shared environment. In Hetherington, E. M., Reiss, D. and Plomin, R. (eds), *Separate Social Worlds of Siblings*, 1–31. Hillsdale, NJ: Erlbaum.

Plomin, R. and Daniels, D. (1987). Why are children in the same family so different from one another? *Behavioral and Brain Sciences 10*: 1–16.

Polan, H. J. and Hofer, M. (1999). Psychobiological origins of infant attachment and separation responses. In Cassidy, J. and Shaver, P. R. (eds), *Handbook of Attachment: Theory, Research and Clinical Applications*, 162–180. New York: Guilford.

Rowe, D. (1994). *The Limits of Family Influence: Genes, Experience and Behaviour*. New York: Guilford Press.

Rutter, M. (1999). Psychosocial adversity and child psychopathology. *British Journal of Psychiatry 174*: 480–493.

Rutter, M. (2000). Psychosocial influences: critiques, findings and research needs. *Development and Psychopathology 12*: 375–405.

Scarr, S. (1992). Developmental theories for the 1990s: development and individual differences. *Child Development 63*: 1–19.

Serketich, W. J. and Dumas, J. E. (1996). The effectiveness of behavioural parent training to modify antisocial behaviour in children: a meta-analysis. *Behaviour Therapy 27*: 171–186.

Shure, M. B. (1993). *Interpersonal Problem Solving and Prevention: A Comprehensive Report of Research and Training* (#MH-40801). Washington, DC: National Institute of Mental Health.

Spock, B. and Rothenberg, M. B. (1985). *Dr. Spock's Baby and Child Care*, 5th edn. London: W. H. Allen.

Sroufe, L. A. (1986). Bowlby's contribution to psychoanalytic theory and developmental psychopathology. *Journal of Child Psychology and Psychiatry 27*: 841–849.

Sroufe, L. A. (1996). *Emotional Development: The Organization of Emotional Life in the Early Years*. New York: Cambridge University Press.

Sroufe, L. A. and Rutter, M. (1984). The domain of developmental psychopathology. *Child Development 83*: 173–189.

Suomi, S. J. (1991). Up-tight and laid-back monkeys: individual differences in the response to social challenges. In Brauth, S., Hall, W. and Dooling, R. (eds), *Plasticity of Development*, 27–56. Cambridge, MA: MIT Press.

Suomi, S. J. (1997). Early determinants of behaviour: evidence from primate studies. *British Medical Bulletin 53*: 170–184.

Suomi, S. J. (2000). A biobehavioral perpective on developmental psychopathology: excessive aggression and serotonergic dysfunction in monkeys. In Sameroff, A. J., Lewis, M. and Miller, S. (eds), *Handbook of Developmental Psychopathology*, 237–256. New York: Plenum Press.

Suomi, S. J. and Levine, S. (1998). Psychobiology of intergenerational effects of trauma. In Danieli, Y. (ed.), *International Handbook of Multigenerational Legacies of Trauma*, 623–637. New York: Plenum Press.

Thompson, R. A. (1999). Early attachment and later development. In Cassidy, J. and Shaver, P. R. (eds), *Handbook of Attachment: Theory, Research and Clinical Applications*, 265–286. New York: Guilford.

Tienari, P., Wynne, L. C., Moring, J., Lahti, I. and Naarala, M. (1994). The Finnish adoptive family study of schizophrenia: implications for family research. *British Journal of Psychiatry 23*(Suppl. 164): 20–26.

Tronick, E. (submitted). 'Of course all relationships are unique': how co-creative processes generate unique mother–infant and patient–therapist relationships and change other relationships. *Psychoanalytic Inquiry*.

Tronick, E. Z. (2001). Emotional connection and dyadic consciousness in infant–mother and patient–therapist interactions: commentary on paper by Frank M. Lachman. *Psychoanalytic Dialogue 11*: 187–195.

Waddington, C. H. (1966). *Principles of Development and Differentiation*. New York: Macmillan.

Winnicott, D. W. (1963). Morals and education. In *The Maturational Processes and the Facilitating Environment*, 93–105. London: Hogarth Press.

Part 2

Chapter 5

Psychotherapeutic work with parents and infants*

Tessa Baradon

This chapter addresses the process of psychoanalytic psychotherapy with parents and infants. Parent–infant psychotherapy works with the relationship between parent (or primary caretaker) and his/her baby, where there has been a disruption or distortion of the normal course of bonding.

The partners in the process of the therapy are the parent(s), the infant(s) and the therapist. Within the constant, predictable 'setting'[1] of the therapeutic partnership a three-way relationship is created. The mother brings to this a constellation of thoughts and feelings. These derive from her own experiences of being a child, her current relationships, and her aspirations for her child and herself as mother of the child. These thoughts and feelings get translated into behaviours in relation to the child at any given moment of the interaction. The mother's feelings and behaviours towards the therapist are similarly shaped by her representations of past and present relationships. The infant meets his mother and the therapist with his constellation of attachment needs and developmental potential – his emerging feelings and thought constructions. These, too, are translated into behaviours that are both presented and responsive to her (mother's) behaviours. Thereby, mother and infant both repeat aspects of past relationships and construct new relationship experiences within the here and now of the session.

The therapist has a unique role *vis-à-vis* the parent–infant relationship. On the one hand she is a clinical 'observer' (Rustin 1989) as parent and infant get on with the business of being together. From their delicately co-constructed interactions, moving back and forth as they adjust to the other's response (Tronick 1997), the therapist deduces their emerging mental models of being with each other. On the other hand the therapist is involved in the raw emotions between parent and infant as they unfold and encompass her. The presence of the baby heightens the countertransferential issues for the therapist. The therapist is faced with shifting,

---

* This chapter was first published in the *Journal of Attachment and Human Development* (2002) Vol. 4 (1) and is reprinted with permission (http://www.tandf.co.uk). For convenience of reading, the parent and therapist are referred to as female and the baby as male. In clinical practice, fathers are always included in the therapy when available. The notion of 'father', whether present or not in the family, is equally part of the therapy.

often contradictory, identifications. On the one hand the adult's narrative is compelling, and the therapist is absorbed with this. On the other hand the baby's vulnerability and dependency create a sense of immediacy and urgent responsibility for, and towards, the baby. The unique contribution of the therapist lies in the constant attempts to understand and represent symbolically, for both parent and infant, their experience of being with each other.

Ordinarily, the infant's dependency on the adult for physical and emotional survival and development is the central 'preoccupation' of the adult. The term 'preoccupation' is borrowed from Winnicott (1956) to denote the particular mental state of the parent in relation to the child, which at the beginning excludes all other interests. Although the mental state is relieved as the infant develops from its state of total dependency, the child remains a primary preoccupation of the parent over time. In attachment terms this may be seen as 'the [parent's] capacity to engage directly, flexibly, creatively, and actively in the solution of interpersonal and intrapsychic attachment problems as they arise' (Bretherton and Munholland 1999: 99). Despite her hopes or intentions, however, a parent may find herself unable to mentally embrace her infant. The infant then meets a parental mind that is in the grip of preoccupation with their own mental state – e.g. depression, fear, delusion. There may be no safe anchorage in that parental mind for the ordinary state of the baby as vulnerable and dependent.

Disturbances of attachment are characterised by a repudiation, often unconscious, of the essential nature of infancy – immaturity, primitive emotions and dependence. In the parent the negation of the state of infancy takes place in relation to her own infant, and thereby ordinary infantile needs, e.g. for safety, comfort, soothing, are not recognised. Often a parent repudiates these very needs in herself, too, because they threaten to unbalance the coping strategies the parent has developed to deal with past and present psychic pain.

An illustration of this may be found in the following sequence:

> The work takes place on the floor. Dad is leaning back, legs outstretched. He is talking with his partner and the therapist about how exhausted – at the end of his tether really – he feels with Joe waking up at night. Joe, age 7 months, crawls over to father and across his knee, apparently heading towards the toys at father's side. Father raises his legs and Joe hangs precariously. Mum calls out 'handstand', sounding bright but anxious, and Dad holds on to Joe by his overalls. He lowers his legs and Joe's body tone relaxes. Dad raises his legs again and again holds Joe by his overalls. On lowering his legs Joe somehow slips and falls on his head. Joe freezes briefly – his body is rigid and he is completely silent. Father and mother watch. After a few seconds Joe lets out a cry and mother moves quickly and picks him up. She soothes him: 'Ah, did you fall? That wasn't nice.' Joe stops crying. Mother says: 'Is that better now?' Joe remains on his mother's lap, now facing outwards.

In this interaction father was *engaging* in spontaneous 'rough and tumble' with his little son. Mother moderated the game by framing it as playful ('handstand'). She was also giving it symbolic representation. Her somewhat anxious tone may have been a cue to father to hold on more tightly, and he *grabbed* the overalls. When Joe fell both parents waited – their responses were cued by his (although possibly mother here was also guided by her partner). Mother immediately gathered him up when he cried, although baby was still by father's side.

> The therapist asked father about his communication to Joe when he fell. He replied: 'that I'm a cruel father.' [The therapist understood that the sarcasm was directed at her for what had been revealed and witnessed in this interaction, and perhaps guilt about his anger with his son, whom he blamed for his exhaustion.] In further discussion father suggested that it had not been a hard fall and that his son, left alone, would have 'pulled himself together' and carried on playing with the toys. The father had previously described his own father as 'unapproachable and intimidating. I always felt I let him down.' Unwittingly, he was repeating the internal working model (Bowlby 1973) of a father who cannot tolerate the dependency and vulnerability of his son, nor those aspects in his 'exhausted' self.

The infant, too, may display behaviour that denies his infantile dependency. An example may be that of a small baby who falls but does not cry to summon comfort as would be expected. The psychoanalytic studies of Spitz (1961) and Fraiberg (1982) examined the defences in infants, as young as 3 months, who had experienced extreme danger and deprivation from their carers. They observed behaviours such as 'closing the eyelids' – an early self-regulating form of withdrawal, avoidance – a total reversal of normal seeking of visual, vocal, tactile contact with mother, and freezing – complete immobilisation. Schore (2002) further elaborates on the mechanism of disassociation the infant may adopt in the face of ongoing (cumulative) relational trauma – frightening emotional volatility in the parent and corollary emotional parental neglect of the baby's state of disregulation. Current attachment and neuropsychological research on defensive self-regulatory mechanisms highlights the mechanisms by which these infants join their parents in co-constructing emergent defensive constellations against their attachment needs (e.g. Beebe 2000).

In parent–infant psychotherapy, the therapist is concerned with the behavioural and affective interactions in the room. These incorporate both the declarative (the narrative, symbolically represented, of parenting and being parented) and procedural (enactive) forms through which relational experience is represented. It is often the earliest relational procedures, derived from the parent's experience of being parented in infancy, that are the basis for the spontaneous attitude and gesture (adaptive or otherwise) of the parent towards the infant. Since this is encoded procedurally, i.e. before symbolic representation, it is outside the parent's conscious awareness ('procedural unconscious'). For example, in the clinical illustration above, the mother scooped her baby into her arms when he cried without recourse to the act of thought – i.e. symbolic representation of his fall and of the required response to soothe him.

More actively excluded from awareness (the 'dynamic unconscious'), but nonetheless potentially acted upon, are feelings, attitudes, behaviours towards the infant that are intolerable (to the parent) to be known about or experienced. In the defensive warding off of affects, as in repression, procedural knowledge – expressed via unconscious action – is maintained while the associated declarative knowledge – the understanding of the action – is lost (Clyman 1991). Thus father, in the above example, was not aware of the bullying element to his subtle withholding of comfort from his son as this entailed the painful, even shocking, recognition of the similarity between his father and himself.

In examining the mechanism by which parents who experienced extreme deprivation in their childhoods come to repeat these same caretaking patterns with their infants, Fraiberg *et al.* (1975) highlighted the mechanisms of repression, where frightening and/or painful feelings cease to available for recall, and identification with the aggressor, whereby feelings of helplessness are mastered by relocating the bully within the self. Her ubiquitous term 'ghosts in the nursery' refers to the unconscious repetition of the past in the present, via the colonisation of the relationship of the parent and infant by repressed pain and sadism from the parent's past. Affect repressed in the parent is not empathically recognised in the infant. Thus, the crying infant in the cradle (unconsciously) represents in the parent's mind not their own little newborn – hungry, cold or lonely – but their own unheeded crying when they were small and vulnerable themselves. The baby in the cradle, representing through its developmental dependency the repudiated baby from the past, becomes victim to the bully within the parent. In such cases 'The parent, it seems, is condemned to repeat the tragedy of his own childhood with his own baby in terrible and exacting detail' (Fraiberg *et al.* 1975: 165).

In the renunciation of their infantile selves and the identification with the aggressor, what in fact is communicated from adult to child is a sense that the world of feelings and thoughts is unsafe and to be excluded from the affective dialogue between them. The observable transactions between parent and infant are consequently full of gaps, where particular affects would normally be found, or are skewed towards emotional falseness (Winnicott 1960).

Case material

Grace, a teenage mother with learning disabilities, seemed unable to prevent her infant son, Seb, from incurring multiple accidents: he frequently fell and hurt himself, he pulled heavy objects on himself. Finally, at 10 months, he was badly scalded and was placed on the Child Protection Register under the category of neglect. Mother and son were referred for parent–infant therapy.

Session 1

Grace and Seb arrived late. When they entered the room, both looked quite anxious. Grace and the therapist settled down on the floor and Seb immediately started exploring the toys – handling and mouthing them. There was no contact between him and his mother. [The therapist was thus immediately alerted to Seb's defensive independence. Normally a child of this age would refer to his mother to help him negotiate the anxiety associated with meeting a strange person and room. Why does Seb avoid this? His internal working model seems already shaped around an unavailable object.]

About 10 minutes into the session, Grace and the therapist were talking about how the referral had come about. Seb was playing with some toys at a distance.

Grace: They [professionals] just think that I overreacted with my son a bit. Even I must say that I did. I have different values than other people have . . . I am the kind of person that believes in freedom and freedom of speech and personality and really and truly my son is a very bright person, very bright, and these things that I taught him [sic] when he was younger, my Mum said to me it was too soon.

[The therapist felt she was struggling at this point to understand Grace's communication. She then wondered whether she was experiencing the kind of confusion Grace may feel at times, and particularly in this first session.]

Therapist: What kind of things?

Grace: Well, basically getting his personality out of him and you know, giving him the freedom and giving him faith and letting him do what he wants to do and do his own thing. I mean, yeah, he's only a baby, I do know, but to treat him like he's only one, only a baby, is two different things. You can't . . . babies at his age know a lot and you can't treat them like they're not an adult because if you treat them like a baby then how do you expect them to learn?

[The therapist understands that Grace does not know how she will be treated in the therapy.]

Therapist: I guess freedom and being treated like an adult who can understand things is something you have been wanting for yourself, that you would be treated in that way too.

Grace pauses, in a low sad voice, barely audible, she says:

Grace: My social worker, she don't think that I'm an adult, she thinks that I'm stupid. [The therapist experienced these painful feelings of Grace's on almost a physical level, like a blow.] That's the only explanation I can come up with. She really does think I'm stupid because I haven't gone to school that much. When I did go to school I was statemented as special needs..

[The therapist thinks that Grace is beginning to put her experiences into words, but the intensity of feelings can still not be represented symbolically, and is experienced in the body.]

A little later in the session the following occurred. Seb was crawling with the toy car in his hand, heading towards the desk. He stopped by a chair and, with his free hand, pulled himself into a standing position, facing the desk. He then turned towards his mother and therapist and tried to walk towards them. In so doing he lost his balance and fell, face down. It seemed a hard bump but he did not cry. His mother cried out: 'Seb, don't do that!' She held her stomach – as though she had received a blow. She did not approach Seb. He lay in his fallen position for a few seconds longer. After that he sat up and continued playing with the toy. His face was blank.

In this first session Grace describes her aspirations for her child – that he should be free to be himself, and the role she wished for *vis-à-vis* him – to draw out his personality. The therapist forms a tentative view that Grace is speaking about herself – as a struggling, burdened adolescent – and her wish to be 'free' of her 'stupid' (vulnerable and needy) self. This repudiated self is projected into the critical adults, thus her implicit question of how she will be treated in the therapy. The therapist also recognises Grace's hope that she, the therapist, will be able to acknowledge and 'draw out' the individual Grace over and above the limitations of her learning disability.

At the same time, Grace is 'careless' in relation to her son, in that she does not protect him emotionally or physically in a strange room with an unfamiliar adult. She also confuses stupidity with immaturity and cannot, therefore, accept his age-appropriate dependency needs. He enacts his sense of being unprotected by falling hard, and yet not crying out. There is a momentary freezing and disassociation of the affect associated with the fall. The therapist recognises the psychic act of severing pain via her own feelings of shock and upset both in relation to Grace's pain ('she thinks I'm stupid') and Seb's uncomforted fall. The task facing the therapy seems, at this point, to be to gather those discarded feelings of pain and shame and outrage within the affective discourse between mother and child. The interpersonal dialogue will also embody the externalisations of internal, inter-structural conflict.

Session 2

Grace and Seb appeared more at ease. Seb approached the therapist early in the session and explored her jewellery, and Grace seemed eager to talk. [The therapist felt that a partnership was beginning to emerge.] About 10 minutes into the session Grace talked of her feelings of fear and loneliness at the time of the birth. As she spoke Seb crawled to her rucksack and pulled out a plastic bag which he held towards his mother. Grace took the bag from him and tossed it aside, without interrupting the flow of her talk with the therapist. Seb sat rigidly for a few moments, then started to whimper. He laboriously crawled over to the bag and held it out to his mother again.

Therapist: [Interrupting Grace] Grace, let's see what just happened here. Seb gave you the plastic bag. What was he saying?

Grace: He wants it.

Therapist: He wants it?

Grace: He wants something in it.

Therapist: He wants something in it? [Pause.] You threw it to the side.
[The therapist was uncertain – Graces demeanour suggested she had not noticed Seb's upset. What was this about?]

Grace: Yeah, because there's nothing in it for him.

[The therapist is wondering whether Grace imagines that Seb thinks what she, Grace, thinks, i.e. whether she recognises him having a different, separate, little-boy mind.]

Therapist: Does *he* know there is nothing in it for him?

Grace: He thinks his crisps are in it.

Therapist: Is he saying 'Mummy, I want my crisps'?

Grace: Yeah, but he ate his crisps already.

Grace turns to Seb, who is still sitting by her side. She opens the bag and takes out the empty crisp packet. She shows him the empty bag, saying 'There's nothing in here. Look. See? There is nothing in there. Look . . . Gone. All gone.' This continues for some moments. Grace's voice is angry. Seb looks at the packet, but not at his mother. His body tone is slack.

[The therapist thinks that Grace feels accused and exposed by Seb and the therapist for not being able to meet his needs/wishes.]

Therapist: You want him to remember that there are no crisps because he ate them. It's his fault, not yours?

Grace: Yeah, exactly. I didn't eat them.

Grace expects Seb to 'know' things quite beyond his age. When he persists in wanting his crisps and not understanding that they were 'all gone' because he had already eaten them, Grace is harsh. Perhaps she experiences Seb's ordinary demands as an attack, as they face her with her sense of emptiness and thus her shame. In particular, Grace insisted that Seb really knew how to keep himself safe, and that when he hurt himself it was a consequence of not using his intelligence. The therapist formed the hypothesis that the emotional state of infancy, of not knowing and being vulnerable and dependent, was intolerable to Grace as it represented that part of her that is regarded as 'stupid'. Seb could not be allowed to be a not-knowing little boy as this narcissistically extended her stupidity to him.

This formulation had implications for the therapy. What representation of herself would Grace find when she looked into the therapist's eyes/mind (in the Winnicottian sense (1967) of finding a representation of herself there)? It was pivotal that the therapist never found Grace to be mentally slow; in fact she was impressed by the unfolding of her psychological thinking.

Towards the end of the second session Grace was asked about her father. She spoke about the loss of her father in early childhood. When asked how she had felt,

Grace exclaimed 'No one has ever asked me that before!' Thereafter, the floodgates were open. Focused, as she was, on her own feelings, it was apparent that Grace could not maintain her links with Seb for long. She described 'cutting off' at home, entering a dark space in her mind. In the sessions Grace at times seemed to 'forget' Seb for extended periods (e.g. 20 minutes), unless the therapist called him to mind. During this period the therapist felt she was holding on to the child in the face of mother's need to obliterate him, in that he represented to Grace the miserable child within her, whom she wished to destroy. Yet the therapist found that Seb, a passive and withdrawn baby, was at times hard to hold on to. It was as though, in an 'analytic enactment' (McLaughlin 1991), in an unconscious emotional collusion between mother and therapist, the child could not be loved. In this instance the therapist's reaction may be seen as a gauge of the force of the projections at work. Grace's rejected aspect of her self – the 'stupid' self – was located by her in Seb. In his blank presentation it appeared that Seb had taken on this attribute – stupid in relation to the world. Indeed, his early experiences of lack of safety and care would have been difficult to process, leaving him confused and sometimes overwhelmed. Thus, his external experiences of neglect, and intra-psychic processes of projective identification (Silverman and Lieberman 1999), converged. The therapist, meeting with the infant's opaqueness, found herself resonating a listless lack of interest in him. She had to prompt herself to think about Seb in order to revive complexity from blandness. Yet the therapist's consistent holding of Seb in mind, despite his tendency to disappear into interpersonal voids, was a first step claiming him back into a relationship with a live object (Alvarez 1992).

In parallel, the therapist noted small changes in Grace's behaviour towards Seb – instances, for example, when she spontaneously reached out to hug him, or when they played pleasurably together. It seemed that there was an unfolding of the process observed by Fraiberg and her colleagues (1980) whereby listening to the silenced cries of the parent can help the parent to attend to their infant, as their identifications shift from the bully to the injured child within.

In the following observation from session 5, mother, Seb and therapist are working together.

Seb had remained at his mother's side after they entered the room and settled. She played with him, pressing the buttons on the toy car and allowing him time to explore the car and copy her actions. Seb's breathing sounded wheezy but he was making no other sounds. This play went on for 3–4 minutes, then Seb started to explore the room with his eyes, still from within his mother's embrace. Grace asked the therapist how she was. Seb angrily threw a toy on the floor. The therapist mirrored his action with a playful rise in her voice [thus capturing his anger but meeting it with humour], and said to Seb that he did not want to share his mummy's attention. Seb threw the toy again, and Grace laughed and hugged him. Seb laughed happily. The therapist had not heard him laugh before.

After 2 months of therapy it was agreed that Grace's mother, Dinah, would join the sessions, as she had started to share the care for Seb with Grace. While Grace experienced her mother's help as supportive, it also reinforced her view of herself as an inadequate and disqualified mother. It also brought up intense resentments towards her mother for not doing a better job of parenting her in the past, and when Seb was born.

Session 12

Seb is playing with the tea-set behind Grace's back. Dinah and Grace are sitting side by side facing the therapist. Dinah is angry with Grace for not helping around the house.

Dinah: Grace, if I don't tell you what to do, you don't do nothing. I don't understand it.

Grace: I'm depressed. I–am–depressed.

Seb, unseen by Grace and Dinah, is waving a saucer and looking at the therapist. The therapist nods at him. He holds her gaze momentarily and then resumes his play.

Grace: That's all you got to say? You never thought, well why am I depressed? What's going through my head?

Dinah: It doesn't matter why you're depressed.

Grace: Yes it does, it does.

Dinah: Depression is depression.

Grace: Mummy, it does matter, if someone is depressed, it matters why they are depressed. Otherwise, if they don't know why they're depressed, they'll never not be depressed.

Seb looks up here but does not engage in eye contact with the therapist. [The therapist feels a bit worried for Seb. She wants him to keep in contact].

Dinah: Well, you know why you're depressed.

Grace: Yeah, but you don't know.

Dinah: Grace, because no matter what I do, you won't tell me anyway.

Seb has started banging gently with a small spoon in a cup. Dinah leans back to look at him. She stays in this position for a few minutes, watching him, but Seb does not look up from his play. [The therapist reflects on Seb's depressed withdrawal. His granny cannot reach him. Seb, too, seems to feel that she does not try hard enough to reach him.] Dinah resumes her seated position with Grace. Grace and her mother are getting angrier and louder. [The therapist thinks that Grace wants her mother to acknowledge some responsibility for her depression, and that Dinah cannot tolerate the implied accusation from her daughter.]

Dinah: You go on and on and on. You're depressed, you know why you are depressed. You don't want to talk about it. I can't change the situation.

Grace's voice here becomes loud – she sounds both desperate and strident.

Grace: No, no, no. For crying out loud, you're not listening to me. You are not listening to me!

Seb, still banging, looks up. [The therapist notices how closely he is attending.] Grace goes on: How do you know you can't do anything about me being depressed if you don't know what I'm depressed about?

Dinah: Well, you don't say. If you would say . . .

Grace: I'm supposed to know, Mummy? I'm supposed come up there to you and say 'Oh, Mum, I'm depressed for this reason and that reason and the other reason'? No, it don't work like that.

Seb drops the cup. Spoon in hand, he crawls between Grace and Dinah. He leans with one hand on his mother's knee but turns to the welcoming face of his grand-mother. Dinah and Seb play together – Seb is thrusting the spoon into Dinah's mouth and she pretends she is being fed. Grace's angry tone has dropped.

Seb is faced with a row between the adults he loves. He seems, initially, to suc-cessfully 'blank out' the intense emotions and focuses on the toys. He manages to sustain the structure of the play for quite some time. As Dinah and Grace become more intense, he attempts to master the emotional tone through his banging, which mirrors the verbal exchange between the two adults. When acrimony increases, however, he becomes more anxious. He initially uses the therapist as his social reference, but then abandons this too. The therapist feels worried for him. Finally, he cannot sustain his solitary solution and seeks out his caretakers, expressing his wish for solace in the feeding play with his grandmother. However, even in this sequence his real vulnerability is denied, in that he does the feeding rather than receiving sustenance from the adult.

For Grace and Dinah, however, this was a ground-breaking discussion, in which each was challenged to 'listen' to the other. 'Listening', in such context, entails opening one's mind to the other's communication even when their pain directly challenges one's own. Certainly Grace was confronting her mother with her (Dinah's) inability to look into her daughter's depression. In this sense, it was Dinah's 'stupidity' – a defensive emotional dumbing down – that was in focus, and Grace chivvied her along: 'if someone is depressed, it matters why they are depressed . . . if they don't know why they are depressed, they'll never not be depressed'. Grace was taking the leap into knowing minds – her own, initially, but also those of others, e.g. recognising her mother's fear of her own depression. The therapist communicated that it was safe to look into the other's mind in this setting by 'holding' the emotions rather than moving too quickly to fix them. Perhaps, therefore, Seb's move towards the adults was not only driven by anxiety but was also his recognition that a new, more emotionally alive, way of being-with-the-other was emerging.

In the final stages of the therapy Grace and Dinah allowed each other the occasional individual session with the therapist. While Grace used these occasions to think abut her current mental states and plans for the future, Dinah wanted to think more about her past. She told the therapist, in a jovial voice and with a broad grin, that as a child she had felt that no one – not her parents nor her siblings nor classmates – ever liked her. The therapist felt unbearably sad as Dinah spoke, and they were able to explore how Dinah made the therapist feel the sadness she had to disavow. They could then link Dinah's difficulty in experiencing her own feeling states with a consequent lack of recognition of disturbing emotions in others. For example, Dinah failed to realise that Seb was missing his mother when she went away for a few days, dismissing as coincidental clues such as his inability to settle in the night and his running to the door each time it opened.

'Cutting off' (disassociation), as a defence against the pain and shame of feeling different and unloved/unlovable, also came into the arena between Dinah and Grace.

Session 27

Seb could not attend the session as he was unwell. Grace started by talking about her fear that harm would come to Seb with his cold. Grace and Dinah were taken aback when the therapist made a link to Grace's sudden loss of her father in childhood – an event that had never been discussed by mother and daughter. Dinah was dismissive of the therapist's idea that this may have had an impact on Grace that carried through from childhood to adulthood.

Therapist:	You think that Grace did not react in any way?
Dinah:	Well, *I* did not react in any way.
Therapist:	Why?
Dinah:	I never do.
Therapist:	You go on as if nothing has happened?
Dinah:	Yeah.
Therapist:	Do you think that is something you've been doing since you were a child?
Dinah:	Anything bad that happened [making dismissive gesture with her hand] . . .
Grace:	[Humorously] So that's where I get this wipe-out thing!

[The therapist notes and welcomes Grace's acknowledgement of what she shares with her mother.]

Dinah:	I don't forget it, I just wipe it out. [Now Dinah is using Grace's term.]
Grace:	You don't want to know . . .
Therapist:	Because it is too painful?
Dinah:	Anything bad . . . I blank it out.
Therapist:	Perhaps there was a reason you developed that particular way of dealing with painful or frightening things, rather than developing another way of dealing with these feelings.
Dinah:	I suppose it was the only way I could deal with things because anything bad was never talked about.
Therapist:	So you were left all alone with the bad thing.
Dinah:	You dwell on it and dwell on it . . . [She made a gesture as though the thoughts could drive one mad.] But, if something traumatic happens, you don't forget.

Grace: You just put it at the back of your mind and close the door. Then every now and then the door is blown open.
Therapist: I was suggesting that we could track the worry about Seb to behind the door that was closed on your feelings about your Dad.
Grace: I actually think that ever since Seb was born [her voice drops to a whisper] I worried that he would die.

How to love a baby you fear you may lose? How to trust in your ability to keep a baby alive when in your childhood fantasy you were not able to keep your father's love/life? Seb's vulnerability and dependency evoked a panic in Grace – mirroring her own discarded self in the face of her mother's depression and later her father's death. Seb, in Grace's mind, was at great risk and she was not going to be able to save him. This repeated the feelings and ideas associated with her father's death, when there was no partner in the dialogue to scaffold what she, as a child, was unable to put into words. Sinason (1992) links trauma and stupidity: 'We have seen that the word "stupid" actually means "numbed with grief". We are all aware of that meaning in the word "stupefy". . .'(p. 30).

Discussion

The intergenerational ghost in this family is the lonely and frightening experience of being a baby whose mother cannot tolerate his cries. The babies – across the generations – have to look after themselves. In the repudiation of their developmentally rooted infantile needs, they have become 'stupid'. As such they are experienced as attacking and shaming of the parents, and evoke their anger and neglect.

Seb's birth threw Grace back into a tangle of emotions she had managed – in a pseudo-adolescent rebellion – to hold at bay. Her own infancy experiences with her mother, at the time a depressed adolescent herself, were repeated with Seb in her lifelessness, neglect and blanking out. The repetition – how I am with my baby is related to how I think my parent was with me – takes place at the procedural level of undigested feelings which are enacted. As Raphael-Leff (2000) writes: 'We see a mother tending her baby but internally she is being engulfed by what is "closing in" inside – unprocessed, acute moments with her own, fallible, early caregivers, now revitalised in the demanding arena of babycare . . . Conducted through sensorimotor preverbal rhythmic conduits, it evokes inchoate memories in the adult' (p. 60). Yet for Grace these complex feelings had no outlet. Dinah's style, which she brought from her own childhood to her mothering, was to foreclose the discourse on disturbing emotions. 'You never ask me why I am depressed' Grace cried, and her mother responded: 'Depression is depression.' The message was not to enquire about the state of the other's mind, as the resonation of its contents may be overwhelming. In the face of this there is an inhibition of the very process of thinking. For Seb it was dangerous to look into his mother's mind because of the negative attributions his mother held. Thus, the very constituents of thinking – being curious, enquiring, making links – were to be relinquished (Fonagy *et al.* 1993). In this sense Seb was, defensively, becoming stupid.

In our clinical work we have found that the affective dialogue is a pivotal 'port of entry' (Stern 1995) for the therapist. The affective dialogue includes all forms of interpersonal communication – verbal, tactile, gesture, expression. As Lyons-Ruth (1999) has suggested, developmental dialogues that are associated with secure attachment and resilience in the child's later development are characterised by truthful and collaborative dialogue. Similarly, change in enactive procedures takes place through participation in more coherent and collaborative dialogue. 'Collaborative dialogue . . . is about getting to know another's mind and taking it into account in constructing and regulating interactions. Without recognition of one person's initiatives or communications by another, no intersubjectivity or dyadic regulation is possible' (p. 583). Grace and Dinah's discussion about 'blanking out' would illustrate the achievement of some mutual recognition of the other's mind, when the dialogue between them at referral was fragmented and overwhelming. This characterises many of the parent/infant dyads and triads who enter therapy with a relationship disturbance.

The locus of intervention is this dialogue. The therapists bring to it the 'mentalistic, elaborative stance' (Fonagy 1999), the constant endeavour to understand and represent the mental experience of mother and of infant, and at the same time to make available her own thinking for exploration by them. While incorporating the narrative of the past, the dialogue is co-constructed in the present between infant, parent and therapist. '[The transference] focuses the patient on the analyst's mental state as he tries to conceive of the patient's beliefs and desires. The repeated experience of finding himself in the mind of his therapist, not only enhances self representation but also removes the patient's fear of looking' (Fonagy 1999: 10).

The recognition of Grace's wish to be treated as a capable adult enabled Grace to withdraw from the grandiose statements about her son's intelligence, which belied her fear of his stupidity, and to recognise his age-appropriate infantile needs in relation to her. The therapeutic work also encompassed Seb as a direct and active participant. The therapist observed the thrust of his developmental needs, his emerging enactive procedures of being-with-the-other to meet, or defend against, those needs, and his 'history' as his mother's 'transference object' (the screen upon which the figures of her past and the feelings towards them were projected). These could be addressed directly, e.g. when the therapist said to Seb 'It is frightening and lonely [his mental state, as represented in the therapist's mind] when you fall and no one comforts you [he is victim to the repetition of the past]. You don't know what to do, if you can call mummy? [his procedures of being-with-the-other].' The therapist was actively scaffolding the baby's emotional experience and anticipating, through modelling, his mother's ability to do this for her child.

Indeed, the changes in Seb were manifestly linked to the accumulating changes in his mother, both in relation to her capacity to construct a coherent narrative for herself and in her responsiveness to Seb. We also know that at his particular age (12–24 months) his psychoneurological development was most sensitively receptive to the attachment transactions between him and mother and to the changes that were taking place (Schore 2001).

The withdrawal of the negative maternal attributions and Grace's greater mental availability freed Seb to experience a broader range of feelings and behaviours with his mother and other adults. With his mother's increasing attention to *his* states of mind, Seb seemed to come out of his blankness and gradually demonstrated a desire to engage with his objects rather than with toys. The example where he moved in between his quarrelling mother and granny and elicited play with Dinah suggests that the early schema of being-with-the-other, which relied on the exclusion of painful *affects*, was no longer the singular mode of engagement. The relationship-focused early therapeutic intervention, matched to a critical period of experience-dependent development in the brain (Schore 2002), facilitated the emergence of a more emotionally flexible and encompassing schema. While the early schema, as mental structure, may persist (Sandler and Joffe 1967) it would appear that Seb was increasingly able to apply the developmentally more adaptive schema to meet his attachment needs.

Notes

1 Parent–infant psychotherapy often takes place in a clinic setting. However, it can be creatively applied, as in the 'therapy at the kitchen sink' of the patient's home (Fraiberg *et al.* 1980) or in the corner of a prefabricated hut in a South African township (Berg 2000). Thus the setting is essentially established by the boundaried therapeutic partnership.

References

Alvarez, A. (1992). *Live Company*. London: Routledge.

Beebe, B. (2000). Coconstructing mother–infant distress: the microsynchrony of maternal impingement and infant avoidance in the face-to-face encounter. *Psychoanalytic Enquiry* 20(3): 421–440.

Berg, A. (2000). Beyond the dyad: parent–infant psychotherapy in a multi-cultural society – reflections from a South African perspective. Presented at the *7th Congress of the World Association of Infant Mental Health*, Montreal.

Bowlby, J. (1973). *Attachment and Loss: Vol. 2, Separation*. New York: Basic Books.

Bretherton, I. and Munholland, K. A. (1999) Internal working models in attachment relationships: A construct revisited. In J. Cassidy and P. R. Shaver (eds), *Handbook of Attachment: Theory, Research and Clinical Applications*. New York: Guilford Press.

Clyman, R.B. (1991). The procedural organisation of emotions: a contribution from cognitive science to the psychoanalytic theory of therapeutic action. *Journal of the American Psychoanalytic Association 39*: 349–383.

Fonagy, P. (1999). The process of change and the change of process: what can change in a 'good' analysis. Keynote Address to the Spring meeting of Division 39 of the American Psychological Association.

Fonagy, P., Moran, G. and Target, M. (1993). Aggression and the psychological self. *International Journal of Psycho-Analysis 74*: 471–485.

Fraiberg, S. (ed.) (1980). *Clinical Studies in Infant Mental Health*. London: Tavistock.

Fraiberg, S. (1982). Pathological defences in infancy. *Psychoanalytic Quarterly 1*(1): 612–635.

Fraiberg, S., Adelson, E. and Shapiro, V. (1975). Ghosts in the nursery: a psychoanalytic approach to the problems of impaired infant-mother relationships. *Journal of the American Academy of Child Psychiatry 14*: 387–421.

Fraiberg, S., Shapiro, V. and Spitz Cherniss, D. (1980). Treatment modalities. In S. Fraiberg (ed.), *Clinical Studies in Infant Mental Health* London: Tavistock.

Lyons-Ruth, K. (1999). The two-person unconscious: intersubjective dialogue, enactive relational representation, and the emergence of new forms of relational organization. *Psychoanalytic Inquiry 19*(4): 576–617.

McLaughlin, J. T. (1991). Clinical and theoretical aspects of enactment. *Journal of the American Psychoanalytic Association 39*: 595–614.

Raphael-Leff, J. (2000). Climbing the walls: therapeutic intervention for post-partum disturbance. In Raphael-Leff, J. (ed.), *Spilt Milk*. London: Institute of Psychoanalysis.

Rustin, M. (1989). Observing infants: reflections on methods. In Miller, L., Rustin, M., Rustin, M. and Shuttleworth J. (eds), *Closely Observed Infants*. London: Duckworth.

Sandler, J. and Joffe, W. G. (1967). The tendency to persistence in psychological function and development, with special reference to fixation and regression. *Bulletin of the Menninger Clinic 31*: 257–271.

Schore, A. N. (2001). The effects of early relational trauma on right brain development, affect regulation, and infant mental health. *Infant Mental Health Journal 22*(1–2): 201–269.

Schore, A. N. (2002). Dysregulation of the right brain: a fundamental mechanism of traumatic attachment and the psychopathogenesis of posttraumatic stress disorder. *Australian and New Zealand Journal of Psychiatry 36*: 9–30.

Silverman, R. C. and Lieberman, A. F. (1999). Negative maternal attributions, projective identification, and the intergenerational transmission of violent relational patterns. *Psychoanalytic Dialogues 9*(2): 161–186.

Sinason, V. (1992). *Mental Handicap and the Human Condition*. London: Free Association Books.

Spitz, R. (1961). Some early prototypes of ego defences. *Journal of the American Psychoanalytic Association 9*: 626–651.

Stern, D. N. (1995). *The Motherhood Constellation*. New York: Basic Books.

Tronick, E. Z. and Weinberg, M. K. (1997) Depressed mothers and infants: failure to form dyadic states of consciousness. In Murray, L. and Cooper, P. J. (eds), *Post Partum Depression and Child Development*. New York: Guilford Press.

Winnicott, D. W. (1956). Primary maternal preoccupation. In *Collected Papers: Through paediatrics to psychoanalysis* (1958). London: Tavistock.

Winnicott, D. W. (1960). Ego distortion in terms of true and false self. In *The Maturational Process and the Facilitating Environment* (1965). London: Hogarth Press.

Winnicott, D. W. (1967). Mirror role of mother and family in child development. In Lomas, P. (ed.), *The Predicament of the Family: A Psychoanalytical Symposium*. London: Hogarth Press and The Institute of Psycho-Analysis.

Chapter 6

The use of fantasy as a psychic organiser for traumatic experience

Marta Neil

In this chapter I describe part of the therapy of Kieran, a young boy who was diagnosed with a brain tumour early on in childhood. The treatment he received for his illness was experienced as a traumatic invasion producing overwhelming affects that threatened the integrity of the psychological self.

I shall focus on his use of fantasy to symbolically represent these traumatic experiences in order to gain some control over them and attribute meaning to them. I hope to show how several core fantasies that emerged during different phases of his therapy enabled him to make sense of the complex layers of affect associated with his illness and treatment.

To an extent these fantasies enabled him to organise his experiences and afforded a means of affect regulation. Nonetheless, traumatic memories and the affects associated with them could not be fully integrated due to the overwhelming anxiety and fear triggered by chance traumatic reminders. In order to cope with the sense of internal collapse engendered by these reminders, he felt the need to exert rigid and, at times, aggressive control.

Despite Kieran's wish for help, it was difficult to engage him in the reflective aspects of the therapeutic work. His angry and frightened responses to interventions indicated that these were felt to be as intrusive as the treatments he had endured. His tendency to experience me as a traumatising other strongly influenced the transference. However, as it became possible to engage him in thinking about his experiences and he became more able to make use of the therapeutic relationship to assist in the regulation of affects, the process of integrating traumatic memories with affects could begin to take place. The subtle changes in his internal representations of self and object made possible through this process have positively affected his view of the external world and his relationships with others.

Referral

Kieran was referred to the Department of Psychological Medicine at the age of 7 years by his neurology consultant who requested treatment for 'needle phobia and anxiety'. Despite the skilled input from the hospital play specialists, Kieran reacted strongly to his treatment, screaming and struggling against the staff who at times had had to hold him down in order to administer treatment. So great was his distress that his parents had resorted to carrying him into the hospital with his head covered in a blanket.

The clinical psychologist who assessed him concluded that he was suffering from a severe traumatic reaction. Perpetually hyper-aroused, he had difficulty regulating his affects so that minor stresses evoked intense anxiety and distress. He often cried hopelessly for long periods, expressing the wish to die. He was unable to attend school because he could not separate from his mother. He also suffered from sleeping and eating difficulties.

The initial neuropsychological assessment identified several cognitive problems which also affected his general functioning. Amongst these were difficulties in short-term and visual memory, abstract verbal reasoning and delayed recall. It was unclear at this point whether these problems were related to his psychological state or were early indicators of the effects of radiotherapy. However, the impact on Kieran was clear. Feeling unable to remember the simplest things and struggling to express himself verbally, he reacted with frustration and despair. The psychologist recommended a desensitisation programme to help him to overcome the needle phobia. However, she was unable to proceed with this because Kieran could not bear to hear mention of his illness or treatment and would react by covering his ears, screaming and crying, or by running from the room. At this point, she referred him for individual psychotherapy. Despite the need for a more intensive therapy this was not practical for the family so we agreed that I would see him once weekly. He was 7 years and 9 months when we began therapy and is now 12 years old. Treatment is ongoing at a reduced frequency.

History

Kieran lives with his parents and two sisters. Sara is 2 years older and Tara 3 years younger. Various members of the extended family live nearby and are supportive to the family. There is a history of depression on the father's side.

The parents married during their early twenties and mother became pregnant soon after. Father worked as a mechanic and prior to Kieran's illness ran his own small business. Mother worked as his secretary. When Kieran was 6 months old, mother returned to work part-time. Mother was pregnant with Kieran's younger sister, Tara, when Kieran was diagnosed with a benign cerebral tumour. He was just 3 years old at the time. He had surgery and local radiotherapy but the tumour was incompletely excised and regrew 2 years later, requiring further surgery and radiotherapy. Regular brain scans now monitor the growth of the residual tumour. The surgery itself caused various problems including right cortical blindness and difficulties with gross motility. The radiotherapy affected his cognitive functioning and produced a growth hormone deficiency that will require treatment until adulthood. These problems are woven into Kieran's fantasies about his illness and treatment, and like the tumour itself represent deep narcissistic hurts.

Following his diagnosis, mother gave up her work to look after Kieran. Father did not support her decision and this caused tension between them. During Kieran's first hospital admission, the parental relationship broke down. Father returned to his parents' home, taking care of both daughters, while mother remained in hospital for many months with Kieran.

Several months into the therapy I learned that Kieran's mother, feeling unsupported by her husband, had experienced considerable distress witnessing Kieran's treatment and had often been too upset to help him cope. She felt guilty about this, believing that her distress had placed an added burden on Kieran. As Kieran's treatment progressed and his prognosis improved, the parents' relationship and family life stabilised. However, both parents have struggled to come to terms with the physical and psychological impact of the illness and treatment on their son. They have each expressed a sense of loss, feeling that the child Kieran once was has gone forever. Father, in particular, has expressed his disappointment in Kieran who, in his eyes, would never become the masculine, competent boy he had hoped for. Kieran's awareness of his parents' feelings compounded his own disappointment, despair and rage. Despite the parents' commitment to Kieran's therapy, however, it has been hard to engage them in supportive work that might have enabled them to think more deeply about these issues and about the impact of Kieran's illness on the family as a whole. It is only relatively recently that the parents, mother in particular, have revealed aspects of their own childhoods that have contributed to this.

The therapy

Throughout the course of Kieran's therapy crucial questions about his brain tumour have influenced his material. What is it? How did it get there? Why was it removed? Will it grow again? These questions have arisen many times, although they have been asked in different ways and represented at different levels of understanding. His material also reflects his struggle to make sense of a treatment which, although life saving, was experienced as a traumatic invasion and, as such, threatening to his physical and psychological self. The fantasies that I shall present emerged at different stages in the therapy. Each fantasy was elaborated over time and became the focus of the therapeutic work extending over a period of several months. While these fantasies provide a narrative form for Kieran's experiences, encapsulating in fine detail the complex layers of associated affects, they are interwoven with various expectable conflicts and anxieties that have brought particular meanings to the illness and treatment. These meanings have helped to shape his internal representations of self and object and have, in turn, impacted on Kieran's view of, and interaction with, the external world.

The dolphin prince and the tumour babies

In our first session, as Kieran listened to his mother describe their lives prior to his illness, he constructed from plasticine a rather beautiful family of dolphins. This 'royal' family, as Kieran described them, comprised a king, a queen, a prince and two princesses who lived in a 'magical underwater palace at the bottom of the ocean'. Expressing, perhaps, his mother's idealised memories of family life before the illness, Kieran showed the family living happily together, parental relationship intact, generational boundaries preserved. In that first session, Kieran stated that he did not want to talk about his illness or treatment because it made him feel 'too upset', and at that point burst into tears. As he lay curled up on the floor under a pile of cushions tearfully, his mother told me that 'the little boy I once had is gone – he is dead'.

In the following sessions, although Kieran allowed his mother to wait for him outside the treatment room, he sat close to the door and played quietly with the dolphin family, nodding or shaking his head in response to my comments. Deeply suspicious of me, he reassured himself that I did not wear 'a white coat' and there-fore I was not 'one of them'. Careful not to overwhelm him, I simply voiced his uncertainty about me and about this strange room in a new part of the hospital. It would be some time before he would allow me to articulate his terror of me and his fantasy of what I might do to him.

In one session, Kieran drew my attention to the facial expression on his dolphin prince and asked if I thought he was happy. I said that he did not look happy and wondered if Kieran could tell me more. Kieran said that the mouth of the dolphin prince was 'opened wide' and his eyes were 'closed shut'. I suggested that his dolphin prince was frightened. Kieran nodded but when I asked why, he shook his head. I commented that perhaps some frightening things had happened that were difficult to talk about. Again he nodded and said that he did not want to talk about those things. I suggested that perhaps he worried that talking about frightening things would make it seem as if they were happening all over again. Kieran agreed and asked to stop. Early on in the treatment his need to keep a tight rein on poten-tially overwhelming affects characterised his interactions with me. However, as this example shows, while he found it difficult to verbalise affects directly, he was able to symbolically represent them. His willingness, albeit tentative at this stage, to allow me to make explicit the affects he implied in his play, indicated his poten-tial to use the therapeutic relationship to help him regulate the overwhelming affects.

Gradually, as he allowed himself to trust me a little, the material began to change. He began to unfold 'a secret' relationship between the queen and the prince, describing exciting and forbidden trysts. During one such tryst, he showed the queen giving babies to the prince because, as Kieran confided, he was her 'favourite'. Kieran went on to describe how these dolphin babies lived inside the head of the dolphin prince where he had to hide them from the king. He ignored my question about what the king would do were he to see the babies, boasting that the dolphin prince would have 'millions of babies for the queen'. He made a sea garden from plasticine for the queen and prince to live together with their babies, 'happily ever after', as he put it. I commented that this boy seemed to believe that everything would be safe if he lived alone with his mother in this magical place. Kieran said that everything would be 'perfect'.

However, terrifying anxieties began to surface, breaking into this blissful, Oedipal garden. In one session, when I wondered how the babies came to be inside the head of the dolphin prince, Kieran explained that the queen had fed him 'special food that turned into babies that grew inside his head'. However, when I asked what it was like to have something growing inside his head he said anxiously, 'the greedy babies grew so big and fat that the prince thought his whole head would explode'. I wondered what would happen then. In a frightened whisper, Kieran said that he would 'die'. He frantically replaced the plasticine in the containers at that point.

Provided I remained within the arena of the story, Kieran allowed me to verbalise the wishes and fears that were beginning to find expression in fantasy such as the wish for a special love between the mother and her son and the fear that he might be replaced by other babies. In one session, Kieran voiced, tearfully, the thought that the queen might not love the prince as much as he had imagined. He went on to suggest that the queen might wish 'bad things' to happen to him: perhaps the food was poisoned, perhaps she wanted him to die? Cautious not to overwhelm him, I focused on helping him to find a way of articulating these frightening thoughts, while containing his anxiety by staying as much as possible within the displacement.

However, some sessions later, when I tried to address his anxieties more directly, putting into words his memories of his head throbbing as though it would burst when he first got ill and being unable to eat without vomiting his food, or verbalising his fear that he got his brain tumour by eating too much, he seemed to fall apart. He covered his ears and screamed, 'Don't talk about those scary things', as he burst into tears and collapsed on the floor. As this example shows, I had moved too quickly and had overwhelmed him. In doing so, I had become a traumatising other who forced him, in a recapitulation of his earlier experiences, to re-experience frightening things. Although he calmed down when I put this into words, he came to the following session announcing that he did not wish to continue with the story.

He did not return to this theme for several weeks but, nonetheless, it slowly re-emerged. In one session he recounted a dream he had had, a dream of 'a mother poisoning her son'. Taking out his plasticine figures, he told me that the dolphin-queen had plotted to kill her son, and that she intended to use his head as a receptacle for 'greedy princess-babies' who would take his place. In an attempt to preserve the wishful fantasy of a blissful mother–son relationship in the face of these frightening thoughts, Kieran re-created the plasticine garden he had made for the dolphin prince and his mother. This threatening aspect of the maternal representation was difficult to avoid and Kieran became anxious. He talked of starving to death the babies inside the prince's head or vomiting them out through his mouth in order to save the prince. In another session he imagined that they would 'grow small, not big, and would slide through his body and out through his bottom . . . then the prince would not die', Kieran assured me.

Gradually, he allowed me to verbalise some of his fears about the tumour inside his head, his confusion about how it got there and what it was. Together we were able to understand how, at times, he imagined the tumour was a special gift from his mother, a symbol of their special love; how at other times he imagined that the tumour was part of a plot to get rid of him in order to replace him with other babies. This condensed representation of the brain tumour, at once gratifying and terrifying, highlighted the irresolvable confusion that lay at the core of Kieran's self and object representations. He was simultaneously his mother's special child, the object of her exclusive love and the displaced child, the object of her hatred and rejection. As we worked on these thoughts and feelings, Kieran allowed me to voice his terror that the tumour might regrow together with his fear of dying. I linked these fears with the feelings of helplessness he experienced. In one session, handing me a toy knife and scissors, he instructed me to cut open the prince's head and dig out the babies. I spoke of Kieran's wish for me to be a magical doctor who would perform the operation that would save his life. Insisting that I was different from the doctors that he knew in this hospital, Kieran said that he trusted me, adding that he, himself, was not to be trusted with knives or scissors. As I took up his fear of both his own aggression and mine, I spoke also of his wish for me to help him with the angry, rivalrous and murderous wishes and feelings that seemed to grow inside him just like the expanding tumour. Kieran agreed that such feelings were felt to be extremely threatening and in an attempt to distance himself from them, he showed the prince behaving solicitously towards the queen, mirroring his own behaviour in the transference. I took up his wish to hide these thoughts and feelings as a way of keeping us both safe and spoke of his attempt to re-create with me the blissful relationship he imagined to have existed between himself and his mother before the illness.

As Kieran became more able to make use of transference-focused interpretations, the affects which had previously left him so overwhelmed seemed more manageable. Gradually, other aspects of the previously heavily defended Oedipal situation began to emerge. For instance, having avoided talk either of his own father or of father figures in his play, Kieran retrieved the dolphin king he had made in our first session which had remained dormant in his box since then. As he played out violent scenes showing the father as aggressor and son as passive victim, it became clear that the treatment he had received for his illness had been experienced as a punishment for wishes and feelings that had emerged in line with his developing emotional life. Under more ideal circumstances such wishes and feelings might have facilitated an expectable reorganisation of his self and object representations. For Kieran, however, whose fantasies had been dramatically brought to life by traumatic events beyond his control, such a favourable outcome had not been possible. These traumatic events and the overwhelming affects they produced meant that his internal representations took on frightening aspects from which Kieran felt there was no escape. Feeling unable to resolve the deep-seated fears that these internal figures evoked, Kieran seemed to feel he had lost everything.

One session in particular brings to light this painful internal situation. Having shown the dolphin prince and his mother sleeping together, Kieran introduced 'evil sharks' sent by the king to attack the dolphin prince. The affective tone of his play changed as he showed these sharks cutting into the prince's head and ripping out the babies inside. When the prince tried to save the babies, the sharks used their spears and arrows to poke out his eyes. Kieran showed the prince screaming and struggling, but to no avail. The babies were killed and the prince was left blind. Responding to his shaking, I commented on how frightening these violent scenes were. Unusually for Kieran, he pointed to his own blind eye and said that this was what had happened to him and that 'them in white coats did it'. He listened as I spoke of how he felt he had been attacked and hurt, just like the prince, and how he imagined that this was because of the confusing thoughts and feelings inside. Kieran nodded and then showed the prince crying inconsolably, adding that the queen did not love the prince because he was 'damaged'. In a moving reminder of his mother's words in our first meeting, Kieran said that the prince was 'dead to the queen'. Expressing profound feelings of loss and despair, he added that there was 'nothing left to live for'.

The snake's tale

Some months later other aspects of his illness and treatment began to emerge. In one session, he introduced a 'little boy snake' to whom all sorts of catastrophes happened. Playing out violent scenes, Kieran showed how this little snake had been attacked by dangerous animals until his whole body was damaged. This time, however, he showed a mother doll watching passively as these terrible things happened, unable or, as Kieran thought, unwilling to protect him. At other times he showed the mother figure screaming as loudly as the snake himself, almost, as I put it to him, as if the frightening things were happening to her. He showed the snake call out to her for help but she was too upset to do so and the snake was left to suffer alone. This material enabled us to talk about Kieran's memories of his mother's distress; how she had been unable to protect him from the horrible things that had happened and how it had seemed that she had sided with the doctors who had hurt him. In one session, Kieran sat in silence while angrily kicking the side of my desk. I verbalised how disappointed and angry he now felt. He denied feeling angry but continued kicking and asked, 'How could she . . . if she loved me?' In the following sessions, Kieran placed me in the position of passive bystander, wanting me to watch as violent scenes unfolded before me, reliving with me an aspect of his own experience. At the same time, however, there was a strong need to repair the betrayal of trust and a wish to be compensated for the painfully felt lack of a strong, protective internal parent. For example, he often demanded that I accompany him to his 3-monthly brain scans and expressed intense anger and disappointment when I did not do so. I took up his wish for me to protect him and verbalised his fantasy that I had the power to stop the bad things from happening. There was also his need for me to be a calm and containing object able to support him in moments of terror in a way that his mother, too frightened and overwhelmed herself, had been unable to do.

As it became more possible to talk about these memories, feelings of ambivalence emerged. In one session, Kieran said that the snake's mother had 'turned evil' and he showed how ferociously she beat the snake with a cane. This beating was associated with great excitement that Kieran seemed to feel was experienced by both mother and son, the aggressor and passive victim. When I asked why the mother was beating him, Kieran said that the 'evil mother' had become angry when the snake lost control of his bladder and bowel. In vivid detail, he described how the snake awoke one day to find 'wee and pooh everywhere . . . on his clothes, in his bed, all over the floor". He added that the snake had 'red cheeks'. In an effort to make explicit the affects implied by this, I suggested that the snake must have felt embarrassed and worried. Kieran agreed and said he would be 'punished' by the mother. This material had revived Kieran's memory of being unable to exert control over his bladder and bowel following surgery and the intense distress associated with this. As we spoke of this, he covered his ears and burst into tears. I verbalised how upsetting and confusing it had been to lose control and, responding to the level of distress he was experiencing at that moment, I said that it felt as if it was happening right now. He nodded and became quiet. This example seemed to indicate a significant move forward. Despite the distress triggered by this traumatic reminder, Kieran was beginning to show a capacity to make use of the other to help him regulate the overwhelming affects which were so intricately bound with these traumatic memories and, as such, associated with the sense of internal collapse. Concurrent with this, it was gradually becoming possible to begin to integrate these memories and affects in an effort to bring about change in Kieran's representations of self and object. At this point, however, Kieran and I were engaged in understanding the ways in which these traumatic experiences had shaped his internal representations and how these representations influenced his current view of himself and his relationships with others. It would be some time before this work began to facilitate hoped for changes.

Some weeks later, Kieran returned to this theme. In one session, he told me that, having 'messed everywhere', the snake was beaten so severely that his 'skin broke'. Kieran described how the 'evil mother', joined by other cruel and overpowering female figures, pulled back the snake's skin, forcing it to break. He spoke of 'blood everywhere' and showed the snake screaming in pain. When I verbalised how painful and frightening this must have been, Kieran spoke of a catheterisation he had had at the age of 4. He remembered how his mother and several nurses had had to hold him down. He remembered also the blood and the pain. In great distress, he voiced his fear that this experience had 'turned him into a girl on the inside'.

As he struggled with these terrifying memories, intense retaliatory fantasies began to surface which were no less anxiety provoking as Kieran struggled to preserve the benign and loving aspects of his representation of his own mother and me in the transference. In the weeks that followed, taking care to protect the 'nice, kind mother', the snake avenged the 'evil mother'. He laid traps so that she would fall into his urine and faeces and he made a cane to beat her. Staying within the displacement, I took up the wish to hurt and humiliate the mother as she had allowed him to be hurt and humiliated. The beating continued and Kieran laughed cruelly when the mother doll's clothes came off and he began beating her on her bare genitals. Soon mother and son figures were locked into intense sado-masochistic battles characterised by pain, fear and excitement.

Interestingly, the more Kieran seemed able to own some of these feelings in his sessions, the more he seemed to take refuge from them in a passive, feminine identification in his external life. At home, his parents worried that he was more interested in his sisters' activities and opted to play female roles in their fantasy play. At school, he avoided the rough and tumble of the playground, preferring to play with the girls. I noted also that at times he appeared effeminate in his manner and gestures. Was this behaviour a way of shielding his masculine self from the fantasised dangerous pre-Oedipal mother or from the vengeful Oedipal father he had shown in the earlier material? Was he acting out his deep fear that he had, in fact, been changed into a girl? Or, painfully aware of his mother's sense that the boy she once had was dead and intensely jealous of his parents' admiration of his younger tomboy sister, Kieran may have felt that the only way to win back his parents' love was to change into a girl. Whichever it was, his fears about the damage done to his masculine self evoked intense anxiety and rage.

The boy genius and the evil scientist

Two years into treatment, Kieran became more aware of the effects of the radio-therapy on his cognitive functioning. The impact of this on his sense of self together with deep feelings of shame, loss and rage began to emerge. Understandably, he tried to compensate for this with wishful fantasies of omnipotent strength and power.

It was during this period that Kieran introduced the fantasy of a 'genius boy' who owned a 'super-computer' in which 'secret information', the source of his powers, was stored. In the story, an envious evil scientist 'messed up the wires' in this computer so that nothing would work as it should. Robbed of his special powers, the genius boy was left damaged and helpless. In one session, with tears in his eyes, Kieran explained that not only was the genius boy not just an ordinary boy without his powers, he was a 'damaged boy'. Kieran imagined that everyone would see this damage and would reject him. I commented that Kieran seemed to understand how that felt. Kieran agreed and said that what had happened to the genius boy reminded him of the times he had spent in hospital – 'but it's upsetting to think about, it's too scary'. I acknowledged these feelings, but pointed out that thinking about such things was not the same as having them actually happen.

Kieran seemed to consider this. Gradually, he revealed the fear that his brain had been 'broken into by evil doctors'. He imagined that the doctors had 'experimented' on his brain and had 'stolen [his] clever thoughts'. When I wondered why the doctors would do such a thing Kieran said that the doctors had been 'jealous' of his 'clever brain'. In another session, we began to explore the flip side of this fantasy. If the doctors had seen his clever thoughts as he imagined, could they have seen his angry, vengeful thoughts also? Kieran was convinced that they had and reasoned that this was why they had 'attacked' his brain with 'poison radiotherapy'. When I queried this he said, imperiously, 'In case you didn't know, radiotherapy is toxic. Toxic is another word for poison. They wanted to poison my brain.'

Although Kieran has since been able to move on from this paranoid position, at the time, realistic explanations about his treatment did little to alleviate his anxiety. The only way forward was to slowly disentangle the tightly woven network of memories, fantasies and feelings that left him so overwhelmed in the hope that a process of integration of memory and affect could begin to take place.

Kieran's genius boy fantasy also allowed us to explore the trauma of having woken up from the anaesthetic unable to speak or to coordinate his movements. In one session, he drew a picture of his genius boy after 'all the wires were messed up in his head'. Kieran cut out this paper figure and walked it across the table to me, pointing out that the arms and legs were 'all wobbly . . . like jelly'. I suggested that this was how Kieran had felt after the surgery. He agreed, recalling his attempts to move his limbs but, like his genius boy, nothing had worked as it should. The treatment that had saved his life had left his brain 'damaged', or 'mad', as Kieran suggested in another session. Slowly, other questions surfaced. If the radiotherapy had shrunk his tumour, did it shrink his brain too? If the doctors had cut out the tumour did they also cut his brain, the memory bit, the clever bit, the bit that would otherwise enable him to ride his bike or kick a ball? As these frightening thoughts emerged, Kieran's anger intensified, enacted in the transference as he crashed the office chair into the furniture or threw objects around the room. I verbalised how frightening these thoughts were and how angry with me he was for helping him to voice them. I spoke also of his fear that I, as he imagined the doctors could, saw inside his mind and could read his thoughts. At times, Kieran shrank from my words, refusing to make a connection with them. At other times, he seemed to experience relief from the thoughts that tortured him. Gradually, we were able to put together his sense of being completely different from how he once was. He recalled often the period before the illness when he had been a 'normal boy' who had ridden his bike and had played football with his father. Now, everything had changed. Ashamed of his deficits and fearful of failure, Kieran refused to attempt even the simplest challenges. For example, he would order me to cut out his pictures or write down his stories. If I questioned this, he would shout in a tyrannical way that he did not want to make mistakes. When I encouraged him to try with my help, he would burst into tears or attempt, get it wrong, and become furious. Mistakes were associated with the sense of internal collapse, confirming his view of himself as hopelessly damaged.

While omnipotent fantasies about his specialness temporarily compensated for the narcissistic hurt that these experiences engendered, this hopeless view of himself evoked profound feelings of loss, grief and despair. In an effort to make sense of these feelings, Kieran played out funeral scenes that seemed to represent his struggle to come to terms with the loss of different aspects of himself. At the same time, he seemed to be striving also to master the anxiety about the possibility of his own death. For example, in one session, Kieran mentioned that he was a 'very religious person' and, while he imagined he would go to heaven, he dreaded losing touch with his family. In another, he enacted the death of a hero boy whose family painfully mourned their loss, vowing to 'remember him forever'. It has been necessary for Kieran to revisit this depressive position many times in an effort to come to terms with what had been lost. However, his painful struggle has been compounded by his acute awareness of his parents' difficulties in coming to terms with the loss of the boy they had hoped Kieran would be. For Kieran this complicated and, as yet, unresolved process of mourning has needed to take place at different levels of representation – his own representation of himself together with his perception of his parents' representation of him.

Some months later, almost 3 years into the therapy, Kieran was diagnosed as having a growth hormone deficiency, a late effect of the radiotherapy, that would require him to have daily hormone treatment in the form of injections. This news revived terrifying paranoid anxieties as he expressed the belief that the injection contained poison that would prevent him from becoming a man like his father. Revisiting unresolved Oedipal dilemmas in his play, Kieran showed the 'evil' scientist-father administer the injection that would keep his already damaged genius boy a small, frail child forever. When I asked Kieran why the father would want to do this, he said that the father was 'afraid that his son would be more powerful than him'. When I suggested that perhaps the son worried about his own powerful feelings, Kieran insisted that 'nothing bad could happen' because he would 'stay a boy forever'. Despite the anxiety engendered by this fantasy, clearly there was also some relief to be gained from the idea that the aggressive feelings within could be held at bay should he remain a boy forever. In the same way that Kieran had previously sought refuge from the sadism expressed through earlier material in a passive, feminine identification, he now sought refuge from the potentially dangerous aggression in the fantasy of himself as a hopelessly damaged boy.

However, his wish to be a powerful, potent man was strong, as were the erotic feelings that were beginning to emerge in the transference. When he brought flowers to a session, a valentine gift for me, we talked about Kieran's 'growing up feelings' and the exciting 'valentine feelings' in the transference. Later in the session, he expressed the wish that these flowers would 'live forever' in my room. He was dismayed, however, to find that they had wilted the following week – 'they're dead'. He flew into a rage and threw things around the room. When I voiced his anger and disappointment with me for not protecting his flowers from dying, he cried. He held a funeral and with great solemnity, buried the valentine letter he had made with the wilted flowers in the sandpit. I said that he seemed to feel his 'growing up' and 'valentine feelings' must die. He nodded. In the sessions that followed we talked about Kieran's fear that something very bad would happen if he were to express such feelings. In one session he said that 'something very bad' had already happened but turned away, reddening slightly, when I asked what he meant. Later he asked if I remembered the day the flowers 'went all droopy', but could say no more. I wondered if he was thinking about something that happened to a very special bit of himself. He nodded. I said that perhaps he thought that what had happened had damaged that special bit of him forever. Again, he nodded and then said that he felt he was not like other boys, his penis was the wrong shape, and it was 'droopy, not hard'. Kieran thought that this meant he was 'half-boy, half-girl'. He feared that his peers thought this too because they called him 'gay'. In the sessions that followed we were able to understand Kieran's belief that the radio-therapy had damaged his body and that this was the punishment for the 'growing up' and 'valentine feelings' he had felt previously towards his mother and which had now re-emerged in the transference.

Kieran seemed to respond to this reconstruction, which was worked on over a period of several weeks and which seemed to further the process of integrating memory and affect. He became less anxious about the hormone treatment and began to adjust to the reality of the situation. Whereas previously he had struggled to make sense of the explanations offered by medical staff about the hormone deficiency and the treatment required, now he was able to understand how the radiotherapy had affected his growth and how the hormone treatment would help to rectify this. His nurse reported that he was coping well with the preparations prior to the start of treatment. However, although he was encouraged to administer the injection himself, he refused to do so and chose to have his father do it. He explained that he wanted his father to inject him because he was afraid of 'cutting' himself with the injection. Since the injection site was in his thighs or bottom, this was, in Kieran's mind, too close to his genitals. While Kieran seemed to have found a temporary solution to his fear of his own aggression, this strategy was not without anxiety as fears about his father's aggression resurfaced. What was begin-ning to become clear, however, was that aggression, in the form of assaults on the body, had become sexualised and therefore associated with feelings of excitement as well as fear. Kieran's way of coping was to place himself in a position of passive submission in relation to his father as aggressor, a strategy that served to keep his own aggression at bay.

For instance, in one session Kieran used animal puppets to play out a scene between the father and son figures. He showed how the father looked after his son, helping him wash and dress. Gradually, caring ministrations became more aggres-sive and sexual. At one point, using my stapler, Kieran showed the father poke the son violently on the bottom and genitals. Kieran explained that the father had to do this 'so the son would know if he was a boy or not'. I verbalised his confusion not knowing if his father meant to hurt him or to help him. Kieran agreed, 'because daddies don't sex their sons bottoms, do they?' When I linked this material with his confusion about the hormone treatment and his concerns about his father administering the injection he used the puppet to punch me on my breasts. I spoke of his wish to attack the very special part of me, just as the very special part of him had been attacked and said that, in doing so, he wanted me to know what it had been like for him. This shift from passive victim to dangerous aggressor continues to characterise the transference relationship and would seem to represent the conversion of traumatic experience into traumatising behaviour (Lanyado 1999). Significantly, such behaviour emerges at those times when Kieran feels particularly helpless and overwhelmed. As the above example demonstrates, the identification with the aggressor functions as a defence against the anxiety produced by the trauma, a necessary alternative to the position of passive victim.

Several months later, just after Kieran's eleventh birthday, a routine brain scan showed that the residual tumour had started to regrow, causing the fluid around it to expand. Kieran was devastated by the news and reacted with angry, aggressive behaviour at home, in contrast with his depressed, withdrawn presentation with me. In the session immediately after the scan, he made a cardboard submarine and talked about the 'slow, painful death' of the Russian sailors inside the submarine that had sunk in the Barents Sea some months before. Expressing fears about his own death, Kieran commented that the worst thing about this disaster was that the sailors 'knew they would die but could do nothing about it'. In reality his prognosis is quite good but the strain of living with the possibility of death, or yet more painful treatment, is a heavy burden to bear, evoking feelings of helplessness, loss and despair. Concurrent with this news, Kieran learned that the growth hormone had triggered an early puberty which meant that he had to manage the changes connected with this in addition to the anxiety about his tumour. Once again, ordinary developmental anxieties became charged with meaning as he grappled with the fear that not only had his treatments damaged his body but so too had his own age-appropriate explorations of his body. The narcissistic impact of this was colossal.

From affect regulation to integration of traumatic experience through the therapeutic relationship

As Kieran's material demonstrates, traumatised children experience great psychological distress and dysfunction that impacts severely on their development and future adaptation. Recent neurophysiological research has highlighted the link between trauma, brain function and physiology, the effects of which may continue long after the initial traumatic event or series of events is over (Perry 1993; Perry et al. 1995). Even in the absence of external danger traumatised children tend to display a heightened state of alertness, and hypervigilance to the possibility of danger. They are often vulnerable to chance reminders of the trauma that produce high levels of anxiety that trigger primitive survival responses. At the start of treatment, even minor stresses aroused in Kieran the same intensity of affect as the major stresses had, leaving him vulnerable to a terrifying sense of disintegration.

The cumulative effect of these earlier traumatic experiences combined with a series of later traumatic events had thus prevented him from acquiring the necessary adaptive capacities that might have enabled him to cope more effectively.

In Kieran's case, various developmental and environmental factors may have increased the impact of trauma. As studies on the effects of trauma have shown, the child's response to trauma is influenced by the stage of development when the trauma occurs (Lanyado 1999). For Kieran, the initial trauma of his illness, surgery and radiotherapy occurred when he was 3 years old, thus leaving him particularly vulnerable, being at a stage in his development when his cognitive and linguistic capacities would have been so limited. Lacking the cognitive maturity to distinguish between the pain and suffering caused by the disease within the body and the pain and suffering imposed on him from the outside, both the illness and treatment must have been experienced as inescapable terrors to which he had to submit passively and helplessly (A. Freud 1952). Also, that the illness and treatment coincided with wishes, fears and feelings that one might expect to emerge in line with his developing emotional life, meant that his internal world of fantasies was dramatically brought to life at a time when Kieran would have lacked the cognitive maturity to distinguish fantasy from reality. In addition, his limited command of language, particularly during the early stages of his illness and treatment, would have compounded these difficulties, making it difficult for him to express his needs, feelings and fears. Combined, these factors would have augmented the traumatic impact of these experiences, thus making the task of self-regulation of the overwhelming affects produced by this almost impossible.

These traumatic experiences also impacted on Kieran's attachments to his parents in various ways which meant that they could not be relied upon as objects of safety and security (Briere 1992). For instance, his parents, mother in particular, had had to bring Kieran to the hospital and to hold him down while painful treatments were administered. He therefore experienced them as unprotective and colluding with the medical staff. This brought about a terrible sense of betrayal of trust, adding to the sense of danger, as he felt abandoned by the adults he trusted most to terrifying experiences against which he could not defend himself. In addition, for very understandable reasons, neither parent could talk to him about his illness or treatment in ways which might have helped to contain his anxiety. In particular, due to her distress, Kieran's mother was not able to provide the assistance he needed to regulate the affects which overwhelmed him. Consequently, Kieran was left to cope not only with his own affects but also with the lack of parental provision and the added burden of witnessing his mother's distress. Such experiences and the affects they produced meant that Kieran's internal representations took on terrifying aspects from which he felt unable to escape. As well as compounding his sense of danger, this frightening internal position shaped Kieran's expectations of the external world, negatively affecting his interactions with others.

The treatment of traumatised children is often a long and painful process and the progress can be slow. As part of the process of helping the traumatised child to face and work through frightening memories and feelings in order that a link can be made between overwhelming fear and its causes, there is the question of how far the therapy should address the actual trauma without exposing the child to the repeated trauma of remembering traumatic events and reliving these processes within the transference relationship (Lanyado 1999). As Lanyado suggests, there is the need for the therapist to be sensitive to the traumatic memories as they erupt in treatment while avoiding the temptation to actively seek out these issues and attempt to address them before the child is ready to do so. Although Kieran avoided talking directly about his traumatic experiences and could so easily be overwhelmed with anxiety and fear, nonetheless he came to the therapy with a wish to make sense of these feelings and experiences.

However, while the core fantasies that emerged during the course of the treatment afforded him a means of symbolically representing these experiences, giving a meaningful narrative form to memories, feelings and thoughts that allowed some thinking about them to take place, the meanings he attributed to his experiences were, in themselves, sources of anxiety that augmented the impact of the trauma.

Significantly, while reality-based explanations about his illness and treatment may have reduced his anxiety, Kieran was strongly resistant to the attempts by myself or by medical staff to clarify various facts about his illness and treatment, preferring to rely on his own which, however anxiety provoking they were, made emotional sense to him. However, as his anxiety lessened, he became more able to absorb information about his illness and treatment and make use of reality-based explanations in line with his developing cognitive, linguistic and emotional capacities. He is now more able to make a distinction between the ways in which he understood the trauma in the past and the way in which he can now understand it, with the result that he copes increasingly well with medical procedures. For example, Kieran is now able to administer his daily hormone injections. Interestingly, when the neuropsychological assessment was repeated 18 months into treatment, various significant changes were noted. Overall, there was a significant increase in verbal IQ, representing a shift from the 'impaired' to the 'average' range. Specifically, there was an improvement in abstract verbal reasoning and there was a significant improvement in both short-term and verbal memory. Despite the slowness in information processing, his most recent follow-up indicates steady improvement on both the verbal and performance scales. His educational attainment is a much-needed source of self-esteem. In general terms, these improvements in cognitive functioning would seem to have resulted from a reduction of anxiety and a lessening of depressive affect.

To some extent, Kieran's fantasies about his illness and treatment encapsulated both his memories of the trauma together with his affective experience in dramatic form. They provided an attempted means of organising his experiences and regulating his affects. However, these traumatic memories and affects were not fully integrated and, when triggered, were felt to be extremely threatening. Initially these powerful feelings were felt to be manageable provided they remained within the play space that Kieran constructed. Outside of this arena these affects evoked overwhelming anxiety and fear. In order to facilitate sufficient recovery from trauma to allow further development and adaptation to take place, there is a need for the therapist to help the child integrate traumatic affects into the representation of the self (Schore 2000). This process, however, is a slow and painstaking one. Schore (2000) emphasises the importance of helping the child to re-experience the trauma and its meaning in 'affectively tolerable doses', so that this integration can take place. He underlines the importance of the therapist creating a sense of safety for the child so that these terrifying affective states can be shared, modified and linked to experience. However, for a traumatised child like Kieran who to an extent continues to perceive the external world and others as potential sources of danger, the establishment of a sense of safety within the therapy is not without difficulty. Although he made a good link with me early on, like many traumatised children, he experienced my attempts to facilitate this process of integration as intrusive and traumatising, as the medical interventions had been. This tension between his perception of me as a safe, benign other and his experience of me as a cruel torturer has shaped the transference, bringing out a variety of pathological responses including the need to aggressively control me and the wish to passively submit to me as aggressor. Understanding and working through these processes within the transference has been an important part of the process of integration.

Various other factors were also involved. For instance, an important part of this process was to help Kieran to make a distinction between thinking about upsetting things happening and actually having those things happen; in other words helping him to distinguish between fantasy and reality. Previously, simply thinking about what he had experienced triggered the same degree of anxiety as the situation itself. Lacking the necessary adaptive capacities to modify his affects, he became overwhelmed. It was for this reason that he could not make use of the strategies offered by the play therapists or the desensitisation programme offered by the psychologist.

Another crucial aspect was my role in helping to make explicit the affects implied in his play or expressed in his behaviour. Interestingly, Kieran rarely labelled affects directly; even in displacement this seemed too threatening. For instance, while he could tell me that the snake in his play had 'red cheeks' he could not articulate the affects of shame or embarrassment. Likewise, he could point out that the dolphin prince had a 'wide open mouth' and 'tightly closed eyes' but could not say that he felt frightened. It was for me to the make the affect explicit. At other times, he would show his affects in his behaviour, such as kicking at the desk when angry, for example, rather than tell me in words. Gradually, as these feelings have become more manageable, he has become more able to do this for himself.

Perhaps the most important component in this process of integration was his willingness and ability to make use of me as a containing other with whom these terrifying affective states could be shared and spoken about. It was of crucial importance that he could perceive me as someone able to tolerate the extremes of affect that his parents, because of their own distress, could not.

In time, I hope that Kieran will fully internalise this inter-subjective experience and develop the necessary adaptive capacities that will enable him to cope more effectively with the challenge of new experiences ahead.

Acknowledgements

I gratefully acknowledge Viviane Green for her thoughtful supervision of this case, and Dr Jill Hodges for her wise input. In addition, I would like to thank Dr Deborah Christie, Consultant Clinical Psychologist, for her work with the parents. I am grateful also to Gwyneth Down, Consultant Family Therapist, and to Hilary Davis, Family Therapist, for their thoughts about this case.

References

Briere, J. N. (1992). *Child Abuse Trauma: Theory and Treatment of the Lasting Effects.* London: Sage.

Freud, A. (1952). The role of bodily illness in the mental life of children. In *The writings of Anna Freud*, Vol. 4, 260–279. New York: International Universities Press (1968).

Lanyado, M. (1999). Traumatisation in children. In Lanyado, M. and Horne, A. (eds), *The Handbook of Child and Adolescent Psychotherapy*, 275–291. London: Routledge.

Perry, B. D. (1993). Medicine and psychotherapy: neuro-development and the neuro-psychology of trauma 11: Clinical work along the alarm–fear–terror continuum. *The Advisor, American Professional Society on the Abuse of Children 16*(4): 15–18.

Perry, B. D., Pollard, R., Blakeley, T., Baker, W. and Vigilant, D. (1995). Childhood trauma, the neurobiology of adaptation and user-dependent development of the brain: how states become 'traits'. *Infant Mental Health Journal 16*(4): 271–91.

Schore, A. N. (2000). Relational trauma of the developing right brain and the origin of severe disorders of the self. Paper presented at the Anna Freud Centre, March 2000. Department of Psychiatry and Biobehavioural Sciences, University of California at Los Angeles School of Medicine.

Chapter 7

Counter-transference, sexual abuse and the therapist as a new developmental object*

Inji Ralph

In this chapter, I describe the development of a therapeutic relationship with a sexually abused latency girl who, in the course of her 2 years of four times weekly psychotherapy, was placed in two different foster homes. The child moved from an initial seductive relationship to her therapist to the use of the therapist as a new developmental object in order to establish a sense of basic trust. This was paralleled by the child's development of a capacity to think and to tolerate affect states. The use of powerful counter-transference feelings in the therapist is seen as the main therapeutic tool in the treatment.

Flora

Flora was 8 years old when she was taken into care following the arrest of her pae-dophile father. Medical examination provided evidence that Flora had suffered from chronic anal and vaginal abuse. Flora, who had not spoken of any parental abuse, was immediately placed with a young but very experienced (short-term) foster carer, Mary, who was unattached and lived alone. Flora's father was sentenced to prison and her mother, while not prosecuted, no longer had access to Flora. A psychiatric assessment of Flora recommended a full care order, a perma-nent foster home, that Flora has special educational support at school and intensive psychotherapy. Supervised contact with Flora's extended family was also to be maintained on a monthly basis. By the time Flora began her four times weekly psychotherapy, her mother had applied for contact and termly supervised visits were granted. However, it remained unclear how and whether Flora's mother knew of the abuse perpetrated on her daughter or whether she herself was involved.

* This chapter was first published as 'Countertransference, enactment and sexual abuse' in the *Journal of Child Psychotherapy* (2001), Vol. 27(3), and is reprinted with permission (http://www.tandf.co.uk).

Personal history and functioning

Although not known to Social Services, Flora had been of concern to many professionals from a very early age. A difficult baby, she developed feeding problems early on. At night, she would not settle and would refuse to sleep on her own, away from her mother. When she was registered at her local nursery at age 3, Flora refused to let go of her mother. Between the ages of 3 and 5 there were toileting problems and frequent visits to the GP for urinary tract infections. Around 5, school refusal began as well as eating problems. A year before the arrest, Flora's behaviour at school became extremely disturbed and fearful. The school noted the parents' lack of cooperation and stated that they were very wary of doctors.

When Flora moved in with Mary, at 8 years of age, she would eat only half a slice of bread and wanted to be spoon-fed. However, she soon became a more settled, happier child, able to concentrate at school. For the first time in her life she made educational progress and learned how to play. She also tried to make friends. Her relationships with adults became more appropriate. Her sleep pattern became regular and settled. She slept in her own bed, unlike the child who had refused to sleep apart from her mother. Thus, given a safe and protective environment, Flora could feel contained and begin to develop. However, in moments of anxiety she often masturbated in public and could behave in a very seductive manner. This often left her carer, Mary, shocked, angry and struggling between wanting to protect Flora and wanting to have her removed from her care. In her therapy, it was clearly going to take time before Flora could start trusting an adult again – in a non-abusive relationship.

When Flora began her therapy, at 9 years of age, weekly meetings were also arranged for Mary with Dr Brown, the case manager. This had the additional advantage that the allocated social worker could communicate directly with Dr Brown, as opposed to the therapist, thus protecting Flora, the therapist and the treatment. The social worker had regular contact with Flora's mother and welcomed the support offered by Dr Brown at moments when the needs of the child and those of the adults became confused and blurred. Termly meetings with Social Services were also negotiated and were crucial in assessing Flora's progress and in clarifying her external reality. Finding a regular space to discuss the therapy and the impact of the abuse on both the treatment and the network was necessary for the therapist.

Surviving the abused child

In 1990 Bion wrote that 'in every consulting room there ought to be two rather frightened people: the patient and the psychoanalyst' (p. 5) There were indeed two frightened people in my room but I had not anticipated how long this would last and how many more projected frightening feelings I was to experience – feelings that I had to 'contain' before Flora could begin to experience them. Throughout the first 6 months of therapy, Flora remained quite wary of me and of any adult in the clinic. She constantly checked whether I could be a safe adult and whether the clinic was a safe place. Her need to test boundaries, and to establish whether or not I would also be an abuser, were the main themes of these early months.

The first session was typical of the weeks that followed.

As we were going up the stairs to my room at the top of the building, Flora insisted that I walked up first. She then asked whether the 'other children' were already there. I was puzzled and wondered whether she thought I saw other children. She did not know. In the counter-transference I felt uncomfortable and suddenly remembered that the abuse had taken place in the family's attic. I was replicating the setting. I felt guilty, horrible and abusive. Flora was tense and very tentative as she entered the room. I assumed she would be relieved to find the room empty but then realised that she would experience the 'special' position she was now in as even more dangerous. Flora kept her coat on, did not sit down and remained close to the door throughout most of this first session. When she did look at me, she looked suspiciously.

Once in the room she grabbed the soft ball on the floor and threw it around for a few seconds. She then looked inside the box of toys I had placed on the table and looked interested in the plasticine. Using brown plasticine she made a 'mask'. She flattened an oval piece on the table and added eyes, a nose and a mouth with her finger. She then proceeded to cover it with white glue, tissue paper and stripes of white paper. It looked quite messy and the contact of the white glue with her hands seemed to bother her as she quickly said she did not want to do the mask anymore. In the counter-transference, the messiness made me feel sick and I felt unable to talk. Was the glue and contact with it a memory of semen?

She asked what the bed was for and decided that it was to be used if feeling unwell or tired. She then climbed onto it and asked whether I wanted to see how she could do cartwheels and head stands. She jumped on the bed, lay flat on her stomach, presented her bottom to me, wiggled it and made moaning noises. She breathed heavily and seemed to be getting highly aroused. In the counter-transference I was shocked, angry, numb, paralysed and unable to think. I remained speechless; she ran out of the room to find her foster carer.

Flora had pushed into me the shock and outrage she was not allowed to express or even to feel (Alvarez 1992).

Over the next few weeks, she continued to present sexualised and seductive behaviour either through re-enacting what she had endured or by deliberately flicking her skirt or presenting her bottom to me. My interpretations that it seemed difficult to hope that I would not hurt her the way others had, were met by her running out of the room. For her, it seemed safer to provoke the abuse rather than have to wait anxiously for it to happen. This became a familiar pattern: like a pre-verbal child, she had no words to express her feelings or to make sense of them. In this first session, she had shown me her main repertoire of relating to people she has yet to trust.

Soon, Flora presented other means of testing boundaries. Her lexicon of swear words expanded and I was on the receiving end of horrific verbal abuse. When I told her that she was showing me how it felt to be bossed around and be sworn at, she would speak over my voice. At other times, she would order me to do something and would threaten to 'smack your bottom and smack your asshole' if I did not respond to her requests. When I innocently said that we did not do such things here, as we did not touch 'private' parts, I realised that she had long ago lost this sense of privacy and that for her my intervention was meaningless.

In fact, during these early months, I became aware of the need to alter much of my vocabulary in order to find a common language. Everything I said felt abusive, even interpretations. Talking about confidentiality implied we were going to keep 'secrets': it is quite possible that over the years Flora has been silenced and taught secrecy. Working behind a closed door was also frightening and Flora usually left the door open or would insist on playing in the corridor. Other clinicians sometimes walked by. Despite her anxiety about other adults in the building, this was also reassuring as she could demonstrate to them how horrible I was by screaming and swearing.

My anxiety about being seen and experienced as an abuser was accentuated by the receptionist asking me what I had done to make this child run around the clinic so much. There was already a transference to the clinic: I had become the abuser and my colleagues the rescuers. Flora needed to check who was in the building, and when she ran out of our room she left her mark in most rooms by throwing other people's belongings on the floor. She was not just testing how I would react but how the entire clinic responded to her presence. Therapists and administrative staff slowly began to dread her arrival.

Flora was in control and this was central during those early months. Her need to be in control as a means of feeling safe was present in her wanting to play the same games session after session and in exactly the same order – almost as if to reassure herself that I would not behave differently towards her from one session to another. We usually played different ball games and she was usually the boss, the teacher or the one telling me what to do. Playing ball kept me at a safe distance. In the counter-transference I felt bored, irritated and increasingly unable to think.

Her need to be in control and the anxiety underlying it also appeared in her obsessional thinking and behaviour, such as when she repeated the same steps or movements. This was painful to watch, leaving me feeling exhausted. I began to dread each session – probably my own defence against having to survive Flora's horrible experiences and projections. It seemed that, as her therapist, I carried for her the dilemma of having to 'think' or 'not think' of her experiences – as if my mind mirrored hers. Often, in those moments, I wished I could turn a blind eye rather than have to face Flora's pain. Hopkins described this process clearly when she wrote that:

it seems that helping a child recover from trauma is liable to involve the therapist not only in sharing the pain but in suffering grave doubts about whether facing the pain so starkly is necessary, and whether the self-protection of turning a blind eye may be preferable.

(Hopkins 1986: 63)

However, she added that

recognition that suffering such doubts is a feature of the therapeutic work with traumatised children may help to make the work more tolerable.

Nevertheless, we *were* surviving one way or another. Flora was attending regularly and her foster carer, Mary, welcomed the support received from Dr Brown. Together we hoped to set up a safe environment from which Flora could begin to explore her feelings and past experiences. In those early months she had prepared me for what was to come every time she felt highly anxious – usually whenever she was in contact with her mother or extended family or whenever there was a slight change in her routine. With time, she would hopefully find the words to express herself rather than continue to externalise her feelings through activity – to symbolise rather than act. However, we had a lot of ground to cover before Flora could begin to experience me as a trusting, safe and protective object – an object who could verbalise her experiences for her.

Basic trust and the beginning of intimacy

Flora continued to run out of the room and around the building, not allowing either of us to think. This attack on thinking left me unable to recall her sessions – her games being repetitive and changing rapidly from one moment to another. I had to find my own space for thinking in order to be able to continue to survive her projections, to 'contain' (Bion 1962) her feelings and provide a 'holding' environment (Winnicott 1960). Winnicott (1949) wrote that 'the analyst must be prepared to bear the strain without expecting the patient to know anything about what he is doing, perhaps over a long period over time'. However, with the help of colleagues, Flora began to respond to boundaries. Whenever she entered another clinician's room she was quickly told that she should be going back to her room and that she was interrupting other's work, which was private. I also began to feel more comfortable in setting boundaries and saying 'no'. There was a greater sense of safety around her and the adults were beginning to be in charge, to protect her and provide a safe base from which her anxieties could begin to be explored.

With the approaching first break, Flora's sense of rejection and anxiety around family contact emerged. She responded by reverting to seductive behaviour, being aggressive, telling me she had a boyfriend and therefore that she did not need me. She was fighting not only her attachment to me but its implications – becoming attached meant accepting dependency and intimacy. This was intolerable. She denied being angry at being left but asked urgently, 'I'll see you again after the break, won't I?'

Flora attempted to negotiate this first separation by playing hide and seek. She was delighted when I could find her but her fear that I would not was high: she hid by standing in front of me! During the last few sessions before the break I was often locked out of the room. Keeping me out of the room was understood as a defence against her aggressive feelings – if we stayed in the room she would be bossy and angry with me. It was safer for me to be outside, a sign of concern for the object.

This allowed Flora to begin to experiment with intimacy and whether it was safe to be physically close to me. When playing close to each other, such as drawing, she would suddenly run out of the room if I touched her arm accidentally – as if threatened by intimacy. Touch brought back horrible memories and Flora was again unable to feel contained. Like the contact with the white glue in her first session, Flora seemed overwhelmed by memories where she seemed unable to put words to her experiences.

As issues of intimacy became increasingly central to her sessions, Flora seemed concerned with what was real and what was not, and would become quite irritated if I did not give her simple 'yes' or 'no' answers. Maybe Flora was beginning to remember some of the abuse and was unsure of what was real and what wasn't. She seemed scared that if we talked of something it might happen – perhaps her fear that if she tells me about the abuse it will actually happen again?

One way of dealing with these anxieties was to introduce an imaginary twin sister – Claire. Claire was used as a way of safely addressing aspects of herself that otherwise felt too dangerous to address. Claire was the ugly one who had only one boyfriend; Flora was the pretty one with several boyfriends. This fantasy of the twin seemed to operate at different levels; first, on a spatial, concrete level where at times the twin felt real. For example, I could not sit on a certain chair as Flora would announce, 'Get up quickly, Claire is sitting there.' The twin resembled an imaginary companion, the kind of figure we might expect from a younger child. Second, Claire was beginning to represent her inner family – she was constructing a small family unit in the form of a twin who occupied a powerful space in her mind. Third, the twin embodied Flora's negative narcissism in that she was ugly and only admired by 'one' boyfriend. Fourthly, Claire was linked to the overexciting father and the part of her that secretly enjoyed the abuse. The following extract presents Claire as the abusing family member.

> Flora wanted to play 'bed time'. She turned the light off and pretended to be tickled by Claire on the bed. She was laughing hysterically, fidgeting and fighting with Claire. She was shouting 'Stop it, Claire, stop it!' She then sat on the floor and said 'Claire, don't touch me!' and was mimicking trying to keep away from Claire by shifting her upper body sideways. Flora then jumped on the bed again; placing her legs against the wall she became increasingly excited and then really quiet. She looked between her legs, waited a little as if

waiting for something to appear and then giggled nervously. She got up and quickly said 'Let's play ball.' I told Flora that I felt all these games made her feel very excited and how scary it was to maybe feel her body could be out of control. She looked away and then decided to pretend she was a dog – resulting in my constantly being faced with her bottom. When I said 'You really think I want to see your bottom?' she stopped and said quietly 'No I don't think that.' She returned to her ball game but seemed calmer.

Through Claire she was showing me the abuse, sexual play and the resulting excitement and humiliation. In addition, at that moment, I was being cast in the role of the observing, powerless mother in the transference, with herself as my daughter. In such moments, Flora seemed to have been unable to process her experience and was overwhelmed. Her capacity for emotional regulation was hindered and, as a result, so was her capacity to have a coherent representation of her affect and of her experiences.

However, this was an important moment in the treatment as I remember becoming aware that, for the first time, I was finding Flora attractive. Prior to that I had found her unappealing; she was now a petite and fragile-looking, pretty girl with rosy cheeks, long curly black hair and sparkling hazel eyes. Seeing a different side to Flora meant that I was perhaps surviving her projections. Alongside this her sexualised behaviour reappeared but imbued with a different quality. Following a session where her fear of being disliked because she did sexy things emerged, she arrived bearing a 'new baby'. 'Tamara', she addressed her, 'this is Inji Brown, come on, let's go downstairs.' This was interesting as Brown was the name of the case manager – she had conflated the two names and in her mind we had slipped into being related. Dr Brown was my mother and Flora began to explore the area of benign mother–daughter relationships. Much material about babies and early infancy began to emerge.

Tamara, Flora's imaginary daughter, was crucial in these sessions. Flora repeatedly told me that her daughter was sick and had a nosebleed. She threw her on the floor, knocking her head against the wall and the doll had an asthma attack and then vomited again. When I observed that she was showing me how dangerous a parental figure can be when looking after a baby, she gave her to me. I interpreted in the transference, conveying my understanding of Flora's actions as an attempt to see how I would respond and whether I would be a safe mother. In turn, Flora wanted to pretend she was herself a baby cared for by me – in a non-abusive relationship. Flora was not only testing my capacity to care for her safely, she also seemed to be trying to live moments she may not have experienced in the past, fulfilling needs not previously met – but this time with a new object. It is this relationship with a new object which allowed Flora to present her own maternal capacities later in treatment.

With the second break approaching, Flora once again had to deal with contact with her family and mother. The prospect of contact set her back. In her sessions, she became needy and feared that I would reject her because of it. Again, she experienced my attempt at setting boundaries as abusive and thinking was attacked. She began to attack me, as a representative of all abandoning adults, by kicking me and hitting me as opposed to running out of the room, destroying the intimacy and the hope of intimacy. In those angry, needy moments, I felt totally powerless and unable to get things right for her. Mary, in her sessions, voiced her despair at dealing with Flora and her wish to have her removed.

A capacity to think and to tolerate affect states

Flora had been in treatment for a year and in Mary's care for 21 months. Mary felt increasingly 'abused' by Social Services for failing to hear her request to have Flora removed from her 'short-term' care. She also spoke openly with Flora about her wish to have her removed. There was therefore continuous uncertainty about her placement. Threatened by separation and being uprooted, she touched everything in the room, the furniture, the walls and me – like a young child needing to touch base and to reassure herself that it was all real, that she was still 'connected'. She regressed to earlier modes of relating, substituting action for thought. Around the same time, Flora's mother was granted monthly supervised contact. Flora now had to deal with the anxiety behind increased contact and her increasing sense of loss of Mary.

> She introduced a new game where we had to giggle continuously. When I wondered whether it was a way of making sure we did not show any tears, she quietly sat in front of me and explained that Mary had told her that one of her shoelaces was not tied properly. She anxiously tied and untied her laces and refused my help; she just had to manage by herself. Flora was in tears; reassuring her that Mary would understand resulted in her slapping my face. In shock, I told Flora that she was showing me how painful it was to get things wrong and to feel humiliated. Through her tears, she cried, 'Why can't I be like any other child, why? . . . It's not fair, all the children get to be with their mum and their dad and I don't, it's not fair.' When I added that it was also not fair that she could not stay with Mary and that I could not make it all better for her, she continued to cry but then hugged me saying, 'I am sorry I hit you.'

Flora was finally able to talk more about her biological family. Acknowledging the reality of her situation allowed her to work through her feelings of sadness, anger and despair. This allowed her to present her view of her own role and responsibility for losing Mary and for the abuse. In the counter-transference I felt very sad; Flora looked exhausted.

Soon, however, Flora began to show progress both in and outside her therapy. With all the changes in her life, I was a constant object who provided some form of stability. She was able to control her aggression; she told me 'I am not going to swear at all today or even hit you because you looked after my pen', referring to a pen she had left behind the previous day. A capacity for humour emerged and she began to accept that being angry with me did not mean we could not stay in the same room. Flora was much more able to *think* rather than dash out without listening or thinking. She could also now be proud of her achievements, making comments such as 'I used to not be able to do that', and would look for my approval. She became increasingly coquettish, rather than seductive, and wished to be normal. Flora was developing a representation of a wanted child with a positive investment in her appearance and body. In those moments, I felt maternal towards her. It seemed that she was establishing an inner family structure consisting of a mother–daughter dyad. She did this through the experience of the therapist as a new reliable object and through the work in the transference. The contribution of the external family structure provided by Mary should not be underestimated.

With these developments, Flora's need for the fantasy twin was diminishing. On arriving for her session, she told me that Claire, her twin, was no longer with us. 'She's not really my sister.' She explained that she had Tamara, her daughter, who had grown up and was a similar age to her. Flora did not need Claire anymore. Instead, she now created her own family, with herself as the mother.

Flora continued to try to make sense of what had happened to her, of her history. Using the baby doll she told me during one session that the doll was fostered because her parents 'did something they should not have done'. When I tried to find out more, she shushed me. Her doll also had to wait 7 years or so before she could be with her parents again, as at that moment it was not 'safe for her to live with her mother'. It was important that I did not interrupt her play, almost as if she was suddenly flooded with memories which my comments threatened to 'wipe away'. Instead, I was to listen and survive the pain and sadness behind her stories. At the end of the session she told me she would need to 'come back to therapy to see you so that she can talk about how she felt'.

With this increased capacity to talk about her history, Flora disclosed to Mary for the first time that her father had sexually abused her. Flora's anxiety was higher as a result of the disclosure and Mary could not contain her. She rang in anger and despair explaining how Flora was no longer manageable. However, Flora continued, anxiously and tentatively, to bring direct material about her father. In the counter-transference I felt upset as her games were unbearably painful to witness. When I interpreted her wish to show me how it felt to be treated badly, she shouted 'My dad did it to me.' She was anxious and told me she did not want to talk about it as 'it makes me angry'.

Memories about her father were associated with her hurt body. We were repeatedly to play at her hurting herself, feeling sick, having asthma, etc. When I linked her hurts to her father, she shouted that I did not know *anything*. When I said that I did not know *everything*, she screamed, 'Did I tell you he touched my mini, no I did not so there, and I don't want to talk about it.' For the next few minutes she was anxious, walking rapidly around the room, keeping her hands between her legs, not knowing whether to hit me or whether to hug me. However, there was a great sense of relief as she ended the session by finally hugging me and telling me, 'I am sorry I shouted.'

During the last few weeks before the summer break, Flora looked tired, uncared for and ugly again. I was dreading her sessions mainly because in the counter-transference I felt so sad. When I cancelled a whole week for being off sick Flora quietly told me 'You should not make promises you can't keep because then little girls get upset inside and get all worried.' When I apologised, taking up her anger with me, she quietly said, 'I am not angry, I was worried.' Maybe she feared she caused my illness but maybe she was showing me that she had developed a capacity for concern for the object. On her last session before the break, she asked what I would be doing during the break, hoping that 'you'll be thinking of me?' Despite her sense of abandonment and rejection, she was still able to think of herself as loveable and 'thinkable of'.

Gaining objects, losing objects

Flora was moved to new foster carers, Mr and Mrs Red, over the long summer break, having been with Mary for 2 years and in therapy for 15 months. Although she knew she was leaving Mary, the ending was sudden and a repetition of the sudden separation from her mother. Mr and Mrs Red had another child in their care – a baby girl called Sandra. Initially, Flora's sessions were chaotic again; she was regressed and sexualised material reappeared as well as obsessional behaviour. Living with Mr and Mrs Red revived memories of living with a dangerous, abusive and rejecting couple and this emerged in the transference.

In addition, while trying to work out why she no longer lived with Mary, Flora was overwhelmed by her own aggression and feared that she might kill herself or that someone would come and kill her or kidnap her. In her sessions, I had to repeatedly bandage her arm or leg as the only means of looking after her. However, she soon became more settled, mainly as a result of Mr and Mrs Red setting very clear and effective boundaries. Flora became much more part of the family, taking part (with Mrs Red's support) in everyday household activities. She was also forming a very strong attachment to Sandra. She was most attuned and caring towards her, often coming to her sessions with her own baby doll. She would spend time changing, feeding and caring for her 'child' in a most appropriate way. Often during those same sessions Flora would also look for care herself, pretending to be the baby that I had to protect and look after. With me, the new object, she seemed to be attempting to make sense of whether or not she was 'parentable'. When I commented once on how well she looked after her baby she informed me that 'I look after her and you look after me.' Prior to breaks or weekends Flora insisted on taking something from the room for her baby. She took sand and plasticine and called them 'therapy-made food'. Her need for continuity was essential.

Flora became increasingly interested in herself, her body and how she looked – all age-appropriate concerns. Through the use of the doll, she could begin to think about her own body. Giving her doll a bath, she filled a tray with water and showed me how to check the water temperature by putting her wrist in the water. She explained that Mrs Red does this for Sandra – she could identify with female figures. She then very spontaneously said that she wanted to have a bath too. She took off all her clothes and sat in the tray for a few seconds. Like a toddler, she seemed to display her non-sexual body, with no sense of privacy. In those moments I felt that for Flora it was very important that I could bear seeing her body so that she could begin to accept it too. Soon after she put her clothes on and proudly explained how she prepares herself in the morning – putting her under-wear on first, then the tights, then the shirt, etc . . . I felt she was showing me her competencies in a non-sexual way.

However, her anxiety about her body being damaged soon emerged. Mrs Red spoke openly with Flora, now almost 11, about sexual development and Flora was understandably confused, curious and anxious. She also seemed to be renegotiat-ing the abuse at this different stage of her development. She came to a session announcing, 'I just had my period', then adding anxiously 'If I don't have my period then I won't have babies?' When I took up her anxiety that she could be dif-ferent from other girls this led to her bursting into tears and running to the toilet. As I spoke of the anxiety behind growing up and her body changing, Flora whispered, 'How is that?' My explanations were met by silence – the thought of her body being out of control was clearly unsafe for her. When I took up her anxiety of not knowing what sort of grown up-girl she was going to be and her fear that she was broken inside, she opened the door and asked 'Inji, can you carry me?' Pointing out that she was showing me, through her wish to be carried, that she could be a baby even if her body was changing and growing, relieved the tension – Flora was giggling.

Flora was settling with her carers, who were very fond of her and keen to keep her in their care on a long-term basis – a major shift since her placement with Mary. Flora was increasingly disclosing abuse to them – she clearly felt safe with them and they felt able to protect her. Sadly, however, 6 months after she moved to Mr and Mrs Red, due to circumstances beyond my control, I had to leave the clinic. While Flora's therapy had to end prematurely it was not precipitous and the termination took place over a few weeks.

A difficult ending

Telling Flora I was leaving was going to be difficult for her and for me. Just as I had first to acknowledge my feelings about the abuse and work with it in the sessions, so I had first to acknowledge my own feelings about my departure before Flora could begin to feel safe in expressing her own feelings. However, before telling her that I was leaving, Flora already sensed something was up. Probably picking up on my guilt and sadness she often asked me in her sessions, 'Why are you looking at me like that?' She would also try hard to keep me involved in her play. The day I decided to tell her I was leaving, she arrived looking sad. The silence at the beginning of the session was very unusual for her and unbearable for me.

> Flora reacted to my telling her that my time at the clinic was coming to an end with a contemptuous 'Yippee! No more therapy! I won't have to see your git

face ever again.' This projection was painful and her sense of rejection was obvious. It was not long before she expressed her fury. She 'exploded' when I interpreted her repetitive games as a mean of stopping us from thinking. She was beside herself, she screamed and shouted. In the transference, I was the abusive father to whom she was finally able to express her fury. She repeatedly said, as she put her hands between her legs, 'You're a bastard, you've hurt me, you've had me, it's all your fault. I hate you, you bastard!' and she continued to cry and scream. She was also coughing and screaming, 'You are making me sick, my throat hurts so much.' In the counter-transference I felt awful and helpless. When I tried to hold her hand, as a response to these powerful feelings, she slapped me with all her strength, resulting in my ending up in tears. My touching her brought back memories of the abuse in the same way that, earlier in treatment, any moment of intimacy was equated with sexual abuse. However, my tears seemed to have calmed her down a bit – maybe she could see that I could feel her pain and that she was not on her own? When it was time to stop, she asked me to go downstairs and wait for her until she was ready. She was giving us both the space we needed.

During the next few sessions Flora tried hard to keep control of her feelings. Obsessive behaviour reappeared as well as repetitive, boring games. My interpretation that it was hard to believe that I might care about her even if I was going away brought a new game. She started each session by playfully having a hand battle with me. She giggled when I interpreted this game as a means of taking revenge on me for leaving her. Interpreting her ambivalent feelings towards me allowed her to ask me questions – was I still going to be a therapist? Was I leaving other children behind? Why was I leaving anyway? Could she ring me?

As the last weeks approached, Flora's anxiety heightened. She was at times very regressed and would bring her 'baby self' to her sessions. During those last weeks, she also missed several sessions either because she was ill or because she wanted to attend school activities – something she had never liked in the past. Most often, however, Flora did not get to her sessions because her escort was not informed she was to bring her or because her social worker forgot to organise transport. It felt as if the whole network was reacting again. The administrative staff and other clinicians were sad that Flora would not be coming. Flora was clearly now a child whom people liked and the change in the clinic from dreading her presence to contemplating missing her was striking.

Gains of therapy

Flora used her last weeks to convey to me what she felt she had gained from her therapy and her sense of hopefulness as well as her continuing worries. She started her sessions by jumping on the bed and holding on to my hand. She seemed to want to touch part of my body whenever she could – like a small child. We repeatedly played at my having to pretend that I had twisted my ankle and Flora, as the teacher, had to look after me. She was extremely caring. She could now be a caring person, a protective mother. Then, reversing roles, she would ask me to carry her. She would smell my neck like a small child looking for comfort and would fall asleep in my arms.

Flora made sure I kept her in mind through different means. She spoke, for instance, of fancying a boy at school and hoping they would go to bed together. She laughed when I said she wanted to show me that I should still be concerned and be looking after her and protect her. She also asked me to pretend I fancied her (she was a boy) and had to come close to her and be 'sexy'. I felt she was trying one last time to check whether I would become abusive. When I interpreted her wish for me to be abusive so that she would not miss me, she reminded me that she would not miss me anyway.

Finally, Flora was able to enjoy comparing herself to me. We spent most of the last week with her comparing her physical appearance to mine: the length of our arms, fingers, and our hair. During these sessions she also desperately tried to reach the ceiling by jumping on the bed. She giggled when, at times when I felt she might fall off, I jumped. She laughed saying 'I love it when you are panicky.' She told me that soon she would be taller than me – 'when I am 19 or 25' – and that we might be able to compare our heights when she reached those ages. When I wondered whether she might want to come and see me then, she informed me that 'I might have a baby by then' and that they might both come.

During her last session, she struggled between wanting to cuddle me and wanting to hit me. She then asked whether she could take the doll with her but then worried that her carer would think she was 'into dolls' again. She reassured herself by saying 'but I need something to remind me of therapy. Maybe if I tell her that she'll understand.' But she also wanted clothes for the doll, the bottle, some food, etc. She wanted so much; it felt no amount would be enough. Just before the session ended, she gave me a kiss on the cheek and then left quickly.

Discussion

In 'Remembering, Repeating and Working Through', Freud (1914) suggested that:

> The patient does not *remember* anything of what he has forgotten and repressed, but *acts* it out. He reproduces it not as a memory but as an action, he *repeats* it without of course, knowing that he is repeating it. . . . Above all, the patient will *begin* his treatment with a repetition of this kind.
>
> (Freud 1914: 150, italics in the original)

When working with children who have been sexually abused, the expectation for the child is that the abuse will be repeated in the consulting room. This has to be allowed into the transference relationship, where the therapist must be available to be perceived as a potentially abusive adult (Sinason 1991). The child's expectation leads him to enact what he may have endured both as a means of presenting his dreadful experiences to the therapist and as a means of projecting onto the therapist the shock and outrage he may not have been able to express.

Lanyado (1999) has pointed out that many authors have stressed that until the therapist has experienced their patient's trauma 'in an attenuated form' (Bergman and Jucovy 1982) within the context of the therapeutic relationship and felt genuinely shocked by what the patient has experienced, the patient cannot start to work on the problem of their own traumatising behaviour. Thus, if the therapist does not get emotionally involved sooner or later in a manner that he had not intended, the therapy will not proceed to a successful conclusion (Boesky 1990). Through this process, the child will be given the opportunity to see that the therapist is being affected by what is being projected, how the therapist may be struggling to tolerate it and, if the therapy is effective, that the therapist is managing to maintain her analytic stance sufficiently without grossly acting out. It is through this process that the child is able gradually to re-introject the previously intolerable aspects of herself that are involved. She is also able to introject the capacity to tolerate them, which she has observed in the therapist (Carpy 1989).

But what is the impact of such projections and enactments on the therapeutic relationship and on the care network surrounding the child? Kolvin and Trowell (1996) describe child sexual abuse as the 'abuser psychically raping the child's mind, that is, a piece of madness is forced into the child's mind so that the child can no longer make sense of his experiences, thoughts and feelings'. They add that 'the same process can happen to those working with the child'. Counter-transference feelings of confusion, protectiveness, rage, sadism, helplessness and an inability to think are aroused, often leaving all those involved with a wish to turn a blind eye. McDougall (1978) describes how the ideas, fantasies, and feelings of certain patients, traumatised at an early pre-verbal stage, can be discerned first in the counter-transference. She adds that 'in these cases it is permissible to deduce the existence of sequelae to early psychic trauma which will require specific handling in the analytic situation. This "screen-discourse", impregnated with messages that have never been elaborated verbally, can in the first instance only be captured by the arousal of counter-transference affect.'

Attending to one's counter-transference, in the first instance, may well be the only available tool for understanding the child's communications, experiences and feelings. Often, however, such feelings are far too powerful to allow them to reach one's consciousness. Thus, the network surrounding the child – including the therapist – is likely to act out or re-enact the abuse. Hughes (1999) stresses that the therapist needs to be constantly aware of both the internal world of the child and his or her current external reality. She adds that the work with children in care demands a particular ability from the child psychotherapist to keep in mind both the internal psychodynamics of the individual child as well as the often complex dynamics of the care network. In this work, our own capacities and limitations are challenged together with our own (resolved or unresolved) issues with regard to sexuality, perversion and abuse. As therapists working with children who have been sexually abused and who have been moved around the care system, we become acquainted with the three roles described by Dyke (1987): 'rescuer, abuser and the one in shock (or the victim)'. These roles are passed around in the network and, as Davies (1996) suggested, 'professionals dealing with such cases are not free agents but potential actors who have been assigned roles in the individual's own re-enactment of their internal drama'. Having a space to think about the processes and mechanisms that are enacted when working with these children is crucial.

Over the course of her 2 years of four times weekly psychotherapy, Flora has been able to make use of her treatment to begin to make sense of what happened to her and to develop a representation of her self. Through her treatment, she presented her different attachment relationships and, with each, her means of regulating her affect states and her representation of herself. It was in a relationship characterised by excitement that Flora seemed to struggle most to make sense of her experiences. In such moments, she felt overwhelmed and seemed to have lost a capacity for emotional regulation. In turn, she seemed unable to have a coherent representation of herself and of her experiences. Physical and sexual abuse has 'cut across' her capacity to mentalise, leaving her unable to differentiate between reality and fantasy.

Over time, through the transference relationship with a constant (new) developmental object, Flora has had an experience of being a wanted child, giving her a sense of a self that is valuable and lovable. Initially, I provided a space for Flora's projections: I had to survive them, contain them and accept them for her, before she could begin to own them herself. As her therapist, it was important that I remained attuned to her mental states and experienced her raw affects for her. At times, I struggled myself to contain her and to hold on to her powerful emotions and experiences. Having a space to share my counter-transference feelings was crucial. With this containment, Flora began to experiment with the idea of the therapist as a benign object, who could both enjoy her and also reject her. She could slowly begin to own her memories and, at times, struggled to keep them alive in order to make sense of them.

However, even with these changes, Flora will continue to need support at each stage of her development – adolescence, a first boyfriend, a first non-abusive sexual relationship, etc. – and with each stage the abuse will need to be renegotiated. Horne (1999) emphasises that if the abuse happens within the family, the capacity to make use of attachments and object relationships is particularly severely damaged and distorted. Perhaps, however, her short analytic experience will have helped to equip her for the years to come?

References

Alvarez, A. (1992). Child sexual abuse: the need to remember and the need to forget. In *Live Company*. London/New York: Tavistock/Routledge.

Bergman, M. S. and Jucovy, M. E. (1982). *Generations of the Holocaust,* New York: Basic Books.

Bion, W. (1962). A theory of thinking. *International Journal of Psychoanalysis, 43*: 306–310.

Bion, W. (1990). *The Brazilian Lectures.* London: Karnac.

Boesky, D. (1990). The psychoanalytic process and its components. *Psychoanalysis Quarterly 59*: 550–584.

Carpy, D. (1989) Tolerating the countertransference: a mutative process. *International Journal of Psychoanalysis 70*: 287–294.

Davies, R. (1996). The interdisciplinary network and the internal world of the offender. In Cordess, C. and Cox, M. (eds), *Forensic Psychotherapy: Crime, Psychodynamics and the Offender Patient, Vol II: Mainly Practice.* London: Jessica Kingsley.

Dyke, S. (1987). Saying 'no' to psychotherapy: consultation and assessment in a case of sexual abuse. *Journal of Child Psychotherapy 13*: 65–80.

Freud, S. (1914). Remembering, repeating and working through. (*Further Recommendations on the Techniques of Psychoanalysis*, II)'. *SE, XII.*

Hopkins, J. (1986). Solving the mystery of monsters: steps towards the recovery from trauma. *Journal of Child Psychotherapy 12*, 61–71.

Horne, A. (1999). Sexual abuse and sexual abusing in childhood and adolescence. In Lanyado, M. and Horne, A. (eds), *The Handbook of Child and Adolescent Psychotherapy.* London: Routledge.

Hughes, C. (1999). Deprivation and children in care: the contribution of child and adolescent psychotherapy. In Lanyado, M. and Horne, A. (eds), *The Handbook of Child and Adolescent Psychotherapy.* London: Routledge.

Kolvin, I. and Trowell, J. (1996). Child Sexual Abuse. In Rosen, I. (ed.), *Sexual Deviation*, 3rd edn. Oxford: Oxford University Press.

Lanyado, M. (1999). Traumatisation in children. In Lanyado, M. and Horne, A. (eds), *The Handbook of Child and Adolescent Psychotherapy.* London: Routledge.

McDougall, J. (1978). Primitive communication and the use of countertransference: reflections on early psychic trauma and its transference effects. *Comtemporary Psychoanalysis 14*: 173–209.

Sinason, V. (1991). Interpretations that feel horrible to make and a theoretical unicorn. *Journal of Child Psychotherapy 17*: 11–24.

Winnicott, D. W. (1949). Hate in the counter-transference. *International Journal of Psychoanalysis 30*: 69–74.

Winnicott, D. W. (1960). *The Maturational Process and the Facilitating Environment.* London: Hogarth.

Chapter 8

Leo: the analytic treatment of an elective mute boy*

Viviane Green

Although silent for most of his treatment, Leo was active, playful either in my presence or directly with me, and above all highly communicative with all the non-verbal means at his disposal. He was also intensely related, moving from an initial intense teasing, triumphant, and sometimes challengingly destructive relatedness, to an eventually calmer capacity for being with me where he could play out and voice his wishes and thoughts.

The challenge of treating an elective mute was that I was thrown back on Leo's non-verbalised transference and my countertransference response in a particularly stark way, as this was literally all I had to go on. I simply had to trust the develop-mental potency of the non-explicit or more precisely non-verbalised therapeutic relationship as the means for forward moves and also as the very explanation by which to account for those moves. I found myself having to be with him in a way that called forth a type of responsivenes reminiscent of particular aspects of the early child/caregiver relationship.

In recounting Leo's analysis I hope to bring to life what it was like being in the room with him. It will not be an exhaustive account but will focus on specific phases throughout the 2 years, a vignette to capture a typical part of the early treat-ment, then the key sessions when he began to talk, followed by an abbreviated summary of the concerns that he was later able to verbalise.

Finally, I will attempt to highlight aspects of the role of the analyst as a 'new developmental object'; these were afforded by the treatment relationship that enabled his development to unfreeze.

When Leo was first seen at just under 5, he would talk to peers but not to teachers or other adults. He also talked at home but not to adults in his wider social circle.

Leo was a planned baby. He had two sisters: one 3 years older and the other 7 years older. Mrs T, originally from South America, had had a painful history marked by unresolved mourning which still overwhelmed her. In recounting the

* This paper is a modified version of the paper presented on 13 April 2000, at the Annual Meeting of the Association for Child Psychoanalysis in Miami, Florida. The original version was published in *Child Analysis* Vol. 12 June 2001 and is reprinted by kind permission of the editors.

details she became distressed and rather less coherent. She attempted to keep her unhappiness and confusion at bay by manifesting a rather rigid coping style. Her emotional state made it hard for her to find pleasure in her son. Mrs T spoke to Leo in her mother tongue, whereas Mr T spoke no Spanish and spoke to his son in English. The au pairs were often Spanish. In the context of this family, where it later became evident that there were considerable strains between the parents, 'speech' became the readily available medium where Leo's difficulties in managing his identificatory conflicts were played out. Speaking English or Spanish meant exclusion of either father or mother's known preference. During Leo's analysis before he spoke, I once asked him how he thought of himself and his reply was to make Chinese eyes as a bid for autonomy and indicating a neat side-stepping of conflicts.

Leo was described as incredibly shy and insecure. He was also seen as having an 'extraordinarily strong will'. His mother found him unmanageable and prone to tantrums, throwing her clothes around, banging doors, throwing chairs, etc. He would also kick and scratch his parents. He had sleeping difficulties, wanting to enter the parental bed in the early hours of the morning. He also had numerous fears, e.g. of wolves and lifts, and displayed a nervous tic: blinking.

Details of Leo's early history were not recalled in any great detail by Mrs T. His birth coincided with a very difficult, preoccupied period for Mrs T, who was embroiled in rows with her family of origin. His speech development was within the norms. However, he had had two health difficulties, the first occurring at a critical time in language development. He had 'glue ear' and recurring ear infections which resulted in intermittent hearing loss. This necessitated two operations to insert grommets, the first when he was 18 months old and then again when he was 3½ years old. Prior to the operations they were told that Leo might have 50% hearing loss but subsequently he was given a clean bill of health. For the brief periods of hospitalisation his mother had remained with him.

Mrs T reported that Leo had no overt separation difficulties when he attended nursery on a full-time basis at 2 years and 6 months. From the age of 9 months until 3½ Leo was close to the au pair. At the time of referral, although she was no longer in the home, the au pair still maintained contact with him. Since then there have been a number of au pairs.

Leo presented as a mischievous, attractive and humorous child, who at the same time could be highly uncooperative, provocative, manipulative, and at moments visibly anxious. Analysis was recommended on the basis of Leo's real, hostile, enmeshed and embattled relationship with his mother and what now seemed to be an aggressively tinged hostile internal world. Work with the parents was also recommended.

In fact, the whole process of engaging the family took place over several months and Leo did not begin treatment until almost a year after the original recommendation. Regular parent work took place to support his forward moves. Interestingly, as Leo got better and was no longer the 'Identified Patient', the family's psychic economy realigned. Mr and Mrs T became increasingly open about their intra- and inter-personal difficulties

Leo began treatment on a four-times-weekly basis at just under 6 years of age and terminated at just under 8 years. Sessions were reduced in the last few months of treatment.

Establishing a sense of safety in the face of rage over separation/individuation and loss of omnipotence

This account of the first phase attempts to convey something of the quality of Leo's hostile, excitable, and controlling relationship with me. During the many protracted periods of frustration, disempowerment and even hatred that we both felt in the therapeutic relationship, something kept us both going. For Leo it was his continuing hope that I was someone worth communicating to even if it was only to pick away at me and the paintwork on the outside of the house until he could convey his feeling of himself as an omnipotently destructive child and could engender a real and familiar engagement through annoyance and triumph. The entity (in me) that he initially sought out and then needed to re-create for himself was the mother engaged through irritation and hostility but who then became overwhelmingly hostile and crazy and had to be kept at bay. Leo communicated this very clearly when early on during on during one session he looked at me intently and thoughtfully, and then made a gesture indicating madness. When I took up his feeling that I was crazy he then pointed in the direction of his mother.

On my part there was the sheer fascination of continually trying to understand what was going on as he found ever creative ways to rile me, looking at me with taunting teasing eyes, and in one session deliberately blocking my toilet with a whole toilet roll. However, even in this phase of treatment there were very brief moments when he would allow himself periods of ordinary non-verbal play and communication with me. The first instance of such a moment occurred a few weeks into treatment. He drew some patterns on a rubber which he used as a stamp, thus making a series of abstract pictures. I spontaneously exclaimed 'Leo, these are really nice.' He then dismantled a picture frame in the hallway and inserted his own drawings instead. Such brief interludes in an otherwise more fraught relationship allowed me to see in a naked way Leo's reaching out for a form of safer, early being-with-the-other until he was once again overwhelmed by intrusive overheated closeness.

In the first few weeks of treatment Leo also made it abundantly clear that he wanted his own space and he wanted literally to physically control my distance from him. I wondered silently how far in the transference he needed to do this to protect himself from not only his mother's physical intrusiveness but what he experienced as the overwhelming quality of her unprocessed thinking. There were frequent occasions when Leo would be involved in an activity, drawing or building structures with furniture and objects, when he would have his back turned to me. If I commented on his absorption in the task and his pleasure in getting on with it by himself and keeping me out he would turn round, then indicate with gestures that I was to leave the room altogether. I was willing to oblige although periodically I would knock to see if he was ready to let me in again. When I was allowed in the room I could witness and silently marvel at the complex 'sculptures' and constructions he made using boxes, chairs and several decorative objects onto which he placed dolls and toy animals. No fantasy content was communicated but he conveyed his sheer inventiveness and wish to appropriate the room for himself.

In the September, following a long summer break of 2½ months, Leo expressed his sense of rage and abandonment at the separation by storming into the consulting room and barricading himself in. The sound of chairs being heaped against the door left no doubt as to his intentions. After 15 minutes had passed I was faced with a technical dilemma: to knock with a request to enter or to just remain shut out. Leo's wish to shut me out effectively protected us both from his rage at me and communicated his own feeling of abandonment. As I stood pondering the dilemma, he appeared a couple of times and removed the chairs so that he could once again bang the door hard. The provocation elicited a feeling of irritation. I knocked on the door and he opened it slightly, allowing himself to stand close by me. I said that he was treating me rather horribly by shutting me out so much and added that when he did that I guessed that he was also feeling I had been horrible to him. He looked at me extremely intently (was he anticipating that I would 'explode'?) I added that however horribly he treated me I would not do the same back. Following this Leo made every possible attempt to provoke further. Here, I think he was wanting to see if I would step in and physically restrain him. However, I did not do so, noting that while he was threatening to break things he never actually did so. Interestingly, while he could spill over in my presence a basic level of trust prevailed. Somehow I never felt he would completely lay waste the room and he knew I trusted him when he was in there alone.

The provocation continued and I began to dread sessions. In one session he rang long and insistently at the doorbell, then when I went to fetch him he had disappeared around a bay window where he was standing and picking the paintwork on the window ledge. I had to be very careful not to get too close to him as when I took a step nearer he backed off, continuing to pick and grinning defiantly and tauntingly. I was very, very irritated. I said that I knew he was trying to annoy me and although he was smiling I didn't believe that is what he really felt like inside. I added that it must be awful to be with me when all he would do was try to make me cross and to feel cross himself. Leo eventually came in of his own accord and proceeded to tip things out of boxes. Here I stopped him, firmly saying I wished he could find another way of letting me know how horrible he thought I was. He took out a piece of paper and spent the remainder of the session doing a drawing. Using gestures he also communicated the full extent of his feelings. He drew a witch-like lady with enormous teeth coming out of her mouth and her tongue sticking out. Out of the nose ran snot. I said this horrible, messy lady was me and here he began to make farting and raspberry noises, elaborating on the full extent of my vileness and no doubt his own. I added I was not surprised he felt this as I had left him over the long summer. As if to underscore the portentous strength of his feelings Leo made a flag out of his drawing and displayed it to his mother in the adjoining waiting room.

Following these sessions Leo would frequently blow bubbles or make unflattering noises at me while engaged in an activity and then one day he let out a high-pitched scream. It was so deafening he had to stop up his ears. I exclaimed, 'My god, you've really got a voice there.' He screamed again but this time with some delight. I added, 'Well, we both know now you have a screaming voice but what has happened to your talking voice?' Leo pointed to the rubbish bin. 'Who threw that away?' I enquired and in response he pointed in the direction where his mother was sitting. I asked him if that was because a lot of angry words were said with that voice and he nodded. He then made lots of other noises, most of them truly repulsive and then gestured that he was eating his snot. I said, 'Are you trying to get me to hate you?' whereupon he nodded enthusiastically then laughed out loud. I then said, 'Well, maybe you are trying to make me hate you so I will shout at you and also become hateful', and again he nodded very emphatically. We had gone through the cycle of his attempting to engage me in an angry and excited interchange with an unmet expectation on his part that it would culminate in a doubtless familiar, explosive climax. Around this time he opened the shutters before leaving the room, indicated that I was to stand there and, as he walked up the garden, he waved all the way to the car. This became a regular separation ritual.

Leo continued to have periods of shutting me out of the room but here there was an interesting difference. Rather than trying to work us both into an acrimonious engagement he calibrated our distance but then made reparative offerings. Once again, I found myself standing by a closed door but this time rather than anxiously thinking to knock or not I felt it was safe to just wait. After a long time Leo came to the door and handed me a pocket calculator enclosed in a sellotaped wrapping. I thanked him for the present. At regular intervals other such presents followed. After the third such present I remarked that although we were apart, I could see he was thinking about me when in the room. After the fourth time, he left the door ajar and it felt possible to enter the room, albeit taking care to keep some distance. With marked concentration, he was doing a drawing. It was a house and I asked him who lived there. Rapidly he drew a figure with hair sticking out and an object at crotch level. The figure had a big smile on her face. It turned out the figure was a witch with a broomstick. I said that she looked quite friendly but as she was still a witch maybe she was also still a bit scary. Leo nodded. Did she do awful things to children? He nodded vigorously and then wrote his name on the back. I then said maybe she was a bit like me, friendly but still scary. Temporarily overwhelmed by the transference, he went and hid behind the couch but shortly after re-emerged, making what sounded like early vocalising sounds. I looked up in surprise, smiled and made some sounds back. He made several burps in reply. Then, extending the vocabulary, I blew out my cheeks and Leo knew exactly what I was going to do and also started to try and make popping noises with his finger. I asked if he could whistle, which he could. At one point he stretched his mouth very wide. I did likewise and at the same time said, 'My name is Viviane.' He then repeated his name. In the last session of that week he did a drawing of me that was amazingly detailed, showing the cut of lapels on a jacket, etc. He gave me a big smile and I remarked on how today the witch just seemed to be a friendly lady adding that just sometimes he and I could be together in a friendly way.

The desire to talk: bridging the gap between self and other

After 14 months of treatment Leo began to talk. In retrospect I saw that several developmental processes had to take place before Leo felt the active wish to relinquish his symptom. Much of his early treatment addressed his need to omnipotently control me as a means of managing his terror of me and his terror of his own rage, particularly in the face of separation. For Leo to give up a certain amount of omnipotence meant the risk of facing us with his ensuing rage. He needed many repeated experiences that we could be safely together without either of us falling back into an overly intrusive and heated merger. He had to repeatedly test whether I was a mad witch-like lady or whether I could maintain a level of sanity. Most of all he had to experience himself in relation to me as someone with a coherent sense of agency, not just as a fragmented, triumphantly angry boy. In an attempt to establish a link with him I had frequently faced a dilemma when he wanted to communicate something. Should I guess and keep guessing until we got there or should I just give up and verbalise the frustration by acknowledging his wish for me to understand him and the frustration for both of us when I couldn't? Ultimately, like Winnicott's good enough mother who has to allow the possibility of frustration to engender a further creative gesture, I had to repeatedly fail him and verbalise the mutual frustration.

In contrast to his previous surreptitious curiosity and attacks on the maternal body (either myself or my room) there began a series of sessions when he would allow himself open curiosity about my room and then proceed to draw my house and the contents. This seemed to herald the consolidation of his move into a more symbolic exploration and representation.

Then in one session he began making lots of urgent noises and hand gestures. Again, I took up how awful it was when I couldn't understand because he wouldn't or couldn't speak to me. His noises became ever more extravagant, with squeaks now included. I finally looked at him and said, 'Leo, that's bird language and I don't understand it.' He then tried a series of noises in a gruffer register, which I identified as some large animal's language. In the heat of the moment, in genuine frustration, I added I was still not understanding and he was not doing much to help me.

In the following session he was brought by his father. Leo began by wandering around the room, pointing to his head to show he was thinking. I verbalised that he was thinking about something. He alighted on the phone and began tapping on the console. I was sitting very close by and he began to mouth some words. I mouthed them back trying to discern the meaning but once again had to give up, verbalising both my helplessness and his urgent wish to communicate. He gave me to understand that he was trying to phone someone. 'Is it your eldest sister?' Head shake. 'Someone in England or Spain?' Leo drew the English flag and mouthed the word 'Granny.' He then searched the room as if he were searching for another means of communication. Finally he found a Dictaphone, which I showed him how to work. He went out to his father, indicating that I should stay in the room. He and father, at Leo's instigation, came out with the following tape-recorded sentence: 'My granny' (Leo) 'lives in' (father) 'Leeds' (Leo). Upon his return he handed me the tape recorder and covered himself to conceal his embarrassment while I listened to the tape. I remarked that now I finally understood what he had been wanting me to know. In the following session (again accompanied by father) he brought with him a paper mouth on which were painted eyes. The paper creature had a telephone number printed on it. Leo brought me the phone and it was clear he wanted to ring the number. Sitting very close to me, he waited while I tapped out the number and handed him the phone. The message requested that the caller leave their name and number, which Leo only felt able to do with his father. For the rest of the session he went back and forth between his father and me. Finally, he got out a piece of paper, indicating that I should write down my number. I said that maybe he wanted to leave a message on my Ansaphone. That evening the phone went, and suspecting it might be Leo I left it on. The first message was a lot of giggles. The second message (with father prompting in the background) said, 'Hello this is Leonard. Have a nice weekend. See you Monday.' According to the parents this had been entirely his idea. Following these sessions he would say 'Goodbye' or 'Hello' through the letter box, but it was to be a while before he talked spontaneously. We learned from the parents that he had begun to talk to unfamiliar adults.

In a session following the next break Leo sat thoughtfully in a chair; I asked what he was thinking about. He started to tell me about the languages he could speak: English, Spanish and a little Portuguese because of his favourite au pair. He then referred to his mother by her first name and listed all the languages she could speak. He went on to talk about the family's holiday plans, explaining all the journeys they would be making. I was aware that this was the first time I was having an ordinary conversation with Leo and, given the fragility of this newly established move, just left it at that. During the World Cup he was full of talk about the matches, describing with some amusement his mother's excitement during matches involving the team of her country of origin. He was identified with father in wanting England to win. In one session he asked hopefully if we could watch a match on TV! Once, in the course of these conversations, I asked why he had not talked before when he obviously had so many things to say. He said that if you didn't talk at school you didn't get told off. But then, hinting at the omnipotent triumphant pleasures offered by his wilful silence, he said that he talked to a teacher's daughter but not to her and that made her very jealous. Like children who withhold their precious faecal gifts, Leo had conveyed a sense of jealously guarding his precious gift of speech until royally and politically dispensing it to the favoured (and safe) few.

Some elaboration of fantasy and internal preoccupations in play and speech

Mr and Mrs T wanted to stop treatment when Leo began to talk, but agreed to a termination period, which turned out to be rich in Leo revealing his thoughts and fears as well as his sense of himself and his objects as 'weird'. In the last term of treatment Leo verbalised in the transference that I was a weird lady who was all wrong and upside down. In fact he suggested that I see a specialist. He also told me that my whole family was gender confused, the boys dressing like girls and that I dressed like a boy, embellishing on this by providing exact details of clothing. Of himself he informed me that he was pleased he was boy because his children and his children's children would have his name but his sisters' children would not. I fleetingly wondered how far he actively wanted to be a girl like his sister but felt that on the whole his bisexual wishes were less to do with gender confusion per se and more to do with his omnipotence, i.e. wanting to be and have it all.

In this period of treatment growing up was very much on his mind. His material showed his preoccupation with attempts to assert a phallic potency and a fear of belittlement. In displacement, through play with dolls, he showed his concern with who was the best and strongest. When I took up with him in play by referring to a doll that it was awful to feel inferior Leo replied, 'Yes but he is proud.' At this point it was possible to take this up with him directly and to link it to his private wish to conceal his feelings of vulnerability.

In one session through projection he referred to his own wish to creep into the parental bed and his conflicts about growing up. The same theme would later re-emerge in his play. Through play with dolls he brought to life the family constellation in various combinations, highlighting a parent–son threesome, then a quarrelsome parental couple, protective brother and sister relationship, and a father–boy couple. It was as if he was sorting out the various dyadic and Oedipal permutations.

After the summer break, during which he had excitedly and anxiously learned to swim, Leo began to make a complex structure which included a bridge and buildings offering shelter. 'Let us just say it is place where they can go to get out of the rain', he offered. Then a figure who walked across the bridge fell into the water and Leo gestured, cutting his throat to show the figure would die. Here he pointed to the blue carpet, saying it was the water. I remarked on the terror of being alone in the water. Leo replied that the child's parents were on the beach. I said, 'Yes, the boy knew this in a part of his mind but he still felt alone in the water', whereupon Leo added 'Yes, especially if he knows his parents don't like him and want him to go away.'

Interestingly, in this period of treatment Leo's parents reported that he would sometimes suddenly volunteer his thoughts about his mutism. In the car, returning from his session he told his father that he thought one of the reasons he did not talk was because he had been scared. He recalled the time he had been at nursery (when he was very little) and how he had hated being left there. One of the teachers had shouted at him and from then on he did not want to talk. I found it poignant that Leo had begun to do his own puzzling out about himself.

In talking to me Leo had to let go of his need to wilfully control himself and me, despite his underlying sense of anger and fear. Attempts at omnipotent control of the dangerous object were no longer enacted through his symptom. Nor were they needed to protect his vulnerable, wounded sense of himself as a weird, damaged boy. There was, though, a move to omnipotence in fantasy that he elaborated vividly. In one session Leo lay on the floor while he spoke about becoming a bigger boy. I asked him if he had thoughts as to what he would grow up to be like. He imagined himself one day as a father with a family. He then began to play around with all the possibilities: 'I can be superman, a doctor, a dentist, a specialist, a warrior, an Olympic athlete . . . .' The list was prefixed by 'the best' and 'the most'. While this may well have signified a persisting defence it was in an altogether different key. When we had to stop Leo said, 'Oh that's a shame.' Alongside the defensive aspect there was satisfaction to be had in his sense that he could express his wishes, recognising them as such. I agreed it was a shame, saying that it was a lot more fun thinking of all these things then having to be an ordinary non-superman boy.

In his last session, using plastic drawers he sellotaped together a large, long boat. In one of the drawers he placed several small dolls. Suddenly a fire broke out. Excitedly, he described the panic and devastation wreaked. I commented on the dangerous situation, wondering aloud what would happen to the people on board. 'Quick, quick, jump!' he exhorted the dolls as he placed them in the sea. At this point I found myself wondering if our ending left him feeling adrift. I asked what would happen and Leo, after deliberating awhile, decided that even if help did not come it would not matter too much because they could now swim on their own.

Leo waved as he left, walking backwards and into the car. He was still waving as the car pulled away.

Psychic changes and developmental processes

For Leo, a new developmental figure meant that he could extricate himself from his previous enmeshment with an internal object threatening to overwhelm him with a seamless stream of angry, hostile and, above all, panicked shadows. He conveyed a sense that not only was his internal object weird but that correspondingly he too was weird. A formidable anal wilfulness was the stamp of his desperate defences against this humiliating self-representation. It was a real conflict built on early deficits. His intermittent hearing loss as a child provided a later channel for tuning in and tuning out, a physical complement to his mother's tuning in and out. This may have lain behind his fascinated compulsion to repeat the activating and stopping various noises made by the console, an alarm clock, etc.

The intermittent hearing loss would also have coincided with a critical period in language development. Psychic growth was contingent upon establishing his sense of himself as an effective, more autonomous agent. It was no accident that he enlisted his father's help when he wanted to talk. It was the expression of an internal shift where a third party was now psychically available.

The mutative experiences wrought by the treatment relationship have long been a subject of interest to psychoanalysis. In Anne Hurry's book *Psychoanalysis and Developmental Therapy* (1998) the theoretical and clinical chapters make explicit and delineate the ways in which the therapist enters the child's developmental stream as both a transference and a new developmental object. The therapist continues to address conflicts and to interpret, but as a new developmental object changes are understood to be effected 'silently' through the new and different experience of an intersubjective vitality offered by the treatment relationship. Embedded in and arising out of these new experiences are altered self and object representations. They are new experiences which promote the unfolding of mental processes. Leo became able to safely experience, symbolically represent and express his feelings. His mind and the mind of the other could safely be discovered.

In a special edition of the *Infant Mental Journal*, 'Interventions that effect change in psychotherapy: a model based on infant research'(1998), the contributing authors hypothesise about particular intersubjective processes in the early infant/child caregiver relationship that seem pertinent. The cornerstone is a view of development where the notion of the importance of an implicit, procedural mode of relating is privileged. It is that which is rooted in non-conscious schemata, which define the 'how' rather than the 'what' of interpersonal behaviour. This nonvoluntary system, as outlined in the chapter by Solms and Turnbull, is implicit, non-declarative and non-reflective. This mode of relating is laid down early and lies outside the field of awareness but is activated in the treatment relationship. A feeling of being known and understood by the other as one experiences oneself offers a moment of mutual recognition out of which arises a powerful sense of fulfilment. Tronick (1998) suggests that moments of reaching out for fulfilment oscillate with moments of dissonance, indifference, mismatching. Where there are repeated experiences of inappropriate engagements with insufficient moments of fulfilment the infant begins to incorporate this maternal view into the self state organization. However, reparative moments enable the cycle of reaching out, perturbation, reparation to resume. As Steele points out in her chapter, 'Attachment, actual experience and mental representations', repeated experiences of reaching out to repair breaches promotes development as much as the moments of fulfilment. The resilient child it is suggested is one who senses that the reparative gestures are worth making. Thinking back on Leo's period of shutting me out I was struck by how we had to live through a very long period of a repetitive cycle where he sought to engage me by attempting to evoke a heightened and familiar mutually angry climax. His compulsion to repeat was his enactment of the 'how to' engage. Having experienced my failure to respond in the way he expected, a new and different outcome occurred, entirely at his instigation, when he sought out and discovered a reparative way to re-engage. I do not think this was based on guilt but rather his drive for fulfilment sought out a different means of re-engaging that could then be matched, giving rise to a different 'fulfilment'. At the interpretative level this was anchored in the object-related affects aroused by separation but I would suggest it was not solely the interpretation per se that was the agent for change. Interpretation was the culminating expression of an experience that rested on the different way of being with and 'knowing' a person and knowing oneself.

Stern (1998) proposes a model of therapeutic change where the accent is on temporary periods of destabilisation or disequilibrium. These moments arise and can be harnessed for therapeutic change. An apparent transgression of periods of shared meaning is mutually enacted, mutually recognised and ratified, following which a new intersubjective state comes into being that can take place at a different, higher level of intersubjective organisation. He refers to this as the 'moving along'. The key aspect is that it is a catalyst for an alteration in both participants' implicit knowledge about their relationship, leading to a progressive complex growth. Well-timed interpretations exert an emotional effect at the level of explicit knowledge but impact on the domain of implicit relational knowing. The therapeutic relationship is the medium within which the 'how to' of relating can be reconfigured. How does this fit in with psychoanalytic understanding in one particular respect, a notion that there is an unconscious that shapes and gives rise to imaginative expression of oneself and one's objects organised by an agency whose mechanisms work along rather different lines than implicit procedural knowledge? Clinicians know that children and adults attribute meaning and give fantasy expression to inter- and intra-subjective experience. Leo's play (as well as his relationship to his therapist) was the symbolic expression, the unconsciously driven preoccupations with sorting out where he was in relation to both dyadic and triadic relationships. Ultimately his sense of himself as a boy shifted and changed during the course of the analysis. He moved from being an angry, explosive and paradoxically withholding boy into feeling more safely potent, with an increased sense of himself as his own agent. The finely grained world of subjective experience as it is embedded intrapsychically is captured in a psychodynamic framework where the full range of both conscious and unconscious life is given room and different affective experiences in their details can be privileged.

References

Fonagy, P. (1998). Moments of change in psychoanalytic theory: discussion of a new theory of psychic change. *Infant Mental Health Journal 19* (3): 346–353.

Hurry, A. (ed.) (1998). Psychoanalysis and developmental therapy. In *Psychoanalysis and Developmental Therapy*, 38–75. London: Karnac.

Stern, D. (1998). The process of therapeutic change involving implicit knowledge: some implications of developmental observations for adult psychoanalysis. *Infant Mental Health Journal, 19* (3): 300–308.

Tronick, E. Z (1998). Dyadically expanded states of consciousness and the process of therapeutic change. *Infant Mental Health Journal 19* (3): 290–299.

Chapter 9

Young adolescents: development and treatment

Willem Heuves

Introduction

In this chapter some of the major developmental tasks of the young adolescent will be discussed against the background of pubertal maturation and some findings from research. It will be stressed that, in contrast to middle and late adolescence, the psychological process of early adolescence remains a rather unexplored area. In view of recent research it would appear necessary to reconsider some theoretical contributions about this developmental phase. The technical difficulties in the psychoanalytic treatment of young adolescents will be addressed and illustrated with some clinical vignettes.

The process of adolescence spans a period of roughly 10 years. Within this time span a variety of psychological developments take place. In the first part of adolescence, rapid and drastic bodily changes serve as an organizer for many psychological developments. In the second part of adolescence, the awareness of having an adult body is a major impetus for further development. The transition from childhood to adulthood may accordingly be separated into early and late adolescence. They are dissimilar and distinct phases of development whereby 'only a semantic accident leads us to call both early and late phases by the same name' (Spruiell 1975: 520). Depending on individual maturation, early adolescence roughly spans from 10 through to 15 years of age.

In the first part of the twentieth century adolescence was not a central focus of interest in the work of most psychoanalysts. Bernfeld (1938), when reviewing the psychoanalytic literature on adolescence, concluded that only a handful of studies about adolescence were available. Due to drastic changes in Western society paralleled by important cultural changes leading to the appearance of adolescent subcultures (Coleman 1961; Rieff 1959), psychoanalysts began paying more attention to this age group. Adolescents became recognized as a group of potential patients, with complaints and disorders, which could only be successfully treated with the help of a proper understanding of this developmental phase. The pioneering work of Anna Freud, Peter Blos, and Moses and Eglé Laufer has greatly contributed to the current psychoanalytic understanding of adolescence and adolescents. However, in reviewing the psychoanalytic literature on adolescence, one is struck by the fact that psychoanalysts are mainly concerned with the second phase of adolescence. Both case studies and reviews about early adolescence or young adolescents are relatively sparse. Since Rutter *et al.*'s (1976) seminal research on adolescent turmoil and Offer and Offer's research (1975) on adolescence, there is an increasing appreciation of the wide range and diversity in normal adolescent development. What is apparently true for some adolescents is not necessarily true for all, implying that the demarcation of normal and abnormal development during early adolescence is quite unclear. The crucial psychological processes taking place during this developmental phase, in which children reach sexual maturity, are only partially understood and poorly explored.

Systematic findings based on clinical experience and more general research on the psychological and psychodynamic development of this age group are relatively sparse, leaving room for scientific myths and speculations about the inner world of the young adolescent.

Most contributions to a psychology of early adolescence adhere to Freud's view that sexual maturation is the central force behind adolescent development. Recent research presents evidence that while there is indeed a relationship between the biological and psychological processes, between sexual maturation and adolescent development, it is not a straightforward one, For Freud, it is the revival of an incestuous undercurrent in the psychosexual development and the incest taboo that propels the adolescent away from the parents toward the peer group to refind the love object outside the family. Subsequently, the notion of adolescence as both a recapitulation and a new developmental phase has remained a central notion in psychoanalytic thinking on adolescence (Jones 1922; Blos 1985; Tyson and Tyson 1990). From a research perspective, however, this process appears not to be as universal as Freud and later authors assumed. The psychological development, the separation from the primal objects and the finding of an object outside the family appears to be a much more complicated process, motivated by many factors about which little is still known. There has been little support from research for the widely accepted psychoanalytic view, which stresses that the increase of sexual impulses is the salient force behind the separation individuation process of adolescence, caused by the reactivation of the incest taboo (Adelson 1980; DeHart *et al.* 2000). There is growing evidence that cognitive development and social factors also play a more significant role in the separation individuation process than hitherto assumed (Steinberg 1993). The turn to the peer group and away from the parents seems to be significantly related to social factors and social expectations and not exclusively attributable to the upsurge of sexual wishes.

This chapter will focus on various aspects of young adolescents and early adolescence in the light of biological, cognitive and psychosexual changes. Case material will be used to highlight and illustrate treatment issues related to this developmental phase and to describe the role of the therapist as a new developmental object.

Biological aspects of puberty

Endocrinal changes

A complex feedback system involving various hormone-producing glands governs sexual development during puberty. What factors cause the onset of puberty is still obscure. Increased secretion of androgens results in the production of live sperm and the secondary sex characteristics: the growth of pubic hair and the lowering of the voice. Increased androgen levels account for some changes in the pubertal girl (hair under arms and pubic hair). Menstruation and breast development result from the female hormones, oestrogens (Sroufe *et al.* 1996). These endocrinal changes are accompanied by additional somatic changes, in skin and sweat glands. The endocrinal changes and growth spurt start for boys 2 years later than girls (Tanner 1990). Although biological factors stand out, clinical experience and empirical research make it increasingly clear that a variety of psychological factors are also involved (Livson and Peskin 1980; Heuves 1991).

The timing and tempo of puberty are not related to each other. The onset of puberty can occur as early as 8 years in girls and 9½ years in boys, or as late as 13 in girls or 13½ in boys. The complete physical maturation process may take as little as 1½ years or as long as 6 years (Steinberg 1993). Peer differences in development or developmental rates are an important source of personal concern and uncertainty (narcissistic vulnerability). Girls and boys who mature late show more stability and have a longer pre-adolescent period, important for the development of coping skills and a firm and adequate defence structure. The early maturers are slightly more at risk of deviant behaviour and substance abuse (Anderson and Magnussen 1990). In addition they engage in sexual activity at an earlier stage. Strikingly, the perception of the young adolescent of his/her maturational timing is most predictive for adolescent behaviour. Adolescents who estimate themselves to be early maturers may see themselves as ready to engage in adult behaviour. Several authors have observed that sexual relationships of young adolescents (especially boys) are often aimed more at satisfying sexual curiosity than at having a relationship (Heuves 1991; Spruiell 1975).

Cognitive development in early adolescence

Throughout the psychoanalytic literature on adolescence the importance of cognitive development is stressed. Cognitive development during puberty consists of a gradual but marked increase in a range of mental capacities. Whereas the thinking processes of children are related to concrete reality, young adolescents are gradually more able to think about possibilities and impossibilities (abstract thinking) and to evaluate their behaviour in their mind. Their growing ability to think about thoughts (metacognition) and the rapid growth of introspection are of particular importance. The young adolescent gradually discovers that human interactions are based not only on behaviour, but also on feelings and thought

(Selman 1980). During the transition from latency to puberty, Sarnoff (1976) notices a gradual shift in fantasy life from thoughts about fantasy objects (such as fairy-tale persons, monsters and amorphous demons) to real objects (such as movie stars, singers, models, robbers and kidnappers).

This dramatic widening of cognitive horizons not only increases curiosity and the search for truth but is often also a frightening experience. Thoughts about the concept of eternity and infinity may take over and confront the adolescent with the triviality of his own existence, which may in turn shatter his fragile narcissism. Introspection opens up possibilities for the young adolescent to become gradually more able to verbalize his feelings and thoughts, evaluate his experiences and empathize with others. Cognitive development provides the young adolescent with the ability to think about his parents and his family. The young adolescent starts to compare his life with that of other adolescents, gradually becoming more able to evaluate and question parental style. The increase of sexual urges is not solely responsible for the detachment from and turning away from the parents (Steinberg 1993). It may be hypothesized that the growing cognitive capacities of the young adolescent contribute greatly to the characteristic de-idealization of the parents. This painful process of de-idealization is felt as a loss. The growing very painful awareness of the erosion of parental omnipotence and omniscience brings in its wake the shattering of the prospect of his own future perfection. The de-idealization of the parents and the erosion of future perfection are strong motives for turning away from the parents.

Cognitive development allows the young adolescent to explore the external reality and increase reality testing. Many sensitive young adolescents also want to explore their inner world. However, due to the rapid physical and psychological changes, young adolescents often find it difficult to know what they really feel, which increases their vulnerability to magical thinking and illusions. The inner world of the young adolescent is very often a *fata Morgana*.

On the other hand (Pincus and Dare 1978), adolescents are able to be painfully frank about their family and the pathology of the parents, and are able to make adequate comparisons with the lifestyle and parenting styles in other families (Elkind 1981). Some adolescents in very disturbed families seem to be able to function quite well, however much they may have suffered from the stress at home. Both the parents' awareness of their own pathology, as well as the child's experience with a significant good object other than the parents, seem to be a crucial contribution to their resilience (Heuves 2000).

Narcissism in early adolescence

For most children, healthy narcissism is safeguarded by the unquestioned love from their parents. However, during this period of development they lose many of the familiarities of childhood both outside and inside themselves. This vulnerable narcissism is experienced as an extreme sensitivity to shame and shaming experiences. Following their cognitive development, young adolescents become smaller in a growing world. This cognitive capacity, the process of separation and the painful experience of de-idealization of the parents and self contribute to the narcissistic crisis of early adolescence, leaving them more vulnerable to shame (Levin 1971). The avoidance of shame and embarrassment becomes a most prominent motive in all relationships. Dramatic bodily changes can make them feel like strangers in their own bodies and contribute to the young adolescent's narcissistic fragility. As the young adolescent has to rely increasingly on the peer group for his narcissistic equilibrium, many young adolescents prefer severe punishment from the parents to deprecation by peers. Relationships during early adolescence often have strong narcissistic overtones, in which young adolescents share many activities, but few thoughts and feelings. Winnicott (1961) stresses that the young adolescent is essentially very much alone: 'Young adolescents are collections of isolates, attempting by various means to form an aggregate through the adoption of an identity of tastes' (p. 80). It is from a position of isolation that a beginning is made which may result in relationships between individuals.

Psychosexual development in early adolescence: changing affects, fantasies and self representation

The crucial task of the adolescent is to integrate in his mind the sexual aspects of his body and to accept that from now on sexuality will play a role in all human relationships.

In 1905 Freud published his now well-known three essays on the theory of sexuality. In his third essay, the theory of the sexual development of puberty, he describes the pubertal changes, which are destined to give infantile sexual life its final, normal shape. A central notion in Freud's work is the necessity for a particular convergence of love and sexuality, an integration of tenderness and aggression in one object relation. Sexual excitement is awakened from three sources: external stimuli, internal organic stimuli and mental processes. Sexual excitement evokes sexual activity leading to orgasm. Sexual excitation is both stressful and pleasurable, introducing the concept of fore-pleasure. Not until puberty is a sharp distinction established between masculine and feminine characteristics. The process of puberty establishes the primacy of the genital zones. During the latency period, children learn to feel for other people who help them in their helplessness and satisfy their needs. Their love is modelled on and is a continuation of their own more infantile relationship with their mothers. Children behave as though their dependence on the people who look after them were in the realm of sexual love. A child sucking at his mother's breast has become the prototype of every loving relationship. The finding of an object during adolescence is in fact a refinding. The barrier against incest is maintained by the postponing of sexual maturation until the child can respect the cultural taboo upheld by society. The sexual life of youth is almost entirely restricted to indulging in fantasies. Freud stresses the incestuous nature of these fantasies. When incestuous fantasies are overcome, detachment from parental authority is completed.

Based on Freud's work and explicitly formulated by Jones (1922), most psycho-analytic authors conceptualize adolescence as a recapitulation of early infantile development in the context of a maturing sexual body. Most psychoanalytic authors (Blos 1962; Freud 1958; Laufer and Laufer 1984) credit the increasing drive pressure, a consequence of maturation, as the motor of adolescent development. Anna Freud (1936, 1958) described in depth the adolescent's internal struggles between his sexual wishes, his defences and superego development.

Several authors approach this developmental phase from the perspective of a separation–individuation process (Blos 1985; Esman 1980; Jacobson 1964), in which the adolescent has to abandon childhood dependence on the parents. According to others (Spruiell 1975; Kohut 1971) the changes in narcissism or the transformations of the self are the central adolescent issues. Many other authors have made substantial contributions to a psychoanalytic theory of adolescence (for an overview see Tyson and Tyson 1990). Most authors emphasize that the body, which until puberty was experienced as a passive carrier of needs and wishes, now becomes the active force in sexual and aggressive fantasies and behaviour. Put differently, the main developmental function of adolescence is the establishment of the final sexual organization. This *ownership of the body* is probably the most important task for the adolescent (Laufer and Laufer 1984). Sexuality is both a central preoccupation for young adolescents and a secretive, much concealed topic.

The primal scene is an anchor-point for the sexual fantasies which promote psychosexual development. Adult sexuality, what adults actually get up to, is at the centre of his curiosity. Masturbation is of great help to the adolescent in helping him integrate the sexual aspects of his life into a new self-image and in diminishing the threats of sexual and/or aggressive acting out. In combination with the new cognitive possibilities, masturbation functions as an important protection of the fragile narcissism of the adolescent and helps to sort out different aspects of his/her sexual desires and wishes. In the more severely disturbed adolescent masturbation often has a defensive function in that it keeps the adolescent away from having to participate adequately in peer relationships. In other disturbed adolescents the masturbation fantasies hold the threat of perverse and sadistic acting out at bay. In some severe cases, masturbation serves as a protection against homicide and disintegration (Laufer and Laufer 1984).

Psychosexual development brings about a gamut of new feelings. For the young adolescent, the intense sexual feelings and excitement can sometimes be over-whelming experiences. The expression and regulation of sexual feelings are a challenge to the young adolescent. Masturbation plays an increasingly important role. However, during the early stages of puberty masturbatory activities often evoke intense feelings of shame and guilt, which may, especially in young adolescent girls (Laufer and Laufer 1984), lead to inhibition. During the early phase of adolescence, these new sexual feelings are not yet exclusively related to sexual situations. During early adolescence all states of arousal may give rise to sexual fantasies. An anxious social situation may unintentionally arouse a sexual response or acquire a sexual connotation. Generally speaking, during early adolescence all emotionally significant object relationships may become sexualized. Furthermore, in peer group interactions a young adolescent may be confused and insecure about whether or not a sexual behaviour is wanted or expected.

Young adolescents frequently express feelings of boredom, which are often related to an agitated dissatisfaction about their own actions. Since sexual feelings are not exclusively related to sexual situations, Fenichel (1937) assumed that this often sultry boredom is related to a forbidden excitement about parental sexuality, accompanied by a restlessness for which the young adolescent does not yet have an outlet, or for which the outlet through masturbation is a taboo. More generally speaking, boredom is often a defence against sexual arousal in a non-sexual situation (Winnicott 1961).

Sexual fantasies and the regulation of desires

For most mildly disturbed or neurotic young adolescents, sexuality and sexual curiosity are of prime importance. In most psychoanalysts' experience, however, young adolescents can hardly directly communicate their preoccupation with sexual fantasies (and to a lesser extent sexual behaviour) during treatment. This is felt to be too embarrassing, too seductive or too dangerous. Consequently, the presumed incestuous nature of their fantasy life is more a construction on the part of the analyst than a clinical fact. The more seriously disturbed adolescents, on the other hand, are more open about their sexual fantasies (Laufer and Laufer 1989) and may talk about fantasies of a perverse and incestuous nature. In normal development, the incest taboo is firmly established during the infantile Oedipal phase. From a clinical perspective one may assume that overt incestuous fantasies and behaviour are more likely in those adolescents who suffer from serious deficits in the infantile Oedipal phase or from pathological Oedipal conflicts. The next vignette describes an episode in the analysis of a young adolescent for whom sexual fantasies played an important role.

Arnold

Arnold is 13 years old and the third son of an intact family with high intellectual standards. He has two older brothers of 16 and 20 years old and two younger sisters. Arnold was an excellent pupil at school, but in the first year at secondary school there was a breakdown. His results at school deteriorated rapidly and he blatantly stole money from his parents. One afternoon he ran away from school and to his parents' great alarm returned home late that evening. He did not want to tell where he had been or what he had done. He sobbed to his parents that he had been unhappy for years and did not think his life worth living.

Arnold was a depressed and shy boy. It soon became clear that he was isolated from his peer group. From the outside he appeared to be a well-adapted boy, always trying his best at school and to meet the demands of the adults around him.

His inner world, however, showed an obstinate protest against and an intense jealousy of his older brothers, whom he thought of as very socially successful. Behind his apparent adaptation, Arnold struggled with intense conflicts about separation and a secretive omnipotence.

He told me that his crisis came to the fore during a school party. There was a girl he liked very much and all evening he took the opportunity to stand close to her, without speaking a word 'of course'. At the end of the party, she left with an older boy and looked at him in a very contemptuous way. This had upset him greatly. Our therapeutic encounter gradually evolved into a typical psychoanalysis of a young adolescent boy. At times we were clumsily bored, often did not know what to say to each other and to avoid protracted silences frequently played chess. I felt that my interventions hardly had any effect at all. In the counter-transference, I gradually experienced the uneasy feelings I grew familiar with in the treatment of other young adolescents: feelings of helplessness, provoked by a thinly concealed contemptuous attitude, the lack of reciprocity in the relationship and the counter-depression.

On a Monday morning in the seventh month of his analysis, Arnold told me about a family reunion in the country. He attended this with his father and sisters. For the occasion the family had rented a series of holiday bungalows. At the end of the afternoon, the family gathered and deliberated who was to share the various bedrooms. It was decided that Arnold would share a bedroom with an uncle he knew very well. He did not object and the family spent a pleasant evening with each other. During the night, however, he noticed that he was right at the edge of the double bed he shared with his uncle. He did not sleep that night. When I asked him whether he had been afraid to go to sleep, he denied this vigorously. The bed had been noisy, the room had been too warm and his uncle was a restless sleeper.

From a classical psychoanalytic viewpoint, we can interpret Arnold's experience as an expression of his fear and defence against incestuous homosexual feelings which were projected onto his uncle. Also I wondered why he was suddenly so confiding about his experience. Was he putting me in a position to rival his father and uncle? Was he seducing me into a conversation about homosexuality? I kept silent for a while, partly because as the psychoanalyst of a young adolescent one is in a difficult position. What can be said – as a male alone in the room with a young adolescent boy – about homosexuality, without being either intrusive or seductive? I asked him how he felt about sleeping in one bed with his uncle, now that he was no longer a boy. Arnold took the opportunity to deride his father by whom he had felt humiliated that afternoon. During the following sessions, I was able to ask him some remaining questions about the incident. Why had he not protested against the decision to share a bedroom with his uncle? He was not a child anymore. Why not stand up for yourself? etc. With some regret, I found myself asking him whether he was afraid of what could happen when two men sleep in the same bed. Questions like this may seriously impede the analytic process and lead to a stalemate, acting out or a precocious termination. There was little progress in the analysis and I noticed, to my dismay, that I understood little of what had, during the weekend, upset him so very much. I was able to find an opening when I pondered aloud that he must have felt alone that night. Not only was he angry with his father, but also struck by his sudden embarrassment that he missed his father during the night, although he was not a child anymore. With the typical philosophical pubertal mind, Arnold talked to me about a fear he had of something that might be bigger than him and in which you may even disappear. I felt we had made a start in understanding this episode, during which his fear of being overwhelmed by sexual feelings and his problems in regulating the sexual tension were crucial.

Anna Freud (1936) writes about the intense anxieties a young adolescent may feel regarding the intensity of his impulses. Some adolescents experience insufficient inner structure to integrate the strong increase of sexual feelings. As mentioned earlier, the young adolescent is confronted with the loss of parental protection offered during latency when parents limit the expression of his wishes and impulses. Anna Freud adds that many adolescents are suspicious of their own sexual wishes, because they feel something they have never felt before. Much of this distrust occurs rather unnoticed because of the conflict between wishes and conscience.

From this perspective Arnold's story was not exclusively about homosexual seduction, based on idealization and negative Oedipal fantasies, but also indicative of an intense anxiety about his intense sexual feelings. Arnold was confronted with the important adolescent task of regulating his potentially overwhelming sexual affects. His mainly passive ways of regulating his affects became more maladaptive as Arnold grew into puberty (Westen 2000). Also, I silently wondered about his uncle's feelings during the night. A young adolescent may elicit strong erotic feelings in an adult. Were they both taken hostage by the same fantasy?

The Oedipus complex: dyadic and triadic positions in early adolescence

The Oedipus complex is not defined by behaviour or interactions between parents and children. It is an intrapsychic constellation, which can occasionally be glimpsed in the behaviour of parents and children, but actually takes place within the representational world of the child. It is precisely this invisibility which gives the Oedipus complex its propelling developmental force. The absence of sexual behaviour between parents and children is an essential condition for this developmental achievement. The actual physical and psychological presence of the primal objects, the quality of the parental relationship, the parenting style and the history of the family are the external conditions of the Oedipus complex.

The Oedipus complex emerges from the child's fantasy about the parental relationship and confronts the child for the first time in its life with the prototype of a new class of relationships, in which a third person adds a new dimension to all relationships. The Oedipus complex is a painful erosion of the childish belief that all people love each other in the same way. It provides the child with the opportunity of being a participant in a relationship while being observed by a third person, as well as being an observer of a relationship between two people. The Oedipus complex brings about a fundamental reorganization of the mind and provides the child with the capacity to reflect on himself during interaction with others. A third position comes into being (Britton 1989).

Contemporary psychoanalysis has stressed the importance of both the father and the mother in the early development of the child. The child's experience of having a relationship with both parents is an important step in his awareness of family life. This experience has been subject to much discussion and to some research about the child's capacity to form triangular relationships (i.e. Abelin 1971, 1975; Sachs 1977).

Klitzing et al. (1999) present the outcome of a longitudinal study on the relational processes of early childhood using the concepts of triadification and triangulation. Referring to the work of Stern (1995), the authors define the interpersonal process taking place during interactions as 'triadification' and the intrapsychic process of experiencing a triad as 'triangulation'. In summary, triadification describes the interaction and triangulation describes the intrapsychic experience.

An important question concerns the internal representation of the triad in the mind of the young infant: is there a direct link between triadification and triangulation? Many psychoanalysts hold that a firm internal representation of a triangular relationship is not very likely to occur before 18 months (Abelin 1971, 1975; Tyson and Tyson 1990). On the other hand, most researchers on infant development would suggest that the infants' early capacities to identify the invariants that describe dyadic patterns would equally operate on triadic patterns of interactions. As yet the research about the relationship between mother–father–child questions the psychoanalytic tenet that triangular relations follow dyadic processes. Many researchers conclude that dyadic and triadic processes are separate but related parallel developments (Burhouse 2001; Klitzing et al. 1999). This may give rise to an evaluation of the difference between pre-Oedipal (dyadic) and Oedipal (triadic) development. It suggests that dyadic and triadic object relationships are two separate developmental lines, which have their own developmental dynamics present from early on in life.

From this one could conceptualize a different view of Oedipal development during adolescence. The classical psychoanalytic view of a linear developmental progression from the pre-Oedipal dyadic relationship to the Oedipal triadic relationship is at odds with recent research and observational studies which point to a parallel development. The concept of the Oedipal development during adolescence has not changed since Freud. The view that the young adolescent finds an adult solution for his infantile sexual wishes after recovering from a healthy regression to pre-Oedipal, incestuous fantasies and homosexual conflicts needs serious reconsideration. One could also view adolescent development as an oscillation between dyadic and triadic positions. The dynamic interplay between these positions accounts for the swings between regressive and progressive shifts in adolescent development as well as the often capricious mood. The dynamic interplay between the dyadic and triadic position is the outcome of the personal history, the infantile organization of the personality, the actual developmental tasks and the actual environment. The dyadic and triadic positions relate to different, i.e. adequate and less adequate, ways of dealing with adolescent tasks, and to different processes in the treatment (see Figure 10.1).

Triadic position	Dyadic position
Normal adolescent development	
Separation from the primal objects	Dependence on the primal objects
Depressive anxieties	Paranoid schizoid anxieties
Acknowledgement of the differences between the sexes	Desexualization of relationships
Active exploration of reality	Preference for fantasy play
Integration of sexuality in body image	Desexualization of own body
Verbalization of inner life	Narcissistic retreats
Adolescent psychopathology	
Conflicts about sex-role identity	Disavowal or negation of sex differences
Ambivalent relationship to reality	Passive turning away from reality
Adaptation of self to reality	Adaptation of reality to self
Separation anxiety	Collusion with primal objects
Identity conflicts	Identity confusion
Treatment of adolescents	
Learning from experience and insight	Avoidance of meaningful relationships
Reciprocity in relationship	Avoidance of reflection
Brings material to the treatment	Keeps material away from the treatment
Acting out as expression of inner conflict	Acting out as a destruction of meaning
Internalization and development of therapeutic relationship	
Verbalization	Projective identification
Therapist as a transference object	Therapist as a developmental object
Therapist has a 'mind thinking about me'	No stable self-representation in therapist's mind
	Therapist has a fragmented mind

Figure 10.1 Dyadic and triadic phenomena in adolescence.

Young adolescents in psychoanalytic treatment

For several reasons the treatment of young adolescents is always difficult. Puberty is a period of secrecy and often, while the adults agree that a treatment is urgent, the young adolescent disagrees (Fraiberg 1955). The therapist is frequently perceived as an extension of the parents, thus strengthening the young adolescent's objection. In all likelihood, one of the core reasons for the young adolescent's resistance to treatment is the feeling of humiliation of needing help from an adult to grow up. Alongside this are the intense fears of going crazy. The question of how to motivate a young adolescent to enter treatment has been dealt with by several authors (Aichhorn 1925; Fraiberg 1955; Freud 1958). However, in addition to these initial difficulties, which may lead to a premature ending of the treatment, other problems may arise. Because of the rapid shifts between triadic and dyadic positions, it is often difficult for the therapist to find the right mode of relationship with the young adolescent patient. During one session the therapist may feel that there is some reciprocal relationship in which the verbalization of feelings is present, whereas the following session the therapist is confronted with a taciturn young adolescent who is unable or unwilling to relate adequately to the therapist and hides behind a feigned stupidity or attitude of contempt. An important reason for these, often rapid, shifts is the narcissistic vulnerability of the young adolescent throughout this developmental phase. The interventions of the psychoanalyst are often experienced as an intrusion, an invasion into the inner world.

In addition, the young adolescent experiences the therapeutic situation as a threatening seduction, due to the young adolescent's fear that all arousal may evoke sexual excitement. In the especially vulnerable young adolescent, merely being in a consulting room with just one other adult may easily be felt as seductive and a motive to act out in a sexual way. In order to ward off this vulnerability the young adolescent often chooses a dyadic position. The therapist is impressed by the young adolescent's detached and remote, or even contemptuous attitude. This dyadic position increases the risk of a pseudo-therapeutic contact with the young adolescent, in which the narcissistic armour may become an unassailable fortress. Rather than saying 'I am in therapy', young adolescents tend to say 'I have a therapist'. In her article on patients who are difficult to reach, as is often is the case with young adolescents, Joseph (1975) assumes that these patients do not come to treatment to understand themselves, but from the need to be understood by the therapist. Due to their narcissistic vulnerability young adolescents are reluctant to think or hear about their inner life (triadic position); they seem more interested in what the therapist may think about them (dyadic position).

From a technical point of view this may mean that interventions aimed at the inner world of the young adolescent put a strain on the therapeutic relationship. To the extent that these interventions are correct, this may even lead to severe acting out. In the more disturbed adolescent who has approached the developmental tasks from a dyadic position, interventions aimed at the inner experiences may increase paranoid fears and evoke acute feelings of shame, which will eventually jeopardize the therapeutic relationship. These patient-centred (Steiner 1993) interventions aimed at the inner world of the young adolescent may have an adverse effect, whereas analyst-centred interventions may demonstrate to the young adolescent the way in which the analyst understands his patient. For a young adolescent who is not yet convinced that an insight may be helpful, the experience of being understood by the therapist is an important development promoting experience. Analyst-centred interventions may strengthen the connection between the young adolescent's inner world and the therapist's mind. Bion (1962) referred to this rapacious curiosity as 'eating a mind' and he assumed this cannibalistic attitude of the young adolescent to be a forerunner of a reciprocal emotional relationship. Closely related to these phenomena are Anna Freud's observations about stealing during adolescence. Many adolescents occasionally steal. Young adolescents like to steal from the adult world. They download music from the Internet, because they feel they are entitled to it. More often than not young adolescents are jealous of the adult world and its privileges, i.e. sexuality, money, independence and intimate relationships. They are especially envious of what they perceive as the adult's peace of mind. For this reason a young adolescent finds it difficult to receive something from the adults around him. It will undermine his fragile feelings of independence and competence. Simultaneously, however, young adolescents feel that they are entitled to the privileges of the adult world. Simply taking or stealing is a way of solving this paradox and adults are often stunned by the ingenious way in which young adolescents may deceive or bribe their superegos.

From this perspective one may empathize with the difficulty young adolescents have being in treatment. On the one hand they need the therapist's interpretation to understand their inner world, while at the same time they cannot accept an adult offering this insight. Stealing an insight from the psychotherapist is a typical adolescent solution. Psychoanalysts do not need their interpretations to be heard by the young adolescent; however, such interpretation needs to be left in the room for the adolescent to take away.

The psychoanalyst as a developmental object

The young adolescent lives in the here and now. As they are close to childhood, thinking about the past always brings the risk of regression. In the transference relationship the young adolescent re-enacts and relives past relationships with the primal objects. Interpretations of these past relationships carry the risk that they will enhance a reinforcement of the young adolescent to the primal objects or may even re-install the pathogenic object relation with them. It is this, in my view, which makes analytic treatment with vulnerable young adolescents such a complicated process. Many aspects of the transference cannot be interpreted but have to be contained within the psychoanalytic situation or dealt with in a different way. The treatment is often more effective if it is aimed at promoting the conditions for development. The analyst continues to take up the negative transference but uses his clinical acumen to determine how directly to do this. Arnold's very passive behaviour, with its homosexual overtones, was best taken up by interpreting his resistance to more mature behaviour (his dyadic position as a defence against a triadic position) rather than directly in the transference to the anlayst.

The concept of the psychoanalyst as a developmental object is of special importance for therapeutic work with young adolescents. Tähkä (1993) and Hurry (1998) have written extensively about the subject. In their approach the psychoanalyst functions as a new developmental object, who supports the ego of his young patients, helps in affect regulation and impulse control, and promotes interactions and reality testing. Interpretations are aimed at separating reality and fantasy, while introducing the use of language to promote reflection and to regulate affect. The psychoanalyst directly addresses the primitive defences and destructive behaviour in order to safeguard the therapeutic relationship. The psychoanalyst provides the young adolescent with a model of a working mind, which can think and talk about inner experiences and modulate affects. The analyst promotes reflection and verbalization instead of magical belief in action. Taking the position of a developmental object may be especially important for the treatment of young adolescents whose psychological life is characterized by fragile mental representation of themselves and others, low frustration tolerance, poor impulse control, low self-esteem, cognitive impairments and other features that are typically related to the dyadic position.

Clinical vignette

Peter

Peter was just over 13 years old when he was referred to me for treatment. His major symptoms were encopresis and constipation, from which he had suffered for many years. It was unclear whether there ever had been a distinct period in his life without the encopresis. He defecated in his pants approximately three times a week, sometimes more and sometimes less. The encopresis only occurred at home and during the day, indicating the psychogenic nature of his complaints. Peter was unaware when he defecated or after it had happened. He did not feel it in his pants, nor did he smell it, in contrast to other family members. After further inquiry, it struck me that he had hardly any feelings in or awareness of his body. The dissociation from his body was quite severe. Hunger was often a diffuse experience and he could not feel when he was satiated. He had difficulties estimating whether it was cold or warm outside. Even when injured he hardly felt pain. He had severe difficulties in anticipating his bowel movements and was consequently rather accident prone.

Peter started treatment at a child psychiatric outpatient clinic. Treatment started with enemas to provoke bowel movement and to increase sensitivity in his bowels. When this treatment failed, a behavioural therapy was recommended. This consisted of a meticulous programme of monitoring Peter's eating habits and defecation, accompanied by a complicated system of reward and punishment. In this somewhat compulsive family these systems were practised with intense rigour. When this treatment appeared to be of no avail and Peter became increasingly withdrawn, family therapy was suggested. The parents, however, had lost their confidence and stopped treatment altogether while they continued with the monitoring system and the reward/punishment schedule. After half a year they again decided to seek help for Peter and he was referred to me for consultation.

Peter was the oldest son of an intact family. He had two sisters, who were 3 and 6 years younger. His mother was a vulnerable, somewhat depressed woman. She came from a family where the father had left when she was 2 years old. She had seen her father only once. The relationship with her mother remained problematic and Peter's mother had never been able to undo the enmeshed ties to her mother. Peter's parents spoke about her in a rather disparaging manner. Peter's father was a somewhat awkward man. He came from a large middle-class family and still idealized his rather dominant father. Both parents were management consultants and valued achievement. There were strict rules at home since behaving well was more important than feeling well. The two girls did very well at school and were a source of pleasure and pride for their parents. This was in sharp contrast to Peter, who was a marked underachiever at school. His intelligence was just below average. It was not difficult to detect father's deep disappointment in his only son. Both parents felt that they were not able to make contact with him. They did not know what was on his mind and worried about his future.

The parents were able to present a detailed description of Peter's development, but not of his first 3 years. They always had great difficulties in understanding his feelings and inner world. Mother recalled that as a baby he had been difficult to manage. He cried loudly and bathing him was often the only way to calm him down. Mother felt that attaining a reciprocal relationship with Peter had always been an effort. He was jealous when his oldest sister was born and soiled more frequently. Mother recalled that she was often angry with him, because she felt he was soiling deliberately. Both daughters had serious feeding problems during the first year. Dehydration and undernourishment led to several hospital admissions. Mother recalled that during these years Peter experienced intense anxiety attacks. She could not remember any feeding problems with Peter, but clearly remembered that she was always very worried about whether or not he was eating enough. With both daughters there were serious battles over eating. Strikingly, Peter never objected to the strict eating rules. He always adapted without any protest. As a toddler and during his latency years Peter made very few friends. Due to his encopresis it was not often possible to go out with friends or to stay overnight. He became quite isolated and gradually lost contact with most of his peers. According to the parents this never appeared to affect him very much. He was never in a bad mood and was always eager to please.

When I met Peter for the first time I saw a young adolescent boy, who appeared somewhat younger than his age. He had a pleasant face, was smiling and cooperative. However, it was not very difficult to see the anxieties and embarrassment behind his facade. His clumsiness and appearance of innocence and naivety immediately made me feel sorry for him.

Peter was always on time and always attended his twice weekly sessions. Superficially, he was very cooperative. He recounted all the events of the past days, but his accounts only dealt with facts and events. His world, in which he could only experience action and behaviour, was purely instrumental. He was able to talk about what he had done, but any sign of an inner experience or mentalization of events was strikingly absent. The encopresis could not be discussed. Any question about it was warded off with stunning indifference and disavowal. There was no awareness of feeling states and my attempts at probing for affects led to a kind of desperation in Peter and to a disorganization of our relationship. He was often in a dissociated state in which there were signs of intense confusion about who he was, what he wanted or hoped for himself. During most of our sessions, Peter was rather tense and closed, but in his painful awareness of my presence would often feel a deep sense of shame. In the treatment these experiences of shame were often, for me, the only sign that he was alive and that we had a relationship. I took this as a positive indication of success of the treatment.

Because of the severe dissociation and symptoms of encopresis, I suspected a possible history of sexual abuse; however, I was never able to find any indications or evidence for these suspicions. In a later stage of the treatment Peter told me about the 12 enemas that he had 2 years ago in a distant manner. He told me that the fluid squirted into the bowels felt like a heavy brick falling inside his belly. Each time, a different nurse administered these enemas. After the enemas he would go home by taxi and on several occasions he had huge bowel movements in the taxi. This was intensely embarrassing for him. I was shocked by his account and I noticed that Peter carefully tried to read my face for my reactions. I assumed that the severe dissociation from his body might partly be a reaction to this trauma.

A major part of our treatment was focused on understanding what was done to him and what the effect was for him and for the relationship with his parents. The dissociation from his body decreased dramatically once he could express himself more freely about the enemas and the treatment in the clinic. In addition, the ineffectiveness of reward and punishment schedules, which were a part of the behaviour therapy, very much increased his enormous sense of shame. In fact, the parents and Peter were very relieved when I suggested that they stop the detailed monitoring and the reward and punishment system which mother had continued to apply even after the unsuccessful termination of that treatment.

Since the mentalization was so primitive and the experience of feelings was still at the level of bodily sensations, my focus during the treatment was Peter developing more adequate expression of his fears and feelings. For instance, after half a year of treatment we made an important step forward when he was able to talk about the experience of being hungry as an awareness of 'having a painful hole inside yourself'. I came to understand that Peter expressed much of his inner life in this way. Due to my constant verbalizations of his primitive emotional states, Peter was gradually able to understand that I had a picture of who he was in my mind. He could become excited if I said, for example, that I recognized something he said or that he reminded me of something he had said before. He enjoyed my recalling and linking what he had expressed about himself during the various sessions. His curiosity about what I thought of him or how I understood what he had said greatly helped the treatment. These integrating forces were sometimes opposed by severe regressions to a level of psychotic disintegration. For instance, one week I had to cancel two sessions and simultaneously he also had a difficult week in school because of disciplinary measures, and also at home when his parents punished him for 'rebellious' behaviour. One afternoon during that week he was found in a bath of cold water, surrounded by floating faeces that he had smeared all over his face. This kind of regression diminished gradually thanks to his growing capacity to communicate about himself. From a compliant boy with severe symptoms he gradually changed into a moody, often contrary adolescent. Gradually he became more confident about expressing himself verbally and discovered that by his verbal communication he was able to make other people understand very accurately what he had in mind. This promotion of symbolization paved the way for the disappearance of his symptoms.

In addition, the computer was of great help as a kind of intermediate and provisional device to communicate with me about himself. He was able to use the computer in a symbolic way. For instance, Peter used video games to make me understand his feelings and what happened between him and other people.

After 18 months of treatment Peter was able to take an important step. Discussing a game of chess on the computer he could think of a black Peter and a white Peter. The white Peter was the compliant, friendly and clean boy, but the black Peter – often concealed – was a different story. He wanted to show me the white Peter, whereas the black Peter was a 'shit' Peter. He fantasized that the black Peter was right behind his left shoulder, but (in an allusion to the devil) you could never turn your head fast enough to see him. For the first time, I felt that Peter was making an important step. Rather than being completely dissociated he was approaching experiencing an internal conflict between different aspects of himself, kept apart by a primitive split, in which the bad aspects of himself were projected outside himself into a black, persecuting figure behind his back. The episode of white and black Peter stimulated a further exploration of his emerging internal conflicts.

One obvious theme in the transference and counter-transference was making me feel helpless and powerless in the face of his severe encopresis. For example, at the end of a session he could say mockingly: 'Do you have an idea already about the cause of my encopresis? What could it be: my food, my drinks?' I told him that he was able to disempower everybody by his encopresis: the nurses, the doctor, his parents and me. Peter, with a big smile, emphatically said '*Yes*.' He counted the numbers: nurses, doctors, his parents, sisters and me. Then Peter added: 'This is nothing compared to people who can really make many people powerless: a one with nine zeros: Hitler and Stalin.'

Not only did we catch a glimpse of his aggressive fantasies, but also the reaction formation of his own powerlessness to control his body and his helplessness in the face of his long history of encopresis and the traumatic treatment with enemas. From this point in the treatment I felt that we were increasingly engaged in a psychoanalytic treatment in which it was possible to address some of his internal conflicts about control and aggression and his secret fight and passive protest against his controlling mother. Although there were occasional setbacks, I felt that Peter was enabled to deal with adolescent preoccupations in a more active and age-adequate way, i.e. from a triadic position.

Many factors have contributed to Peter's problems. From what was known of his early childhood his parents remarked that he was a hard-to-manage child. They found it very difficult to understand his feelings. Beebe *et al.* (1997) emphasizes the importance of the intersubjective process of co-constructing an adequate relationship. From this perspective Peter's inadequate mentalization was built upon his mother's inability to understand his feelings, and vice versa. His crisis in adolescence brought about a timely therapeutic intervention which then made it possible for Peter to change this pattern.

The first part of Peter's treatment may be understood as an example of developmental therapy. During the first years of his treatment I mainly served as a developmental object. Interventions were aimed at the development of better reality testing and promoting of symbolization and reflection. Peter lived in a two-dimensional world with little feeling and thought, which hampered the solution of his severe symptoms. As a result of the therapy, Peter became more able to experience himself and other people from a triadic position. Throughout the treatment, I was impressed that Peter was able to overcome his paranoid fears about psychotherapy after his earlier traumatic treatment. His growing ability to reflect on himself and to make a reciprocal relationship with me helped him to better understand his inner world. Treatment terminated when Peter was almost 17 years old. We could discuss his wish and fears to leave home. He wanted to become a soldier and seriously considered applying for training. It was not difficult to see that Peter longed for a safe, well-structured environment. He did not find it very difficult to leave the treatment. He assumed that he would miss me, but he felt that should he need to he could come back.

References:

Abelin, E. L. (1971). The role of the father in the separation–individuation process. In McDevitt, J. B. and Settledge, C. F. (eds), *Separation–Individuation*. New York: International Universities Press.

Abelin, E. L. (1975). Some further observations and comments on the earliest role of the father. *International Journal of Psychoanalysis 56*: 293–302.

Adelson, J. (ed.) (1980). *Handbook of Adolescent Psychology*. New York: Wiley.

Aichhorn, A. (1925). *Wayward Youth*. New York: Viking Press.

Anderson, T. and Magnussen, D. (1990). Biological maturation in adolescence and the development of drinking habits and alcohol abuse among young males: a prospective longitudinal study. *Journal of Youth and Adolescence 19:* 33–42.

Beebe, B., Lachmann, F. and Jaffe, J. (1997). Mother–infant interaction structures and presymbolic self and object representations. *Psychoanalytic Dialogues* 7: 133–182.

Bernfield, S. (1938). Types of adolescence. *Psychoanalytic Quarterley* 7: 243–253.

Bion, W. R. (1962). *Learning from Experience*. London: Maresfield Reprints.

Blos, P. (1962). *On Adolescence: A Psychoanalytic Interpretation*. New York: Free Press.

Blos, P. (1985). *Son and Father: Before and Beyond the Oedipus Complex*. New York: Free Press.

Britton, R. (1989). The missing link: parental sexuality in the Oedipus complex. In Britton, R., Feldman, M. and O'Shaughnessy, E. (eds), *The Oedipus Complex Today*. London: Karnac.

Burhouse, A. (2001). Now we are two, going on three. *International Journal of Infant Observation* 4 (2): 51–67.

Coleman, J. C. (1961). *The Adolescent Society*. New York: Free Press.

DeHart, G. B., Sroufe, L. A. and Cooper, R. G. (2000). *Child Development: Its Nature and Course*. New York: McGraw-Hill.

Elkind, D. (1981). *Children and Adolescents: Interpretative Essays on Jean Piaget*. Oxford: Oxford University Press.

Esman, A. H. (1973). The primal scene: a review and a reconsideration. *Psychoanalytic Study of the Child* 28: 49–81.

Esman, A. H. (1980). Adolescent psychopathology and the rapprochement phenomenon. *Adolescent Psychiatry* 7: 320–331.

Fenichel, O. (1937). Zur psychologie der Langeweile. In *Aufsätze. Band I*. Olten: Walter.

Fraiberg, S. (1955). Some considerations in the introduction to therapy in puberty. *Psychoanalytic Study of the Child* 10: 264–286.

Freud, A. (1936). Triebangst in der Pubertät. In *Das Ich und die Abwehrmechanismen*. München: Kindler.

Freud, A. (1958). Adolescence. In *The Psychoanalytic Study of the Child, 13:* 255–278.

Freud, S. (1905). *Three Essays on the Theory of Sexuality. Standard Edition*, Vol. 7. London: Hogarth.

Heuves, W. (1991). *Depression in Young Male Adolescents*. Leiden: Academic Press.

Heuves, W. (2000). Non-traditional families and psychological development. Paper presented at the International Colloquium of the Anna Freud Centre, November 1999.

Hurry, A. (ed.) (1998). *Psychoanalysis and Developmental Therapy*. London: Karnac.

Jacobson, E. (1964). *The Self and the Object World*. New York: International Universities Press.

Jones, E. (1922). Some problems of adolescence. In Jones, E. (1948), *Papers on Pyscho-analysis*. London: Karnac.

Joseph, B. (1975). The patient who is difficult to reach. In *Psychic Equilibrium and Psychic Change: Selected Papers of Betty Joseph*. London: Routledge.

Katchadourian, H. (1990). Sexuality. In Feldman, S. and Elliot, G. (eds), *At the Threshold: The Developing Adolescent*. Cambridge, MA: Harvard University Press.

Klein, M. (1963). On the sense of loneliness. In *Envy and Gratitude and Other Works*. London: Hogarth.

Klitzing, K. von, Simoni, H. and Bürgin, D. (1999). Child development and early triadic relationships. *International Journal of Psychoanalysis* 80: 71–89.

Kohut, H. (1971). *The Analysis of the Self*. New York: International Universities Press.

Laufer, M. (1982). The formation and shaping of the Oedipus complex: clinical observations and assumptions. *International Journal of Psychoanalysis* 62: 51–59.

Laufer, M. and Laufer, M.E. (1984). *Adolescence and Developmental Breakdown.* New Haven, CT: Yale University Press.

Laufer, M. and Laufer, M. E. (1989). *Developmental Breakdown and Psychoanalytic Treatment in Adolescence.* New Haven, CT: Yale University Press.

Levin, S. (1971). The psychoanalysis of shame. In Socarides, C. W. (ed.), *The World of Emotions: Clinical Studies of Affects and their Expression.* New York: International Universities Press.

Livson, N. and Peskin, H. (1980). Perspectives on adolescence from longitudinal research. In Adelson, J. (ed.), *Handbook of Adolescent Psychology.* New York: Wiley.

Offer, D. and Offer, J. (1975). *From Teenage to Young Manhood.* New York: Basic Books.

Pincus, L. and Dare, C. (1978). *Secrets in the Family.* London: Faber and Faber.

Rieff, P. (1959). *Freud: The Mind of a Moralist.* Chicago: University of Chicago Press.

Rutter, M., Graham, P., Chatwick, O. and Yyle, W. (1976). Adolescent turmoil: fact or fiction? *Journal of Child Psychology and Psychiatry 17*: 35–56.

Sachs, L. J. (1977) Two cases of oedipal conflict beginning at eighteen months. *International Journal of Psychoanalysis 58*: 57–66.

Sarnoff, C. A. (1976). *Latency.* New York: Jason Aronson.

Selman, R. L. (1980). *The Growth of Interpersonal Understanding: Developmental and Clinical Analysis.* New York: Academic Press.

Spruiell, V. (1975). Narcissistic transformations in adolescence. *International Journal of Psychoanalytic Psychotherapy 4*: 418–435.

Sroufe, L. A., Cooper, R. G. and DeHart, G. B. (1996). *Child Development: Its Nature and its Course.* New York: McGraw-Hill.

Steinberg, L. (1993). *Adolescence.* New York: McGraw-Hill.

Steiner, J. (1993). *Psychic Retreats.* London: Routledge.

Stern, D. (1995). *The Motherhood Constellation.* New York: Basic Books.

Tähkä, V. (1993). *Mind and its Treatment.* Madison, CT: International Universities Press.

Tanner, J. M. (1990). *Fœtus into Man: Physical Growth from Conception to Maturity.* Cambridge, MA: Harvard University Press.

Tyson, P. and Tyson, R. L. (1990). *Psychoanalytic Theories of Development.* New Haven, CT: Yale University Press.

Westen, D. (2000). Integrative psychotherapy: integrating psychodynamic and cognitive-behavioral theory and technique. In Snyder, C.R. and Ingram, R. E. (eds), *Handbook of Psychological Change: Psychotherapy Processes and Practices for the 21st Century.* New York: Wiley.

Winnicott, D. W. (1961). Adolescence: struggling through the doldrums. In *The Family and Individual Development.* London: Routledge.

Zeanah, C. H., Anders, T. F., Seifer, R. and Stern, D. N. (1989). Implications of research on infant development for psychodynamic theory and practice. *Journal of the American Academy of Child and Adolescent Psychiatry 28*(5): 657–668.

Chapter 10

Developmental considerations in an adult analysis

Marie Zaphiriou Woods

In this chapter I describe how a woman, in her late thirties, used her analysis to develop emotional and cognitive capacities paralysed during a childhood characterised by neglect and emotional abuse. Early deficits, combined with ongoing trauma and conflict, had resulted in a developmental impasse, a 'standstill', which brought her to treatment as an adult. Always watchful, she had, until then, kept people at bay in a way that was matched internally by rigid defences against thinking and feeling. This way of coping had ensured survival in the face of complex internal and external dangers, but precluded live engagement with her inner, emotional, imaginative, sexual self or the world outside.

Neuroscientists have written extensively about the effects of trauma and abuse on the developing brain, particularly the right hemisphere, 'the locus of the emotional and corporeal self' (Schore 2001b), which adapts to the environment provided by the caregiver. 'The developing infant is maximally vulnerable to non-optimal and growth-inhibiting environmental events during the period of most rapid brain growth. During these critical periods of intense synapse production, the organism is sensitive to conditions in the external environment, and if these are outside the normal range a permanent arrest of development occurs' (Schore 2001a: 220). 'Any deprivation of optimal developmental experiences (which leads to underdevelopment of cortical, sub-cortical, and limbic areas) will necessarily result in persistence of primitive, immature behavioural reactivity' (Perry 1997: 129).

Perry et al. (1995) have shown that abuse gives rise to two separate psychobiological responses: hyper-arousal – a state of fear-terror – and then dissociation, if the threat persists. The repeated experience of unmediated stress that occurs in 'early relational trauma' (Schore 2001a) leads to sensitisation of the neural response patterns that are then elicited by quite minor stressors; a 'state' has become a 'trait' (Perry et al. 1995). The infant/young child remains in a 'persisting fear state', focusing on non-verbal cues, and unable to learn. Furthermore, persistence of the vegetative state, which acts to shut down metabolic activity, renders the child inaccessible to attachment communication and interaction regulation which would contribute to more sophisticated right brain development. This has long-term effects on affect regulation and attachment (Schore 2001a).

Schore (2001a) has explained toddlers' disorganised/disoriented ('D') attachment patterns as 'overt manifestations of an obviously impaired regulatory system, one that rapidly disorganises under stress' (p. 216). He links their typical behavioural response of freezing (becoming 'silent, blank, and dazed', 'excessively still, staring into space as though completely out of contact with self, environment, and parent' (Main and Solomon 1986: 119 and 120)) to the simultaneous activation of hyper-excitation and hyper-inhibition. The development of the 'D' attachment pattern was originally linked to frightened or frightening behaviour on the part of the caregiver (Main and Hesse 1990), but it is now thought that 'all experiences in infancy which strongly activate attachment behaviour without terminating it will result in disorganisation of the attachment system' (Hopkins 2000: 337). Such experiences, which include neglect and all forms of abuse, 'have in common the violation of the attachment system's inherent expectation of protection and security' (p. 337), necessitating powerful defensive strategies.

The analysis undermined Ms A's long-established avoidant defences, reviving her early experiences of neglect and abuse, and showing how they had become represented at, and organising of, subsequent phases of development. By offering insight into old patterns of being and relating within the context of a new relationship in which feeling, thinking, wishing, and imagining could occur safely (Hurry 1998), it potentiated the mental processes that had become arrested, distorted, and inhibited. This facilitated the building up of stable complex representations and contributed to the emergence of a sense of agency and competence, enhanced by positive interactions outside as well as inside the consulting room. This in turn helped modify her distorted self image and world view originally constructed on the basis of her wholesale identification with her disturbed mother and her own life experiences.

Focusing on the developmental movement of a 4½ year analysis puts an inevitable gloss over the many hours when Ms A and I felt stuck and despairing. I was helped during these periods by my observations of young children*, which regularly confronted me with the ebb and flow of normal development, toddlers' delight in provoking and frustrating their parents, and the occasional frozen child, with a history comparable to Ms A's, who could in time respond to sensitively attuned and playful interventions in a secure setting. It seemed natural that, when the analysis ended somewhat prematurely, Ms A should, like the children observed, follow the move from dyadic to triadic relationships with a group experience.

Background to treatment

Ms A sought analysis because she felt at a 'standstill'; her depression, fears, and 'sense of inadequacy' were such that she 'could not go on'. A therapist, whom she

---

* in an Anna Freud Centre toddler group and the Nursery

had started seeing once a week, supported the referral. The clinic consultant who assessed her concluded that Ms A had a hysterical personality accompanied by a defensive identification with her narcissistic mother – a religious fanatic and man-hater.

Her mother had dominated her provincial childhood. Leaving her father when she was 2 or 3, she took Ms A and her five siblings to live with their grandparents, who subsequently fell ill and died. The mother combated their abject poverty with a relentless regime of duty and prayer, and permitted only minimal contact with the outside world. When thwarted she had violent outbursts, regularly beating the oldest boy, who was mischievous. An older sister was a model child, and another brother was sickly, absorbing any available caring. Ms A was reportedly a fat baby who could be left in her pram for hours. She 'got through' school and was, like her two younger siblings, compliant, 'no trouble'. She rarely saw her father, who worked night shifts and died of a heart attack when she was 6.

At the start of the analysis, she was totally isolated, having quarrelled with her one childhood friend. She had failed to complete a professional training and had an unrewarding job. Deeply ashamed of the way she lived, she concentrated on presenting an impenetrable front to her workmates. She concealed her face under layers of make-up, her body in tight, unflattering clothes, and her unhappiness behind a hard, brittle manner. She had a number of physical symptoms, for which she had sought medical help.

The mummified baby, the toddler on a cushion, and the straitjacket

Three different but related images contributed to the understanding of Ms A's standstill:

- The mummified baby first appeared in a dream occurring during Ms A's previous therapy. The analysis revealed that layers of rigid maternal identifications cut the patient off from inside and outside experience in a way that had once been adaptive, even protective, but then became obstructive to further development.
- The toddler on a cushion referred to a piece of the patient's early history, according to which she would literally stand still, leaning her head against a cushion, whenever her mother left the room. The analysis showed how her disorganised, disoriented attachment to her unavailable and frightening mother, her hyper-vigilance, and tendency to dissociate manifested themselves at every level of development. On a fundamental level, the separation–individuation process had been compromised, contributing not just to her failure to develop a solid sense of herself, separate and different from her mother, but also to difficulties in exploring and learning about the world (Mahler *et al.* 1975; Furman 1992).
- The straitjacket of which Ms A complained in her first analytic session

provided additional control in the face of her fears of object loss, madness, and death, as well as humiliation and condemnation. It exacerbated the inhibitions that paralysed her and contributed to the curtailment of mentalisation and representation (Fonagy 1991).

Having found her previous therapy helpful in beginning to think about the role of her past in her present difficulties, Ms A approached her analysis in a very positive state of mind. She was prepared to use the couch, but admitted in our preliminary meeting that she was apprehensive; she liked to have her 'feet on the ground', and to keep a careful watch on people.

Divested of the means to do this, she was immediately anxious about being watched, caught out and criticised. She felt she had been in a straitjacket all her life and that her fear of condemnation made it difficult to do anything or be with people. As if to demonstrate this, she began to come late to her sessions and to finish talking early; she could not help herself and thought I must be furious with her. She was afraid of taking up too much of my time and of giving me ammunition with which to condemn her. She became frightened of making the smallest move on the couch, convinced she should 'stay in the corner' and 'not move or even breathe'.

Matter of factly, she described how, as a child, she had been permanently on her guard, separate from whatever was going on around her and anxious to avoid drawing attention to herself. At school, she had been terrified of the cross teachers, and at home of her big sister, who teased, bullied, and told tales. Her mother was initially described as doing her best; she had to keep the children quiet in the early years because their father slept in the day. There had, however, been the constant threat of physical violence, and, ultimately, of eternal damnation. Since God was omniscient, and thought was equated with deed, even fantasy was not safe. Ms A's solution had been not to think, which had infuriated her mother and teachers. When, in desperation, the school recommended home input into her learning, Ms A became mute with terror. On one unforgettable occasion, she had so enraged her mother that she threatened to stick a red-hot poker down her throat.

Ms A's idealisation of her mother was threatened by the emergent memories of her traumatic outbursts. She shifted to detailed accounts of the previous day at work, but the issues there were much the same; in particular, her boss, who had uncontrollable rages, bullied and humiliated her. Her therapy had enabled her to limit his abusive behaviour, which was consciously likened to her sister's. She told me triumphantly that she had 'turned the tables'. She presented as organised and in control, externalising onto others her denigrated image of herself as contemptibly vulnerable. She even kept hold of essential office information in the hope of rendering her boss and a colleague, with whom he was having an affair, as ignorant and helpless as she had always felt herself to be. Ms A dismissed the idea that she could be jealous of their sexual relationship, reminding me that her boss had propositioned her in the past. However, she was, in time, able to acknowledge that she felt excluded by their closeness in the way she had once felt excluded by her sister's special relationship with their mother.

The approach of the first long summer break undermined Ms A's brittle defences. Her story-telling began to falter and dry up and she fell silent in her sessions, telling me afterwards that she had felt blank and dazed. She became panicky, thinking that I must be getting impatient and angry. Her inability to think and speak reminded her of how she had been as a child. She had always assumed this was because she was stupid, as she was frequently called. More recently, when these states had prevented her from achieving further training, she had become convinced she had a brain disease. As she began to dread her empty weekends, she realised that she spent them in a similar stupefied state. She barely moved off the sofa, mindlessly staring out of the window, or watching television for hours. She felt she neither should, nor could, move.

She brought some significant fragments of history. Her mother had told her that she had taken away her bottle on her first birthday because the oldest boy, P, had shamed her by hanging on to his. Moreover, when she had had to leave the room, she would put Ms A by a chair, and she would rest her head on a cushion, not moving until her mother returned, no matter how long she was gone. Her other siblings had also told her that she had been terrified to walk, shaking with fear, and that they had had to teach her.

We then understood that Ms A experienced the breaks as the premature removal of her analytic feed, clinging to her sofa as she had once clung to the chair cushion and not moving until I returned. She was terrified to take independent steps, and never thought of protesting. I, like mother in the past, was too busy to spend time with or even think about her. She assumed she dropped out of my mind when she was not there, and realised she felt 'lost in space' when on her own. Suddenly, she began to cry, expressing horror at this display of emotion; even as a child, she had never cried, she was 'as cold as ice', i.e. identified with her cold, hard mother who had deplored demonstrations of affection and never touched her.

In a desperate bid to escape the repudiated pre-Oedipal longings emerging in the transference, Ms A developed a crush on a flirtatious older colleague. This brought her close to breaking point, since she felt totally unable to regulate her physical arousal, fearing loss of control, discovery and disgrace, and suffering intense guilt. When the confusion between her longings for closeness and adult sexuality was addressed, she associated to her mother's condemnation of even the most innocent of childhood friendships, and the recent confidence that mother had been sexually abused as a child. She was then able to acknowledge her 'child feelings' about my going away, sobbing bitterly that she had never, consciously, had such feelings before.

She found the first long analytic break 'harrowing', and said, when she returned, that it was as if she did not know who I was, as if she had never been here before. Over this and subsequent breaks, she 'lost' me completely from her mind and, in so doing, she lost herself, becoming hopeless, helpless, dazed and disoriented. Interrupting the analysis was like removing the chair and cushion; she lost the external structure that supported thinking and feeling and had no internal structure on which she could rely to represent her experience.

For the first of many times, Ms A recalled her earlier dream of a mummified baby falling through space. It seemed to refer to the way in which she had dealt with the 'unresolvable paradox' (Main 1995: 46) of needing her unavailable and sometimes terrifying mother, by identifying with her, the 'lost object' and 'aggressor' (Anna Freud 1936). In so doing, she had repudiated her needs and wishes and adopted her mother's paranoid view of the world, fearing and mistrusting people, perceived as intrusive and threatening. This view coincided with her own experience of her mother, compounded by her projected impulses. At this point in the analysis, she externalised onto her mother (and me in the transference) her wish for complete devotion. No other relationship could be countenanced (frequent phone calls home demonstrated this) and it was terribly 'selfish' to need or want anything else. She was so anxiously focused on pleasing and placating her objects that there was hardly space to explore her own mind. She said she had very little curiosity or imagination.

Realising that she might, after all, have a right to some life, Ms A developed a crush on another colleague, a widower of about her own age, who had shown her some interest. This infatuation gave us access to central Oedipal and pre-Oedipal conflicts and enabled Ms A to use the analysis to embark on a process of separation–individuation, much as toddlers practise in action, and adolescents in daydreams and masturbation fantasies, their first moves away from their primary objects.

To the extent that she found Jim physically attractive, Ms A was again flooded with sexual thoughts and feelings. She was 'heart-broken' whenever he spoke to a beautiful female colleague and worried about becoming too thin to compete, since she was finding it so difficult to eat or sleep. I interpreted the underlying wish to make herself less attractive because of her conflicts about being sexual. It emerged that she cut off all feelings for him, rebuffing his friendly attention and telling me 'my mother would be proud of me'. In line with her mother's view about men, the projection of her sexual wishes on to him made him at times a terrifying figure in her mind, a stalker or a sex maniac. The few sexual encounters she had had in her life had been with men who fitted the stereotype of being 'only after one thing', either terrorising her or desperately needy and disturbed. She had felt nothing and used no contraception. She had been celibate for some years.

Ms A was more inclined to feel rejected and to dismiss Jim following breaks from the analysis, after which her mind was again blank. She admitted that she felt angry with me for cancelling, since this proved that I did not want to be there for her. Via Jim, who, like mother in the past, actually was very busy with children, we saw that she felt that I too preferred to be with others. While she feigned indifference, she was in fact watching his, and my, every move, as she must have once watched her mother from her cushion, longing for a glance and then withdrawing and sulking when disappointed. Ms A was shocked to discover the extent of her wishes for exclusive attention ('110%!'), concluding 'I must be a very demanding person.' She was afraid that if she were to express her needs, I (Jim in the present, and mother in the past) would go completely mad or desert her. So she froze, blanking out her thoughts and feelings and becoming a 'non-person'. She said that she felt 'buried alive' and brought dreams of dead or dying people whom she saw as reflecting herself.

Ms A then understood that her mummification, with its defensive cutting off from herself and people, had been adaptive in the past, but was 'crippling' in the present, blocking her chances of developing real relationships. She decided to repair her relationship with her childhood friend, whom she now saw she had ruthlessly cut out of her life when the friend, married and with children, had become too busy to satisfy her inordinate expectations of unconditional support.

The discovery of father and a mind of her own

Ms A had always told me that she had not known who her father was when he visited in the period up to his death; she had only been aware that her mother was frightened of him, shaking and refusing to come to the door. She had assumed that her mother's loathing of men was based on her experience of him, and that he had beaten her, in the way he, and then she, had beaten P.

Ms A's repudiation of her father was so total that any attempt to take up her infatuations with her male colleagues in terms of her unconscious longing for a father made no sense to her. She was, however, deeply moved when Jim singled her out for a small favour, contrasting his goodness with her boss's bullying behaviour. When she recalled that her father had once done something similar, I suggested that she might once have similarly contrasted her father with her mother, feeling guilty both for her disloyalty and for being favoured. This did make sense. Ms A brought more memories of being singled out by her father, for instance when he sang her a song based on her name. She realised that she had assumed that she was the cause of his departure, which would have been fitting punishment for her Oedipal wishes. Regretfully, she reflected that her life would have been totally different if he had lived, since he was sociable and took them on visits. She expressed intense sadness at his loss.

The installation of a third object in her mind opened up the possibility of thinking more about difference and alternative identifications. Ms A became painfully aware of the extent of her mother's and sister's disturbance ('miserable and crazy'), and the consequent need to 'stand on her own two feet', to develop her own separate identity, and to find new objects. She said she could only conceive of doing this because I had never lashed out at her in the way she had always feared I would. However, she was still afraid that I would experience any move away from me as her turning her back on me, and that I would retaliate by going mad or stopping the analysis. She recalled her mother's threats that she would end up in the local psychiatric hospital if any of the children disobeyed her. She alternated between seeing her mother and sister (and me in the transference) as hugely powerful or terrifyingly fragile. She was tempted to return to her previous inertia. In the counter-transference, I felt as if I was carrying a great weight, verbalising her wish to be picked up. When Ms A saw that 'staying on the cushion' would not induce me to take over in the way her mother had always done, she was saddened but also relieved to have the chance to explore her own resources.

Her 'first steps' consisted of a new friendship with a kindly older woman at work, and some preliminary research into evening classes and a holiday abroad. She phoned her mother less often and stopped showering the family with presents. These tentative moves were accompanied by intense anxiety. Following a news bulletin about Yugoslavia, she dreamt that some people in Sarajevo were standing about outside, feeling hopeless, and waiting to get killed. She linked the dream to her attempts to get out in the world. She feared her mother's and sister's retaliation, and the loss of protection of always being told what to do. She added that once she moved out of her mother's orbit, she would never get from her the special relationship she so wanted.

As the second long summer break approached, Ms A complained of working too hard and not eating or sleeping sufficiently; she was becoming 'just skin and bone'. She recognised the reproach to me for leaving and not feeding her over the break. She was identified with both her mother's martyrdom ('the more you suffer the better you are') and the sickly brother who had taken her mother's attention. She realised how angry she was with me for neglecting her, the fat baby, who had been left for hours without protesting. Horrifying dreams in which corpses moved demonstrated her terror of allowing herself to come alive, to know her feelings, her rage in particular: 'rage wipes out everything good'. As she repeatedly lost track of her thoughts and her sentences trailed off, we had dramatic evidence of the way her fear of knowing her mind interfered with her thinking.

Ms A had always been afraid to think and to know, anticipating her mother's (and God's) blanket condemnation of any sexual or aggressive thoughts and feelings she might find within. She had also been afraid to explore the world outside, partly because she had lacked a secure base, but also because here too she might come upon forbidden knowledge. She told me that her mother had banned all secular reading matter and beaten the children for any interest that might be construed as sexual. More specifically, Ms A had felt she was not supposed to know the daily physical abuse of her brother taking place in another part of the house; she had heard terrifying noises, but had not allowed herself to think what they were until her brother told her recently. Weeping, she recalled how P had once crawled into the room following a beating. He was comforted by her littlest brother, while she remained 'indifferent', cut off.

She felt her mind was compartmentalised, and enumerated other secrets in the past and present that contributed to this. She had to recognise their full impact on her thinking when she discovered she was walking an extra 10 minutes to her session because she had not thought to wonder where her bus went on to. She was shocked to realise: 'I pull the wool over my own eyes', telling me that bandages had covered the mummified baby's eyes. To let herself see, inside and outside, would involve a violent separation from her mother and sister, who were experienced as wanting to keep her wrapped up in them. She had two dreams in which bodies were torn apart following a car crash. She associated to her loyalty conflict between me and these prior attachment models (Hopkins 2000), which we saw reflected her own internalised conflict about individuating and thinking for herself. In this context, the straitjacket was like a safety belt, protective but also restrictive.

The adoption of her mother's fundamentalist beliefs had precluded curiosity and learning. Ms A's thinking was often circular, with her tending only to see what fitted her theories and to ignore what contradicted them. This sealed system was slowly infiltrated as the real aspects of the analytic relationship percolated into her consciousness; I neither lashed out at nor dropped her, nor did I intrude or tell her what to do. Her experience of a new way of relating was extended into her workplace, where she began to allow real communication to take place, and so became acquainted with additional perspectives. She came to rethink her ego-centric and paranoid interpretation of events and became more aware of the impact of her behaviour on others.

In the analysis, she had to take on board that her repeated collapses into inertia affected me, when I used my feelings of being rendered helpless, blocked and frustrated to elucidate the transference–counter-transference situation. I said she was perhaps letting me know how she had felt as a child, while she, like her mother, was restrictive and guilt-inducing. She did not respond immediately except to express puzzlement that she could make me feel anything.

A few days later she came back to this interpretation, saying she had felt great afterwards – 'such a change from feeling helpless, like putty in people's hands'. She used her new sense of agency to tell Jim that she wanted to go out with him. They managed to have an ordinary, albeit inconclusive, conversation. That night, she dreamt that she was getting married, but then realised that she did not know the groom or anyone at the wedding, and that the dress was far too big. Reluctantly, she recognised that she did not feel ready for an adult relationship, fearing being taken over or abandoned, and that Jim had similar difficulties. In identification with her new confidant's kinder attitude, she was able to feel some sympathy towards him (and herself).

The building of stable complex representations

Having established some benign objects in her mind, Ms A became able to explore the darker aspects of the transference. Following her cancelling a session, she had a terrifying dream in which she was being driven by someone horrible. Her life was in danger and she had to be very careful – 'a bit like in here when I'm afraid to move in case you'll lash out'. Further associations, to cruel hypocritical tyrants and murderers (Saddam Hussein, Slobodan Milosevic), deepened our understanding of the maternal transference. I was the horrible driver, who was really furious with her for cancelling, and her mother, superficially calm and dutiful like me, had been responsible for savagely beating ('killing') P, the most independent-minded of the children. This had been perceived as punishment for daring to have a mind of one's own, but more fundamentally militated against developing one, because it was too terrifying to contemplate the murderousness in her mother's (my) mind

(Fonagy 1991). When we finally came to terminate the analysis, she was able to use the transference to elaborate the fantasy that her mother had wished her dead.

The anal–aggressive aspects of their relationship were explored when it was time for Ms A to reassess her contribution to the analysis. She felt completely unable to work out her budget, repeatedly postponing the task, and then wanting to name some random amount in the unthinking way she used to produce messy, careless homework. She became terrified that I would turn into a rage-filled monster, like her mother and teachers. She was even more afraid that if she were to calculate and let me know how much money she had, I would feel entitled to take every penny. I reconstructed a toilet-training battle, in which I was experienced as a terrifyingly powerful parent, determined to empty her of her body contents; she had no recourse but to obstinately withhold everything and reduce me to helplessness. Ms A then informed me that she had been constipated all her life; to defaecate had felt like moving, and so incurring her mother's rage. As she became dazed and switched off again in her sessions, it seemed that the only way she could feel safe was to hold everything in: motions and emotions, money and words. This kept out objects (mother/me) experienced as terrifyingly invasive, while at the same time inducing some continued involvement. She told me for the first time that in the dream of the mummified baby there was an image of her mother's hand letting her fall terrified through space.

As we worked on these issues belonging to the second and third year of life, Ms A reported the beginnings of object constancy. She said that she no longer felt surrounded by empty space and that she was beginning to trust me and maintain a link with me outside sessions. She felt this was important and precious and, for the first time, had a 'calm and happy dream', in which I told her I was having a baby. Ms A thought that she was the baby, starting again through me. She felt less frightened and alone, more confident and energetic. She started to attend evening classes and to socialise with colleagues during breaks. She finally worked out her budget, raising her fee and keeping enough money to spend on luxuries. She said the straitjacket was loosening, giving her a new sense of freedom.

The mobilisation of her resources brought fears of loss of control, of her rage, in particular, which, like her money, was equated with faeces. She pictured something grey and moving inside, like a bomb, potentially explosive and omnipotently destructive ('God help the world'). Her dreams and associations returned to smiling dictators who committed atrocities, and this time she was able to recognise that they referred to her self as well as her objects. Nervously, she confessed that she was afraid her anger could kill me. We saw that her distancing herself from people was as much for their protection as for her own.

Following this work, Ms A seemed to have attained sufficient object constancy to keep me in mind over the long summer break. She returned to report that she had enjoyed herself, going abroad and meeting men who were friendly without being overbearing. Eager to meet some more, she went clothes shopping and chose evening classes that would improve her qualifications.

Ms A's new aspirations brought conflicts on every level. She collapsed regularly into an exhausted, unthinking state, unable to get to her bed or her sessions on time. Her terror of my envy and jealousy came to the fore. She recalled a particularly traumatic incident, when, aged 25 she had come home late after a date. Her mother had gone berserk, pulling her around the room by the hair, and punching her, until a younger brother had woken and intervened. Crying and shaking, Ms A thought she must have 'switched off', she had been so unable to defend herself. She had relinquished the boyfriend without a thought. As she used the analysis to process this and similar incidents, Ms A thought she could now differentiate me more clearly from her mother and feel with some certainty that I would not attack her for being sexual.

However, the disorganisation in her life continued to escalate. It was understood as a negative therapeutic reaction, arising partly out of her envy and wish to coerce me into doing more for her. She told me her mother had decided everything for her. I felt invaded by her passive control, and said that she was treating me and wanted me to treat her as if we were not separate persons with minds of our own. This made her thoughtful, and she subsequently reported feeling less watched and followed. Through dreams, she brought her desperate wish to hang on to me until her pre-Oedipal needs to be held and attended to were satisfied. She remembered being taken to her first day of school on the back of her mother's bike, dreading the prospect of a long day away from her. Ms A recognised that she had been attached to her mother, but that associating attachment with unmanaged and unmanageable separation and loss, she had denied it. She expressed the wish that, unlike her mother, I might 'hold her hand' for her to go out into the world. She said she could not think if I was not there.

Further progress was not possible, however, without the exploration of the perverse gratification involved in the sado-masochistic transference. Through Ms A's fascination with media accounts of violence and torture and the constant implicit reproach to me that I was torturing her by expecting her to come to early-morning sessions, we were able to approach her masochism. I interpreted our interactions in terms of her sadistic intercourse fantasies. Ms A denied that she got any masochistic gratification from her suffering, or that she had a conflict about masturbation, which I had suspected might be the cause of the late nights. However, she told me that she had once joked with her sister that her mother must have been a 'rape victim' or knocked over the head for their father to have had sex with her. And that she herself had 'lain like a corpse' in her first sexual relationship, with a man who had used and abused her for over a year, becoming violent when she ended their contact.

Ms A was then able to think about leaving her job, in which she felt similarly maltreated. Acquiring the necessary skills and updating her CV revived all her conflicts over thinking and learning. Ms A angrily accused me of not understanding the dangers of daring to use her mind. Through dreams and associations, her terror of madness and loss of control were worked through. She became able to move beyond the narcissistic hurt of earlier failures to more neurotic conflicts about competing and succeeding, and then to the uncertainties and frustrations inherent in learning. She realised she no longer believed that there was a God sitting in judgement over her, waiting to humiliate and punish her for any signs of independent thinking. The straitjacket had loosened and there was now space to move and think her thoughts. Regretfully she listed all the subjects she had missed out on at school and would now like to be taught.

She began to go for job interviews, expressing curiosity about what was 'out there' in the world, excitement about exploring it, and confidence that she would not lose me nor I her during the approaching long summer break. Having lived through the long period in the transference, when I was her mother or God, filled with aggressive thoughts and feelings, she became free to wonder about me and the contents of my mind. She had a dream that she needed to go to the toilet. She went to the other rooms in my house, coming across me in my bedroom asleep, and then in a meeting in my front room. She now recognised that I did have a personal and professional life outside the consulting room, and brought her curiosity and jealousy regarding my other patients.

Sexuality and Oedipality

The next year of analysis was the last, for a number of external reasons on her side and mine. Although anxious and angry, and at times more stuck on the cushion than ever, Ms A was able to respond to the time limit with more progressive moves, most notably in the area of her sexuality.

Ms A had begun to take on board that she had a sexual body some 2 years into the analysis when she had to undergo a minor gynaecological intervention. She initially found it hard to even name her genitals, because to do so was to admit to a sexuality that was both wrong and disgusting; in fact, she viewed her condition (which became life-threatening in her mind) as deserved punishment for having gone against her mother and having had sex with men.

By the fourth year of analysis, she had reached sufficient awareness of her sexual body and acceptance of her sexual desires to buy herself attractive clothes and join a dating agency. These active moves towards a triadic relationship brought intense conflicts. Mournfully, she contemplated the loss of the exclusive dyadic relationship with me ('just you and me'). She still thought it was only possible to have one person at a time in her mind because she had to give all her attention to that person. She considered stopping the analysis straight away, because she needed me less and I would not tolerate a third. She tested this theory by going to see a hypnotherapist, expressing her astonishment that I did not become furious with her. I took up her showing me that she wanted something that I could not provide – ultimately, a man with a penis.

Ms A began to go out on regular dates for the first time in her life. Initially cautious and critical, and occasionally terrified of being chopped up and murdered (when one man showed too much interest in her), she was able to recognise her projections and externalisations and the extent to which she had so idealised her father that the men she met could not match up. She relaxed her expectations of them and of herself and began to enjoy visits to the theatre and cinema, developing her own taste and interests. This increasing sense of herself brought further conflict. She bought herself an expensive winter coat, but then felt as if she had stolen something. I interpreted her claiming ownership of her mind and body from her mother/me. Ms A said that she no longer felt invisible, and knew that she occupied a space in my mind. She wondered what I thought of her. She thought about sitting up and facing me as an equal; she was 'tired of the child position'.

It was in this state of mind that she first met S, to whom she was immediately attracted. Terrified, she was tempted to pour scorn on him or run away. Oedipal and pre-Oedipal conflicts were worked through, and Ms A reported that, for the first time in her life, she had enjoyed some sexual play. Becoming aware that she wanted S to mistreat her, she finally recognised the masochistic pay-off in her previous sexual relationships, and her sadistic conception of intercourse. She had interpreted her mother's beating of her brother in primal scene terms, sexualising her terror and rage at being excluded. Her parents' sexual relationship had been similarly distorted in her mind, and she learned from her mother that her father had never beaten her.

S was consistently warm and protective. Ms A confessed she was 'falling for him'. Frightened and bewildered, she reminded me that she was not used to 'this'; her mother had rejected tenderness, closeness or 'whatever you call it'. She concluded that her attitude was 'twisted', and perceived S as more like her father and me, calmly supportive of development. She hoped that, unlike us, he would stay around long enough to enable her to fully disentangle herself from her mother. She still feared that becoming sexual, that is fully alive, meant rupturing the symbiotic tie that sustained her and her mother, and could only lead to madness or death; also, that S might die in the way her father had done, realising for the first time her unconscious belief that her mother had killed her father by breaking his heart.

Ms A and S went out for some months before they had full intercourse. Although Ms A had, for the first time in her life, anticipated the event and made proper contraceptive arrangements, her fear of getting pregnant marred the experience. This would be the disgrace she deserved for disobeying her mother, but also the only justification for having sex. Ms A confessed that she would now love to have a baby. For a period, she resisted penetration. I took this up as an envious attack on S's masculinity/penis, which had broken through her barriers, in the way that she feared his sperm would penetrate the contraceptive barrier. Since they had decided that they were too old for parenthood, it was also a last-ditch attempt to resist accepting that she could have sex purely for pleasure.

Their sexual relationship began to flourish, and Ms A became increasingly able to express warm, tender feelings to S, and gratitude to me. Realising that she could hold more than one object in mind, she understood that we could too; I became able to have a family, and S to have other relationships and interests, without immediately forgetting about her.

In the last months of the analysis, there were more external changes. The relocation of her work, and the break-up of her flat share, enabled Ms A to hand in her notice and accept S's invitation to live with him, which meant moving to another part of London. From feeling at a standstill, Ms A now felt that everything was moving. She felt 'excited and enthusiastic', even at times that the analysis was an inconvenience that took up too much time and energy. However, she also felt potentially overwhelmed by too much change, and that if I were to leave her in this state she might return to her cushion or 'get lost on the way to the door'. She wanted me to stay still a little longer while she continued her explorations.

I agreed to see her once a week for a transitional period following the termina-tion of the analysis, during which she would be moving in with S and finding a new job. Once this was decided, the last weeks of intensive treatment were charac-terised by a multitude of dreams that recapitulated many of the central issues of the analysis in the context of the final separation, which Ms A feared could only be traumatic, like the premature removal of her bottle. As they were worked through, Ms A reviewed her progress. She concluded that she was 'living proof' that analysis worked. She felt better in and about herself, and that she had a right to get what she wanted, demonstrating this in her negotiations for redundancy pay and holiday entitlement from her job (as well as the modified terms of our termination). She felt this sense of herself was established and would see her through difficult times. Before her penultimate analytic session, she dreamt that in a supermarket bag full of rubbish, she found a baby duck or bird which was alive and moving, but with a pin through its leg. Here she felt rejected and hurt by our ending, but not devastated, and that she was still alive and moving.

In her once-weekly sessions she had another dream about a bird that could fly but kept bumping into a wall. This seemed to refer to her continued discomfort with new people in a work or social situation. Following considerable discussion, she decided to give up the difficult journey to my consulting room and embark on a period of group analysis. This seemed an appropriate form of treatment for her residual problems, and one that she could manage after over 4½ years of individual work. In one of our last meetings she said that, for the first time ever, she could visualise herself at two, lifting her head from the cushion, taking a step away, and seeing that the chair was still there. When we finally said goodbye, she was very sad, but not overwhelmed. She returned some weeks later with a gift of a large round glass bowl in which some small but healthy plants were growing, thriving in the protected environment provide by the container – a metaphor, perhaps, for her analytic experience.

Understanding of Ms A's development

In her early years, Ms A was deprived of the pleasurable parent–child interactions that constitute the basis of secure attachment. It seems likely that she was left alone too long, and not touched, held, or attended to sufficiently, and that when her mother did have time for her their interactions were not based on sensitive attune-ment, but on the mother's dutiful care of her as a passive, almost inanimate object, to be fed and dressed, but not played with or enjoyed. This lack of mutuality and pleasure was compounded by the mother's outbursts of rage when the demands upon her became too much (or perhaps when she was confronted with situations which took her into her own areas of unresolved trauma and conflict (Main and Hesse 1990)). These frightening, perhaps frightened, episodes, puncturing the more chronic neglect, must have aroused overwhelming feelings in Ms A, since her mother was the cause of them and not available to help her contain and modulate them. Together, these experiences laid the foundation for the subsequent deficit in Ms A's mentalising capacity (Fonagy 1991).

When the analysis reactivated Ms A's longing for attachment, she behaved remarkably like the toddlers described by Main and Solomon (1986). Like them, she felt faced with an unresolvable dilemma: that of needing an object who was at the same time experienced as dangerous, due to traumatic disappointment, real threat, and her own projected aggression. Like them, she escaped into inhibition, immobility and invisibility.

Ms A's readiness to resort to dissociation would seem to bear out the neuro-biologists' comments about sensitisation, while her characterological stance of hyper-vigilance, combined with dissociation from both her inner world and the world outside, confirms their contention that early coping responses, which start off adaptive, may persist throughout life in a rigid and maladaptive fashion. It would seem from the analysis that Ms A tended to deal with the many interferences and conflicts that arose in later phases of development according to this fixed pattern, and that the recurrent images of the mummified baby, the toddler on a cushion, and the straitjacket, all reflected her internal immobilisation in the face of danger. The long-term damage done to her personality was evidenced in her ego deficits (or 'defects', Pine 1994) in the areas of affect regulation, thinking, and learning, as well as in her difficulties in making and holding on to relationships. Her restricted ability to represent affects contributed to her tendency to somatise.

These deficits were compounded by the lack of a father (or caring older sibling) to provide her with alternative positive experiences, to facilitate separation–individuation, to moderate her aggression, and to enable her to reach some Oedipal resolution. The early tendency to dissociation may have predisposed her towards adopting the hysterical solution of repressing her sexuality, along the lines first described by Breuer and Freud (1893–95). The regression to a predominantly masochistic mode of relating arose out of the all-encompassing identification with her mother, which was promoted by their early painful relationship, the denial of aggression felt to be omnipotently destructive, and sadistic intercourse fantasies complicated by the actual beating of her brother (Novick and Novick 1996). It contributed to her 'addiction to near-death' (Joseph 1982), which provided perverse excitement at the expense of real relating, felt to be too dangerous.

An early intervention, ideally during the critical period of brain development and before subsequent conflicts were internalised, would have been timely. However, Ms A's ability to move on from her entrenched position demonstrates that psychoanalysis, even in adulthood, can address early developmental disorders and their sequelae, and effect considerable change. This was achieved classically by analysing defences and interpreting conflicts stemming from the past, in the context of a new relationship that repeatedly disconfirmed transference expectations. While transference–counter-transference interpretations and reconstructions contributed to Ms A's being able to discover me as a 'new object' (Baker 1993), it was a two-way process; the experience in treatment of a safe, non-intrusive, non-retaliatory object made possible the analysis of the more terrifying aspects of the transference, contributing to the establishment of self and object constancy. Loewald (1960) pointed out that cases with obvious ego defects magnify the integrative processes occurring in any analysis. In Ms A's case, affective attunement ('right-brain-to-right-brain', Schore 2000), combined with the consistent verbalisation and linking of inner and outer experience, led to increased mentalisation and a corresponding diminution in her physical symptoms (McDougall 1974; Fonagy 1991).

Schore (2001b) has suggested that the therapeutic relationship can act as a growth-facilitating environment for structures that never grew in the first place. While it cannot erase trauma, it can provide the context in which higher, i.e. regulatory and reflective, structures can develop. This is consistent with Hurry's view of analysis as a developmental therapy (1998); also with the work of Pine (1994), and the ideas of Fonagy et al. (1993) about 'engaging previously inhibited mental processes within the psychoanalytic encounter'. The analytic work freed Ms A to use the relationship with me to think and feel, to become curious and imaginative, and eventually to form relationships in the world outside, which reflected her growing awareness of her affective and instinctual self, and her confident expectation that she could be loved and desired by a reliable and caring other. It did not enable her to find more challenging work, and it remains an open question whether more analysis could have helped her to achieve this, or whether the early deprivation left her with irreversible damage in the areas of thinking and learning.

References

Baker, R. (1993). The patient's discovery of the psychoanalyst as a new object. *International Journal of Psychoanalysis 74*: 1223–1233.

Breuer, J. and Freud, S. (1893–95). *Studies on Hysteria,* Standard Edition, Vol. 2. London: Hogarth Press.

Fonagy, P. (1991). Thinking about thinking: some clinical and theoretical considerations in the treatment of a borderline patient. *International Journal of Psychoanalysis 72*: 639–656.

Fonagy, P., Moran, G., Edgcumbe, R., Kennedy, H. and Target, M. (1993). The roles of mental representations and mental processes in therapeutic action. *Psychoanalytic Study of the Child 48*: 9–48.

Freud, A. (1936). *The Ego and the Mechanisms of Defence.* London: Karnac.

Furman, E. (1992). *Toddlers and their Mothers: A Study in Early Personality Development.* Madison CT: International Universities Press.

Hopkins, J. (2000). Overcoming a child's resistance to late adoption: how one new attachment can facilitate another. *Journal of Child Psychotherapy 26*(3): 335–347.

Hurry, A. (1998). Psychoanalysis and developmental therapy. In *Psychoanalysis and Developmental Therapy*. London: Karnac.

Joseph, B. (1982). Addiction to near-death. In Feldman, M. and Bott Spillius, E. (eds), *Psychic Equilibrium and Psychic Change*. London: Routledge.

Loewald, H. (1960). On the therapeutic action of psychoanalysis. *International Journal of Psychoanalysis 41*:16–33.

Mahler, M., Pine, F. and Bergman, A. (1975). *The Psychological Birth of the Human Infant*. London: Hutchinson.

Main, M. (1995). Recent studies in attachment: overview, with selected implications for clinical work. In Goldberg, S., Muir, R. and Kerr, J. (eds), *Attachment Theory: Social, Developmental and Clinical Perspectives*. Hillsdale NJ: Analytic Press.

Main, M. and Hesse, E. (1990). Parents' unresolved traumatic experiences are related to infant disorganised attachment status: is frightened and/or frightening parental behaviour the linking mechanism? In Greenberg, M. T., Cicchetti, D. and Cummings, E. (eds), *Attachment in the Preschool Years*. Chicago: University of Chicago Press.

Main, M. and Solomon, J. (1986). Discovery of a new insecure–disorganised/disoriented attachment pattern. In Brazelton, T. B. and Yogman, M. (eds), *Affective Development in Infancy*. Norwood, NJ: Ablex.

McDougall (1974). The psyche–soma and the psychoanalytic process. *International Review of Psychoanalysis* (1): 437–460.

Novick, J. and Novick, K. K. (1996). *Fearful Symmetry: The Development and Treatment of Sadomasochism*. Northvale, NJ: Jason Aronsen.

Perry, B. D. (1997). Incubated in terror: neuro-developmental factors in the cycle of violence. In Osofsky, J. (ed.), *Children in a Violent Society*. New York: Guilford Press.

Perry, B. D., Pollard, R., Blakeley, R., Baher, W. and Vigilante, D. (1995). Childhood trauma, the neurobiology of adaptation and 'user-dependent' development of the brain: how 'states' become 'traits'. *Infant Mental Health Journal 16*: 271–291.

Pine, F. (1994). Some impressions regarding conflict, defect, and deficit. *Psychoanalytic Study of the Child 49*: 222–240.

Schore, A. (2000). Relational trauma of the developing right brain and the origin of severe disorders of the self. Paper given at the Anna Freud Centre, London, 8 March, 2000.

Schore, A. (2001a). The effects of early relational trauma on right brain development, affect regulation and infant mental health. *Infant Mental Journal 22*: 201–269.

Schore, A. (2001b). Paper and discussion at conference on Attachment, Trauma and Dissociation, London, 7–8 July 2001.

Index